ON DIRECTING AND DRAMATURGY

'A theatre which is able to speak to each spectator in a different and penetrating language is not a fantastic idea, nor a utopia. This is the theatre for which many of us, directors and leaders of groups, trained for a long time.'

Eugenio Barba

On Directing and Dramaturgy is Eugenio Barba's unprecedented account of his own life and work. This is a major retrospective of Barba's working methods, his practical techniques, and the life experiences which fed directly into his theatre-making.

An inspirational resource, *On Directing and Dramaturgy* is a dramaturgy of dramaturgies, and a professional autobiography from one of the most significant and influential directors and theorists working today. It provides unique insights into a philosophy and practice of directing for the beginning student, the experienced practitioner and everyone in between.

Eugenio Barba (1936, Italy), after working with Jerzy Grotowski for three years in Poland, created Odin Teatret in 1964 in Oslo and moved with it to Holstebro, Denmark, in 1966. He founded the International School of Theatre Anthropology (ISTA) in 1979. He has directed more than 70 productions with his theatre and the intercultural ensemble Theatrum Mundi. His previous books include *The Paper Canoe: A Guide to Theatre Anthropology*; *Theatre: Solitude, Craft, Revolt*; *Land of Ashes and Diamonds: My Apprenticeship in Poland* and, in collaboration with Nicola Savarese, *A Dictionary of Theatre Anthropology*.

ON DIRECTING AND DRAMATURGY

Burning the house

Eugenio Barba

Translated by Judy Barba

Routledge
Taylor & Francis Group
LONDON AND NEW YORK

Every effort has been made to seek permission to reproduce copyright material before the book went to press. If any proper acknowledgment has not been made, we would invite copyright holders to inform us of the oversight.

First published 2010
by Routledge
2 Park Square, Milton Park, Abingdon, Oxon OX14 4RN

Simultaneously published in the USA and Canada
by Routledge
270 Madison Avenue, New York, NY 10016

Routledge is an imprint of the Taylor & Francis Group, an informa business

Typeset in Goudy by
RefineCatch Limited, Bungay, Suffolk
Printed and bound in Great Britain by CPI Anthony Rowe,
Chippenham, Wiltshire

British Library Cataloguing in Publication Data
A catalogue record for this book is available
from the British Library

Library of Congress Cataloging-in-Publication Data
A catalogue record for this book has been requested

ISBN10: 0–415–54920–5 (hbk)
ISBN10: 0–415–54921–3 (pbk)
ISBN10: 0–203–87029–8 (ebk)

ISBN13: 978–0–415–54920–2 (hbk)
ISBN13: 978–0–415–54921–9 (pbk)
ISBN13: 978–0–203–87029–7 (ebk)

TO THE SECRET PEOPLE OF THE ODIN

Learn to predict a fire with unerring precision
Then burn the house down to fulfill the prediction.
Czeslaw Milosz: *Child of Europe*

CONTENTS

ACKNOWLEDGMENTS

'Advice to a Discarded Lover' from *Poems 1960–2000*, by Fleur Adcock, published by Bloodaxe Books, 2000. Reprinted by permission of Bloodaxe Books.

'Requiem' from *You Will Hear Thunder*, by Anna Akhmatova, translation by D M Thomas, published by Secker and Warburg. Reprinted by permission of The Random House Group Ltd.

'For My Birthday' from *The Selected Poetry of Yehuda Amichai*, by Yehuda Amichai, translated by Chana Bloch and Stephen Mitchell and reprinted by permission of University of California Press.

'Fall' from *The Hour of Sand* by Ana Blandiana, published by Anvil Press. Reprinted by permission of Anvil Press Poetry Ltd.

'Purity' from *Questions about Angels*, by Billy Collins, © 1991. Reprinted by permission of the University of Pittsburgh Press and Sterling Lord Literistic.

'The Road Not Taken' from *The Poetry of Robert Frost*, by Robert Frost, edited by Edward Connery Lathem, published by Jonathan Cape. Reprinted by permission of The Random House Group Ltd.

Vincente Huidobro, excerpt from 'Altazor' from *Altazor* © by Vincente Huidobro and reprinted by permission of Wesleyan University Press.

Klein, George., *Pietà*, pp. 39–40: 'The Seventh', poem by Attila József, translated by George Klein, © 1992 Massachusetts Institute of Technology, by permission by The MIT Press.

'Child of Europe' from *New and Collected Poems 1931–2001* by Czeslaw Milosz (Allen Lane The Penguin Press) © Czeslaw Milosz Royalties Inc., 1988, 1991, 1995, 2001. Reproduced by permission of Penguin Books Ltd and HarperCollins Publishers.

Excerpt from *A Tale of Love and Darkness* by Amos Oz, published by

Chatto & Windus. Reprinted by permission of The Random House Group Ltd.

'The Canary Songbook' from *The Canary Songbook* by Karen Press, published by Carcanet. Reprinted by permission of Carcanet Press Limited.

Excerpt from 'Returning Birds' in *View With a Grain of Sand*, copyright © 1993 by Wislawa Szymborska, English translation by Stanislaw Baranczak and Clare Cavanagh copyright © 1995 by Houghton Mifflin Harcourt Publishing Company, reprinted by permission of the publisher.

'Scenes of a Floating World' from *Open World* by Kenneth White, is reproduced by permission of Polygon, an imprint of Birlinn Ltd (www.birlinn.co.uk).

PROLOGUE

> The work of art in theatre is no longer the text of a playwright,
> But an act of life to be created, moment by moment, on the stage.
> Luigi Pirandello: *Introduction to the History of Italian Theatre*

For years I have imagined a performance that ends with a fire. I knew by heart the succession of scenes; I modified them and changed their order in my head. I lingered over the details, retouching them and looking forward to the inevitable grand finale of flames.

I have not put this idea into practice because I knew that the fire could not be a stage effect. Did I want to risk burning the theatre and all the people in it? But this image hammered itself into my mind. To exorcise it, I jotted down some notes.

> It ends with the red of the blaze. It begins in black and white. The performance starts at a gallop with a lynching. A poor black man, a 'nigger', is surrounded by the immaculate white cloaks and hoods of a small group of Ku Klux Klan executioners. They beat him up, prod him with their torches and hang him. They quickly disperse. The victim dangles from a branch. Silence and solitude. A black corpse, like so many others. A mere news story.
>
> From fact to legend: luckily the rope breaks and the body falls to the ground. Barely visible signs reveal that he is still alive. Slowly he recovers. A grotesque scene follows: he believes himself to be in the Next World. Is it Hell? Is it Heaven? Who will appear? The Guardian of the Celestial Door? Or Satan? How come the Next World resembles our world?
>
> The Poor Black Man recovers and explains rationally to himself what has happened. They hanged him, he died and has risen from the dead, like Jesus. It's obvious: he is the poor Christ. Just like the white one, who was also resurrected. He thanks the Father, forgives the assassins and steps out into the world.

Voices of people chatting and playing cards. The first people the Poor Black Man meets are the inmates of a home for the elderly. Men and women, all white. He introduces himself: 'I am Jesus, and have come for the second time. I am the black Christ and I love you all. Don't be afraid. The white Christ had predicted my return. Here I am.' Moved, he tells the story of the white Christ who freed the slaves and helped them to cross the Red Sea of blood unharmed. There, the enemy with the covered faces, frightening hoods and flowing cloaks perished together with their horses and rifles.

When they get over their amazement, the inhabitants of the rest home make signs of complicity to one another: nobody laughs! He must be taken seriously, this crazy ex-slave. They want to have fun with him: not through spite, but to cheat boredom.

The old people pretend to be respectful and venerate him. They beg him to perform miracles. And he does so, because they make it easier for him by acting them out. A cascade of tricks begins. A 'blind' man sees again when the black Jesus lays some mud on his eyes. An old 'paralytic' woman in a wheelchair stands up when he caresses her legs, and the 'virgin who hadn't known a man' (an ex-alcoholic whore) strips off her clothes, rekindling desire and rivalry. The black Christ laughs joyfully and gives his blessing: love one another.

The old people become more and more skilled in conjuring. A woman levitates. A beheaded man gets his head back on his shoulders. Water turns into wine. A luxuriant tree withers as soon as he curses its lack of fruit. The inmates of the rest home stage these wonders which delude the Poor Black Man into believing that he really is the Saviour, alive once more. He believes himself to be the protagonist of the story, whereas in fact he is the mocked onlooker. The 'actors' are the amused spectators.

This performance of magic art is punctuated by the black Christ's sermons. He repeats distorted fragments of the Old and New Testaments. At times he speaks like a heretic, a follower of a gospel yet untamed. The Poor Black Man is ludicrous and ignorant, but very handsome. The old people, male and female alike, deride him yet fall under his spell. Who is deceiving who? Who sets the trap in this world of deceptions? The plot starts to crumble. Then three endings follow, one after the other.

The Poor Black Man obliges each single resident of the rest home to kneel and confess the most ignoble action of their life. They obey, a prey to their own game: ridiculous, fearful, hating themselves. Consternation: one of them collapses with a heart attack.

Around the coffin with the corpse, the old people incite God's black child to enter the darkness and bring Lazarus back to life:

'Step in, embrace the dead body, infuse into it your warmth and vital breath.' The black Christ lies down on top of the cold corpse, kisses it on the lips, squeezes and shakes it. He becomes frantic, uttering one cry after another, while the old people nail the cover on the coffin and bury him amid the stench of putrefaction.

They rush with the coffin to the bottom of the garden, deposit it on a pile of firewood, sprinkle petrol on it and light a match. Then they all run away and lock themselves in their rooms, right behind the spectators. Darkness. The Poor Black Man, scorched and deathly pale, advances holding a torch in his hand. He sets fire to everything. The whole theatre burns. He is the only one to leave in peace.

This, roughly, was the embryo of the impossible performance which I noted down almost as a game and then put aside. Yet, I have often referred to this performance as if, unable to let it grow, I wished to preserve it as a seed. Some fragments of it appeared in *Talabot* and in *Andersen's Dream*. A small fire glowed at the end of both of these performances.

I know that I could never burn, even metaphorically, my and my companions' house – Odin Teatret. But it is as if I had a double. One of me tries to explore its architecture. The other attempts incessantly to set fire to it.

* * *

In this book, the verbs are almost always in the past tense. When saying what I do, I write: *I did it*. When saying what I'm thinking, I write: *I thought*.

It is unfair but necessary.

It is obvious why it is unfair. When I say *I thought*, the reader might believe that I have changed my mind. I have not changed it. It is even worse when I switch from opinions to facts. When I write *I did so and so*, the reader risks seeing me as a speaking corpse. When I write that 'we of Odin Teatret *did so and so*', this funereal misunderstanding also includes my actors.

Reading the typed copy of this book, Ana Woolf, an Argentinean actor and director who has translated some of my texts, was hurt by my distorted use of the verbs. She wrote to me: 'Why do you always speak in the past and never in the future? How can you talk in the past of performances that your actors are playing at this very moment? How can you possibly speak of your new performance, which you have just started rehearsing, in the past? Here they are, all your actors, at seven a.m. on the dot, beside you, still willing to work after so many years, ready to give their all. Don't they deserve to be referred to in the present?'

She is right. My way of forcing the tenses erases the present, sounds artificial and nurtures misunderstandings. Above all, it risks giving the impression that I am detached or separated from my actors. But I feel this temporal misrepresentation as a duty and a necessity. I would like the reader to consider the pages on technique like the description of an antiquated craft from the Middle Ages, and feel free to do what they want or can with them.

I don't distance myself from my actors, my spectators or my life. I distance myself from my readers. I am here, very much alive, in my theatre, among my collaborators, making plans and fulfilling dreams. It is my unpredictable readers who are not with me, here and now. Are there no more of them? Will there be more?

* * *

I don't write to transmit, but to give back. Much has been given to me by masters who didn't know they were, nor wanted to be, my masters. Most of them had already died when I came into the world. Reading their words, coincidences and misunderstandings have aided the discovery of a knowledge that has guided me towards myself.

I know that similar coincidences will happen to some of my readers. But it is not this hope which motivates me to write. It is something I must do although I have a thousand reasons to oppose it. I consider it a duty. I am simply in debt. And I don't want to leave any debts behind me.

* * *

I know that my theatre and that of my companions was an abnormal theatre.

I know that readers who have never seen one of our performances will consider many of my examples obscure or incomprehensible.

I know that even the elementary professional obligations on which our work at Odin Teatret was based will appear incongruous or exaggerated impositions to many people who do theatre or plan to do so. They will wonder why these constrictions seemed to us to be absolute conditions about which we refused to compromise. Perhaps they will realise that the hope of outstanding artistic results is not enough to explain and motivate all the commitment we have invested in our theatre craft.

A theatre which always makes performances with the same people and the same director for a lifetime is not normal. Now, as I write, this state has lasted 45 years. It is not normal, but it is not a handicap either. We have fought and continue to fight so as not to become our own prison.

The fact that our theatre was not normal has had far-reaching consequences. Under our special conditions, so different from the usual ones, all the rules of art and craft assumed peculiar characteristics: from training to dramaturgy, from the ways of establishing ties with the spectators to those of shaping and varying the relationships within our group, mixing anarchy with an iron self-discipline.

We were an island. But we were never isolated – even in the apparent loneliness of our first months in 1964. The very thing that separates one island from another – the sea – is the best means of communication. Where there is no sea to unite and separate, communication may become ambiguous and draining.

It follows that it is necessary to trace a circle and enclose oneself within it, remaining constant and intransigent in order to be worthy to come into contact with the vast and terrible world outside, as Kim and his Tibetan lama said. It is easy to understand this, almost obvious. But when we try to do it, we risk swinging continually between megalomania and self-pity. Doubts and dreams deposit themselves like crusts: we are proud of our diversity and yet we live it as a handicap.

From this point of view there is no great difference if the circle is constituted by a clearly defined tradition, consolidated through the contribution of several generations and easily recognised by the spectators. Or if, on the contrary, it is a 'small tradition', born from the intertwinement of a few biographies and shared experiences. It is the tradition of a handful of people which will disappear with them, just as the fist vanishes when the hand opens.

From all other points of view, the difference is enormous.

* * *

It is undeniably a subjective book. The knowledge acquired on my island is the only one I can talk about with the certainty of things experienced, suffered, enjoyed and partially understood by me. It is a knowledge closely linked to my biography and that of my companions. But even those who have spent a whole lifetime together with me, who have chosen me and still continue to accept me as their director, would not know how to put into practice my way of directing. Every head is a different jungle. It is more than enough if each of us succeeds in opening clearings and paths in our own particular one. Therefore I cannot, nor do I wish to, pass on a style, create a school or a method, or – to use a word that I don't like – define a personal aesthetic that others might share.

But I can recount. In this book I restrict myself to reporting my principles as a director. My desire for clarity has at times suggested a 'you should do so and so' instead of 'I had to do so and so'. I beg the reader to correct this linguistic expression that I have not succeeded in eliminating.

Whosoever writes must strive to be clear. But while I gave myself this aim, I could not help remembering what one of my fellow countrymen by adoption said: 'What is the contrary of truth? A lie? No, it is clarity.' I speak of the physicist Niels Bohr, whose coat of arms and motto – opposites are complementary – appear on the headed paper of Odin Teatret.

So, after having written that at Odin Teatret we began work at seven in the morning, tomorrow at seven I will hurry to our theatre's blue room to confront the present. There, my actors and I are preparing our new performance, whose title is *The Chronic Life*.

* * *

The future?

I am sure that there will always be people – a few or many depending on the waves of history – who will practise theatre as a sort of bloodless guerrilla war, a clandestine revolt under an open sky or an unbeliever's prayer. They will thus find a way to channel their dissidence along an indirect path without converting it into destructive acts. They will live the apparent contradiction of a rebellion which is metamorphosed into a sense of fraternity and a craft of solitude which creates bonds.

I am sure that theatre will always have men and women among its spectators who will look for the indirect exposure of wounds similar to their own. Or wounds which, although apparently healed, have an obscure need to reopen themselves.

I imagine that these people will sense, in these pages, a homely atmosphere, a smell of burning. Like the one I smelt in Poland, when I was a young man with the ambition to become a director. I wanted to change society through theatre. In reality I was driven by an explosive impatience, the desire for pleasure and the wish for power, as well as an uncontrollable and potentially self-destructive need to escape from my past. It was in Poland that I met Jerzy Grotowski. He was only a couple of years older than me and had seen a hundredth of the world I knew. But in that narrow world of his he had experienced the indifference of history, the lack of liberty, a pride in his cultural identity which was continually threatened and always at risk of being disowned. Once more, in my four years in socialist Poland, I sensed the luminous ways in which the individual's spiritual dimension grafts itself onto the grand sweep of history and small individual histories; and how cowardice conceals itself at the source of courage. And vice versa.

It is probable that those people who are attracted to theatre for the love of art and originality will not recognise themselves in my stories. It will depend on chance and luck. Maybe (whether through merit of the book or its reader) something will succeed in perforating the cloud of indifference and misunderstandings that banish other people's stories into silence. I will therefore end this prologue by repeating what I have already said: I am not writing to convince, teach or transmit anything, but to give back. What? And to whom?

There is an ancient saying: *ars longa, vita brevis*. The idea that life is short depends on how we see it. That our attachment to art is long-lived is something we cannot change. And to work just for the beauty of theatre is not worthwhile.

INTRODUCTION
THE FIELD OF POPPIES

> A sound as solemn
> as a small girl walking along a dark corridor
> in her grandfather's shoes.
>
> Karen Press: *The Canary Songbook*

There is a drawing in which a painter is frenziedly working with five brushes: one in each hand, one between the toes of each foot, the fifth in the mouth. Each brush is painting independently of the others. We witness the growth of five parallel, autonomous and coherent worlds. Is the painter showing his working method? Or is he bringing visibly to the surface the inner turmoil or deliberate disorientation which may generate bonds, encounters, plots and unforeseen tensions?

The drawing is by Katsushika Hokusai, author of 30,000 prints and paintings with continuous breaks and variations in style. For every new change of style and technical approach, he assumed a new name. (How many names would Nietzsche, Picasso and Bob Dylan have had? How many Meyerhold or Grotowski?) Hokusai's variety of names is the map of his attempts at renewal and of his escapes.

He was also a calligrapher and a poet. In old age, he enjoyed writing and publishing erotic, even obscene poems. He died in 1849 at the age of 81 and this is one of his last haikus:

> I write
> Erase
> Rewrite
> Erase again
> And then a poppy blooms.

I often quoted these lines, which recalled many situations from my rehearsals and allowed me to place side by side artistic techniques and floriculture. There are flowers which, once they are cut, survive for a long time.

Or, transplanted, they can grow in a different earth from that of their origin. And there are flowers which, once transplanted or cut, fade and die. If we try to seize the dazzling beauty of poppies and transport it into a vase in our house or a flowerbed in our garden, it withers away in a few minutes.

There are technical procedures which can easily be passed from one person to another and be condensed into clear principles. In our craft, these constitute the field of objectivity. At the opposite extreme there is the personal heat that distinguishes every individual, an inimitable temperature which belongs only to him or her and which, when imitated, turns into parody.

In the middle, between the two, lies the field of poppies. Here we find techniques with a double character. On the one hand they have all the features of a set of data and skills which define technical know-how. On the other, they depend to such an extent on the milieu in which they have developed that we cannot extract absolute precepts from them.

The techniques of directing belong to this type.

In every artistic discipline there is a deeply subjective component. There is, however, also a part that can be separated from the biography, from the working conditions and from the artist's personal style as objective knowledge, the base which makes it possible to build a personal oeuvre.

Directing is peculiar in so much as it is a practice that can be defined only *in relationship to a particular theatre milieu.* What is a director? In some contexts the director is a person who takes care of the critical-aesthetical representation of a text; in others, one who conceives and composes a performance from nothing. In certain cases it is an artist who pursues her own image of theatre materialising it in different performances with changing collaborators; in others she is a competent professional capable of harmonising the performance's heterogeneous elements. There are milieus where the director is a wandering artist, looking for companies to be provisionally ruled; and there are others in which she works systematically always with the same group of which she is often the leader and also responsible for the actors' training. Many consider the director an experienced coordinator. Others identify her as the performance's true author, the first spectator who also has the last word in every decision.

Today, for me, the director is rather the expert of the theatre's subatomic reality, a man or a woman who experiments with ways of *overturning* the obvious links between the different components of a performance.

One of the great achievements in twentieth-century theatre has been the growth of independent models, of theatre enclaves which developed through diversity. Today, there is not just one tradition, but there are many *small traditions*, not a continent, but an archipelago in which theatres with discordant styles and values dwell. These theatres differ in techniques, organisation, economic conditions, social recognition and ethos. Often the goals they pursue cannot be compared, nor can their spectators.

I speak on purpose of spectators. Until now, I have not used the term 'audience'. Grotowski sustained that the actor should not play for an audience, but for each spectator. The word 'audience' made him think of a sociological abstraction or of the psychology of the crowd which replaced the independence of judgement in the single individual. These affirmations entailed a rebellious stance in the 1960s. Moreover, they were expressed in Poland, a country with a socialist regime whose political ideology insisted on making the behaviour of its citizens uniform as well as their conscience. But over and above the historical circumstances, Grotowski's vision was prophetic and concerned the destiny of the theatre.

From the mid-twentieth century, theatres no longer have the possibility to turn themselves into courts against the vices and the injustices of their time, as claimed by Schiller. They no longer sway opinions or represent shared beliefs and feelings. Other types of performance have the voice which today is necessary to harangue the people, affect their choices, awaken their conscience or fanaticism, educate or deceive them. Theatre no longer possesses a voice capable of reaching the ears of an entire city. It doesn't frighten anyone as a possible enemy of power and public morality. And no reasonable person expects that its effectiveness can stir up a general change of mentality.

The theatre's prestige is similar to that of the living museums of the arts. At times the theatre can be a minute extra-territorial zone where it is possible to live far from the eyes that judge us. Such theatres can have an impact, but this depends on subtle energies. These subtle energies stem from human beings, from actors who don't address themselves to everyone in the same way, but who know how to bring to life emotions, thoughts, open-eyed dreams, secret loves and forgotten wounds, dormant nostalgias and repressed fears in each single spectator.

A theatre which is able to speak to each spectator in a different language is not a fantastic idea, nor a utopia. This is the theatre for which many of us, directors or leaders of groups, trained for a long time. At first we were not conscious of it and believed we were investigating the secret source of art. Then we became aware that we were exploring the catacombs of a *not-violent* rebellion.

And now I return to the geography of the archipelago and to theatre as the practice of diversity.

We theatre directors have many demands in common. Yet the exclusive mark – the personal method deciding the result's quality and identity – cannot withstand transmission. The same thing happens as with some unique wines which I have tasted in southern Italy: they don't tolerate transport. After travelling for only a few hours, the wine already tastes of vinegar.

Vinegar instead of wine – this is what occurs with the transmission of a method. Something is handed down, it is authentic, yet undrinkable. It can only be used differently, for example as seasoning.

At times I have said that I had no method. *It's not true* because I knew and applied systematically various techniques, principles and conventions which I was able to explain effectively. *It is true* because the core of a method does not consist of indications which may be formulated and applied, but of a nebula of impulses which have to be unearthed and awoken in us. My apprenticeship made me retrieve them: they were often hidden under a cloak of obviousness and common sense. These impulses were linked to my personality and biography, produced by those dark forces which provoked my refusals. *My wounds, the burning winds, my superstitions* were all part of my method.

These impulses were the rope which I grabbed to prevent myself from falling into an abyss of inanity. I gave names to these impulses. At times they became words which enflamed my imagination. I was a trapeze artist who oscillated in the air. I imposed a sense and a rigour on this movement and I called it theatre. I didn't dare to call it circus. There the trapeze artist risks his life. In theatre, only my vanity was at stake.

This oscillation, so bound up with my personality, has been my method. It was not the reproduction of the oscillation – of the method – of another person, nor can it be repeated by others. It was my process of individualisation, of growth, of escape from my origins and my revisiting them as a fugitive. A dialogue with people inside me whom I didn't know. Taking a stand.

Is a personal method, then, impossible to transmit? This is not true either. It can be passed on through a long process of symbiosis with another person, still alive or dead, and involving contradictions and apparent betrayals. If the method is transmitted, it becomes unrecognisable. When it is recognisable, it is an illusion, a crutch or a parody.

1

THE EMPTY RITUAL

Borges: a book is made of many books.
Canetti: a man is made of many men.
Ergo: a performance is made of many performances.

Word bridges

Often, at the origin of a creative path, there is a *wound*. In the exercise of my craft I have revisited this intimate lesion to deny it, question it or simply be near it. It was the cause of my vulnerability and the source of my needs. It had little to do with aesthetics, theories, with the wish to express myself or to communicate with others. This *wound necessity* has acted as an impulse to remain close to the boy I was, and from whom time removed me, pushing me in a world of constant change.

I have often told my actors that a magnificent performance doesn't change the world, but a performance which leaves one indifferent and seems generated by indifference makes it uglier. I was well aware that my performances didn't have the same impact on all my spectators. But I wanted to emphasise a useful superstition: 'behave as if a horrible performance makes the world uglier. But keep your feet on the ground, because it is not with just one performance that you will transform it. And above all, don't let the tendency to be satisfied by the first result seep into your work.'

My sentence is valid only from the point of view of the ethos of the work. A mediocre or indifferent performance doesn't make the world more obscene than it is. For the spectators, nothing is removed or added, and it soon fades from their memory. But a lukewarm commitment remains indelible in my and my actors' memory and nervous system. It becomes a conditioned reflex in our future days of work. If I dilute my longing for *excellence*, for the peak of Annapurna, I erode and impoverish my working process, the capacity for discovering energies buried within me and reacting to the surrounding reality. In such a case, the tepid work tarnishes those who perform and accustoms them to the indifference of the world.

I don't know if this attitude has emerged while working in theatre or whether it has accompanied me since childhood. In the beginning, on the path of the profession, every stone reminded me of the wayfarers who had preceded me. To each of them I asked the questions that I asked myself: What were you running away from? What was the initial impulse – the intimate motives, appetites, obsessions, fortuitous meetings – that triggered your first step? Which house did you burn within you?

I started to do theatre while trying to find out, in a physical, technical and emotional way, what 'doing theatre' involved. Composing performances taught me, as an *autodidact*, to ask myself questions about the history of theatre as it is usually written, to question well-known or insignificant facts, to weigh and translate for myself the professional terms which I heard and read, to conceal in my working process a performance which had fascinated me or which I reconstructed with my imagination. My insecurity and the limits of my knowledge incited me to search again and again among the procedures of *how to do*.

There existed dark forces within me which influenced my choices. They rode me suddenly, they sensed an affinity with a person just met, they persisted in refusing reasonable solutions. Much more than ideas, aesthetics or conceptual categories, these forces have steered me through the tangle of circumstances. They have forged lasting loyalties with dead and living people, with ideals and dreams, with places and books; they have distilled *superstitions* which I have justified to myself and to others with logical, political and artistic arguments.

These forces constituted the secret magma which infiltrated my professional life, the technical meticulousness and the creative storm of my work as director, my craft's ethos and my obstinacy to remain a foreigner.

With the years I have become more and more aware of this intimate magma. I was no longer intimidated by it; I considered it less intangible and translated it into words. Each of us who does theatre possesses a handful of terms which sieve our personal intuition and professional know-how. These terms have accumulated in our pockets, almost without our will. Work and habit have made them smooth like pebbles.

I have always felt the need to question again and again these *word bridges* between the concrete practice of theatre and my secret magma, to scratch them with naive questions in order to chip their surface and affect their solidity. I have treated these words as annoying and malevolent fetishes.

When I have tried to translate my tacit knowledge into concepts, assimilated through years of practice, misunderstandings and errors, I resorted to my *word bridges*. These seemed neutral terms, clear and comprehensible to everybody. For me they were vacuous words demanding to be filled with *my own* sense. They concerned what for me was the essence of the theatre: *revolt*, *empty ritual*, *dissidence*, *vulnerability* (which is the reality of solitude), *transcendence* or, as I like to say today, *superstition*. Others were technical words referring to aspects of the craft which had always fascinated me: *sats* (impulse), *kraft* (power), *organic effect*, *energy*, *rhythm*, *flow*, *dramaturgy*, *dance*.

I had met some of these words unintentionally and they had confronted me with experiences buried deeply within me, with needs that I was incapable of explaining to myself. Perhaps these were the experiences and needs on which my diversity was rooted. *Diversity* was one of the vacuous words which I tried to fill with a sense of my own. More of these words: *refusal*, *craft*, *floating island*, *barter*, *emigration*, *wound*, *origin*. And also *serendipity*.

From this heterogeneous handful of words, I have chosen two: *dramaturgy* and *origin*.

Where do I come from?

We have many origins because many are the lives in our life. We meet our origins on our path, just as we meet our identities and our true family. Narrating a life demands leaps of perspective, repudiating the idea of only one origin which is unravelled in a chronological thread.

Where do I come from?

I come from a world that fell to pieces and found its normality in that fall. 1940–1945, times of war: many houses became empty, others filled with evacuees. Still others collapsed under the bombs and I woke in the morning to see them shattered, like obscene creatures exhibiting their shames. Sometimes their ruins were shaken by laments. The adults spoke of people being buried alive, of survivors being miraculously unearthed, of unrecognisable corpses. Day and night, a voice could be heard from under the rubble. Only after a couple of days did it fall silent.

For the child who listened to these stories, they were like those of fairies and heroes imprisoned in trees. Like the fairy tales, the stories of the heaps of rubble also turned by night into dreams and fears.

It was the end of Mussolini's dictatorship and of his mirage of a fascist empire. Bari was invaded by the army – Americans, Canadians, Poles, Moroccans. The school in front of our house was a barracks for coal-black Sudanese soldiers. Leaning over the balconies they nibbled at white bread, laughing at the girls who waited at the front door. At home, my father, a high-ranking fascist officer, was very ill. The family whispered to my brother and me to play quietly.

On some days my mother and I played a secret game together. She called me aside, combed my hair, made sure that I was tidy and properly dressed, embraced me and then sent me out into the nearby streets, on the seafront. The game was this: I had to hold out my hand and ask for money. I begged. But my mother and I called it fortune-seeking. Those were days when our home lacked even the few coins to pay for food and medicine.

I come from this solitary fortune-seeking.

My father's family enjoyed a certain prestige in Gallipoli, a small fishing town deep in the Gulf of Taranto in southern Italy. We went to live there among relatives who treated my mother as a stranger. The windows and balconies of our house overlooked the harbour and I watched the fishermen rowing out to sea at dawn. At night I counted their lampare, *the lamps they used to attract octopus.*

We had no running water, so we used the rainwater channelled from the roof into a cistern in the courtyard. It was my job to draw water and each time I was warned: take care not to catch the eel. It swam at the bottom, in darkness, feeding on bugs and parasites. If it died, the water would become undrinkable. I pulled up the bucket with closed eyes, held my breath, opened them again and, relieved, saw only water.

I come from the fear of trapping the sacred animal in the darkness of the well.

Gallipoli was an islet, connected to the mainland and the suburbs by a long, windy bridge: whichever way I turned, the sea looked different. Our house was in the old town. We were besieged by damp, the north wind and winter's gloom when we spent the evenings indoors around glowing braziers, our hands devoured by chilblains. In summer we protected ourselves from the sun in the faint light of closed shutters, opening our windows to the sky only after sunset. I didn't get bored. I played with buttons kept in a cardboard box where my mother had her sewing things. For entire afternoons I lined up buttons on the floor, and they became fleets of pirates, squadrons of airplanes, Roman legions, pioneers' caravans.

I come from that box of buttons.

I come from a night that lasts a lifetime.

For three years I studied in a military college. At 14 I found myself in a barracks with a flock of other teenagers. We ate, slept, washed, went to school and even to the latrines together. I sank into an autistic form of refusal and I was punished with long periods in prison. I had few friends.

One day in the second year, my company's captain summoned me to his office. Standing to attention, I was expecting the usual scolding. He went, instead, to a glass-fronted locker full of books, drew out a small key, opened it, took a volume and handed it to me. He gave me permission to read it in study time when normally any reading, with the exception of school manuals, was forbidden. Il fu Mattia Pascal *by Pirandello fell into my head like a brick and I saw stars. After that, I longed to see more stars. I went to the office where the captain opened Ali Baba's cavern with his tiny key and handed me a jewel.*

I come from this glass-fronted locker which Captain Rossi opened with a doll's key.

I dreamt of wrenching myself from the stagnant waters where I grew up. Of my mother's two children, one cultivated the cult and the nostalgia for his southern roots along all his wandering life in Europe, America and Asia. He spoke constantly of the Bourbon dynasty, Gallipoli, and the military college in Naples where we had studied.

The other son displayed detachment and forgetfulness. Or rather, repression and reticence. I am the second son.

I come from that umbilical cord severed by my own hands. Does this also mean burning the house?

I have always kept up a conversation with my father, that unknown yet so intimately familiar man, whom at the age of 10 I saw in agony for hours until the final silence. I return every year to visit his grave in the small cemetery at Gallipoli. I would not call it a dialogue with my roots. It is more like talking to an old friend. We are the same age now, in fact I am older. I bring him news of his grandchildren whom he has never seen, of my life and work, of my worries of the moment and of trivialities that would make him laugh. I ask his advice, listen to his opinions. It is a dialogue with closed mouth, at times murmuring, as certain people do when deafness makes them loquacious.

I have become accustomed to talking with those who came Before me, instead of with the One on High. Is it the origin of my professional inclination to converse with the books of the masters? In front of the One on High we feel ourselves to be believers or unbelievers. In front of those who came Before we feel like children. And for children, intelligence coincides with the capacity to make mischief.

I come from a father who had no time to grow old and suffer because of an estranged son.

When we tried to appraise our genealogical tree, my brother and I didn't speak of roots, but of the family flaw. It was the urge for suicide. We recalled our grandfather and our three great-uncles. Lucid and daring suicides, all successfully accomplished with a baroque imagination. My brother is dead, but not by his own hand. The same is true of my father. But there are many ways to refuse life.

I come from the family flaw.

Roots, origins: the more they are personal and sincere the more they seem the result of chance. I pursue symptoms, signals, fragments of memories, and images which are unable to fade completely into oblivion. There must be a reason – I tell myself – if they surface now and then in my mind.

It is not only the mind which remembers. There is also a memory in that knot of impulses in the small area between the coccyx and the solar plexus. It is a region which those who do theatre must learn to know, mapping out an empirical and personal science, an awareness and a superstition. Burning winds blow from this region to the nerves, the marrow and the so-called eyes of the mind.

I come from this region, from this knot of impulses.

Engraved in my nervous system are Eigil Winnje's actions in his welder's workshop in Oslo: his artisan's pride in a well-accomplished job, and equality without privileges in the distribution of the tasks which he, the owner, shared with us. His acts without words transmitted knowledge and values through humble work.

My nerves remember the Norwegian writer and beloved friend Jens Bjørneboe: the embodiment of the necessity for excess. Without contradictory surges and mutiny even against the ideas in which he believed, life – for him who was a rebel thirsty for absolute justice – risked being reduced to unconscious defeatism.

I find in my backbone the imprint of the way in which Grotowski, in Akropolis, *directed his actors in the physical action of looking, which was characteristic of the inmates in an extermination camp. It was a particular way of observing the surrounding world and history, squeezing the eyelids half-shut in incomprehension and lifting the eyebrows in amazement, with no light in the eyes.*

There still lives in me the profoundly kind action, all solidarity and assent, with which Sanjukta Panigrahi refused one of the tasks I proposed to her with a stubbornness so unshakable as to appear pacific.

I cannot forget the day when, in rage against an actor, I abandoned Odin Teatret*, intending never to set foot in it again. And the silence and the concentration of my actors, on the following days, when they met at seven o'clock in the morning as usual to train and continue rehearsing Brecht's* Ashes *without me. Alone, until the moment I changed my mind.*

These attitudes were deeply rooted within all these people. They were their roots, and have pushed their way into my personality. They are not the past or memories, they are the present. To have common ground means this: that roots which have grown elsewhere can reach into me and actually become me.

In this way I could answer the question 'where do I come from?', by quoting names and facts from the vast forest of shadows which populate the present.

A plurality of dramaturgies

'What sort of dramaturgy do you want to direct?' I had no hesitation. 'Sophocles, Ibsen, Chekhov and of course Brecht.' My answer came easily at my exam for admission to the State Theatre School in Warsaw in January 1961. Dramaturgy, at that time, was the business of writers.

For years I rarely used this term in my daily practice. My efforts were concentrated on understanding my craft as director and the best way to develop it. In other words: how I could provoke personal reactions in the actors and orchestrate these in a performance which didn't imitate life, but possessed a life of its own. 'Life' was the word which came to mind when I observed and judged the actors' results and my own choices while rehearsing.

Did the actors' actions and relationships emanate life? Did they give the sensation of being organic? Did the actors possess a convincing scenic presence? 'Your actions have no *kraft*,' I told them. *Kraft* is a Norwegian word and means strength, power, energy – like electric and psychic energy – or like the waves we perceive when we are close to a child who plays or to a happy adult.

At the end of the 1970s, particular circumstances made me reflect upon my experience of the actor's 'presence'. I had the opportunity to detect and systematically compare some technical principles belonging to actors and dancers from various genres. This field of study, which I called 'theatre anthropology', was developed within the framework of the International School of Theatre Anthropology (ISTA). Trying to explain in my own words the technical terminology of my own theatre tradition, I defined 'dramaturgy' according to its etymology: *drama-ergon*, the work of the actions. Or rather: the way the actor's actions enter into work. For me, dramaturgy was not a procedure belonging only to literature, but a technical operation which was inherent in the weaving and growth of a performance and its different components.

Usually, in the European tradition, dramaturgy is understood as a literary composition whose model is: proposition of the theme, development, peripeteia or reversal, and conclusion. Dramaturgy is a horizontal narrative thread which holds together the handful of glass beads which is the performance. During my many years as director, however, dramaturgy had little to do with a pre-established written text, a narrative composition or a scenario.

I had the impression that it indicated a field which was vital for my activity, yet at the same time I didn't know what were its precise characteristics and boundaries. It had become a familiar expression that I applied as though I knew precisely what it meant. After having seen a performance, for example, I commented that there was something lacking from the dramaturgical point of view. I had an idea what I was speaking about and it seemed quite clear to me.

Dramaturgy became vague as soon as I tried to define it. I had the impression of alluding to an invisible structure which had to blend the heterogeneous elements and the different parts of a performance in a fascinating, unusual and effective manner. This was not enough. I was dissatisfied, as if by digging in this field I might also uncover something else, a small buried treasure.

I found it useful to start establishing the difference between result and process. I understood that from the point of view of the process it is not important to ask *what* dramaturgy is. There were other questions I needed to ask in order to break the smoothness of this term: as a director, *how* did I interfere in the actors' actions?

It is difficult to understand one's own work, how it unfurls and functions, without falling into theoretical constructions which are both complicated and abstract, and whose innumerable details ramify in a thousand sub-sections like a cabbalistic architecture.

Gradually I began to assume that what I called dramaturgy was not the thread of a narrative composition, the horizontal sequence of the various phases in the evolution of a theme. My dramaturgical work began with a particular way of looking which focused upon the *layered nature of the performance*. My dramaturgy also dealt with the multiple relationships between the many parts of the performance. But it concerned the relationships between the various components in a *vertical dimension*. It was a way of observing the different layers or levels of the work, independently from the performance's meanings. I distinguished these levels and developed them separately, as if they were unrelated.

It was the biologist's way of thinking which helped me to understand my own work. In biology it is necessary not only to distinguish parts and components of an organism (for example, its different organs such as liver, heart or brain; or its systems such as the blood circulation, the nervous or respiratory systems), but also levels of organisation. In the first case we divide the organism into parts which are reciprocally coordinated. In the second, we reason in *layers*, distinguishing the levels between which relationships are established according to different logics. Thus we have a level of organisation of the cells which is at the base of that of the tissues, which in turn is at the base of that of the organs which are coordinated at a higher level in the unity of the living organism.

For me, the performance too was a living organism and I had to distinguish not only its parts, but also its levels of organisation and, later, their mutual relationships. 'Dramaturgy', then, was a term similar to 'anatomy'. It was a practical way of working not only on the organism in its totality, but on its different organs and layers.

What interested me was not the definition of the different levels of organisation according to the biologists. I was looking for the effectiveness of a way of seeing which took into account different and overlapping logics. And that above all recognised as concrete a reality which cannot be materially isolated: a single level of organisation, in fact, is not a *thing* which we can see by itself on the anatomical table. It is a *logic*, a concrete substance of the thought or the look, similar to that of a person who reads a musical score horizontally and vertically at the same time.

On the one hand we have the dramaturgy of the performance as plot, as a weaving of different threads in a concatenation and simultaneity of different actions or episodes; on the other, we have the simultaneous presence in depth of different layers, each endowed with its own logic and peculiar way of manifesting its life.

In a performance, the three evident levels of organisation which have interested me were the following:

- The level of *organic* or *dynamic dramaturgy* – this is the elementary level, and concerns the way of composing and interweaving the dynamisms, the rhythms and the physical and vocal actions of the actors in order to stimulate sensorially the attention of the spectators.
- The level of *narrative dramaturgy* – the intertwining of events which orientate the spectators about the meaning, or the various meanings, of the performance.
- The level of *evocative dramaturgy* – the faculty of the performance to produce an intimate resonance within the spectator. It is this dramaturgy which distils or captures the performance's unintentional and concealed meaning, specific for each spectator. It is a level which we have all experienced, but which cannot be consciously programmed. My actors and I, in fact, have not always succeeded in achieving it.

Each of the three levels has its own logic, its demands and objectives. For me, it has been fundamental to be able to isolate these artificially and think about them separately.

At the level of organic or dynamic dramaturgy I worked with physical and vocal actions, costumes, objects, music, sounds, lights and spatial features. At the level of narrative dramaturgy I worked with characters, stories, texts, events and iconographic references. The evocative dramaturgy had a different nature from the other two. It was a goal. It designated the work necessary to make the same performance reverberate differently in the spectators' biographical caverns. I recognised it only from its effects: when it succeeded in touching the personal superstitions, the taboos and the wounds of the spectators, as well as those of the director, the first spectator.

The organic dramaturgy is the performance's nervous system, the narrative dramaturgy is its cortex and the evocative dramaturgy is that part of us which lives in exile within us. The organic dramaturgy makes the spectators dance kinaesthetically on their seat; the narrative dramaturgy releases conjectures, thoughts, doubts, evaluations and questions; the evocative dramaturgy makes us live a *change of state*.

The articulation on several levels was first of all a means to multiply the logics as well as oppose the performance's univocal nature and the plot's explicit relationships. It permitted me to exploit the mechanisms of sensorial appeal beyond the meanings and the story. Nevertheless, the capacity to distinguish these levels has not helped me to solve the problem of how to develop them in an artistically efficacious way. In solving this problem, preferences, procedures and choices are always personal and vary according to circumstances.

My work as director/first spectator pivoted on these three dramaturgies, making me perceive the performance with the same senses and see it with the same eyes as other spectators. But this first spectator needed to master the technical skill to intervene in the actors' creative process and sharpen the power of the performance to incise in depth.

This active participation of the director, however, gave another meaning to the word 'dramaturgy'. It pointed to that aspect in my work which focused on relationships. *Dramaturgy, then, concerned my decisions to re-forge and amalgamate the relationships which had emerged from the organic and narrative dramaturgies*. The purpose of this blending – or montage – was to distil *complex* relationships, capable of *overturning* the obvious ones.

According to this second meaning, my dramaturgy was primarily a technique to shape, merge, multiply and then *overturn* the relationships which gradually surfaced in rehearsals. In this way I tried to transform simple and often gratuitous interactions into ambiguous and contradictory sequences enabling me to provoke in the spectator what was essential for me: the experience of an overturning of the evident relationships. It was a subjective and very personal use of the term 'dramaturgy', denoting that zone of my work where I was alone. It was the phase in the creation where I seemed to demolish, disarrange and destroy logics and links suggested by the texts, my actors and my own themes. But it was also thanks to this 'earthquake' that I succeeded in discovering unforeseen threads and in interweaving them into relationships characterised by ambiguity and density.

Often my best allies in overturning the obvious relationships were the constraints and limits imposed by the outside: material conditions, economy, actors and sudden circumstances. At other times, I voluntarily imposed restrictions and problems on myself which forced me to find unplanned solutions. These constraints didn't bring about original inventions. They generated something which in my eyes was even more valuable: a potentiality of links and approaches different from those already existing, imagined and imaginable until then.

Dramaturgy, in this case, meant the creation of a complex web of threads instead of simple links. It was also a particular way of thinking. It implied a propensity to freely release a process of associations and to blend, wittingly or incidentally, pre-established facts and components in order to overturn them, make them appear strange to me and difficult to identify. I deliberately outlined situations which I was unable to recognise. Thus I had to discover a new coherence for these facts and components and transmit it sensorially to the spectators through the actions of the actors.

During rehearsals, my process of reversing facts, visual and auditive elements and relationships could be simple, even mechanical as long as it was a point of departure. It sufficed to establish a net of constraints and obstacles which respected rigorous rules: for example, to start from a situation opposite to that which I wanted to tell, to radically limit the space, to miniaturise around a table a scene acted out in a wider area, to let the actor's footsteps and gaits tell what her arms or hands had told. This deliberate process of obstruction on the actor's actions or during a scene opened up new perspectives which extended my possible choices.

It was not important in the beginning that the work on reversing be *intelligent*. In the final phase, however, it had to turn into a startling cloudburst which disrupted the flowerbed of my certainties, uncovering in the earth the scales of a dragon. Such a result surfaced in spite of my wishes or those of the actors. It was not the conscious consequence of ideas, theories, analytical or psychological logics. Often it was an effect of the effort to *remain faithful* to my point of departure.

The principle of overturning alone was not enough. A kind of emotional coherence had also to guide my mental process, decide its turnarounds and watch over this need to overturn. Coherence towards what? Towards an image, an association, a memory – towards an ever-present shadow which should not be too detectable in the performance.

The *fidelity* towards this incongruous coherence, which also bewildered me, was fundamental, although it was a burden while rehearsing. I paid the price by losing my bearings and by a prolonged state of uncertainty. During my work on a performance, I was accompanied by the constant feeling of falling in a void, with the anguish that the parachute might not open.

Anguish has not decreased with age. My only consolation was my belief that the night has 12 hours, and then dawn arrives. I was sustained by my faith that if I worked without giving in, after some months I would meet the sphinx: the performance. Once again I would experience the emotion of seeing it approaching from far away, independent and with a proud life of its own.

Fidelity and need to overturn went hand in hand.

But I still had a *third perspective* from which I looked at my activity. And this too I used to call dramaturgy. In the course of the years my actors began to create materials for a new performance in an ever more autonomous way – each with his logical threads, associations and work on the organic and narrative level. Only in a later phase did I link their results, orchestrating them in a flow of sensorial stimuli and meanings. After a long period of rehearsals, the various materials blended in such a way that the spectator was unable to distinguish them.

This practice has gradually made me consider the performance, not as a *mise-en-scène* (of a text, a story, a plot, an idea), but as a *theatrical composition resulting from a plurality of executions*: that of the actor, that of the director and that of the spectator. I also began to define these *executions* as dramaturgies, multiplying the meanings of this term. Today, while writing, I am aware of the confusion generated by using the same word for different points of view and in different fields of activity which, for me, were very clear in the practice.

So, I called this third perspective *dramaturgy of the actor, dramaturgy of the director* and *dramaturgy of the spectator*. Thus I explained to myself to whom the eyes and the logic giving a sense to the performance belonged. It could be the eyes and the logic of the actor as well as those of the spectator or the director.

My director's dramaturgy consisted in elaborating the actor's dramaturgy in order to set in motion the dramaturgy (the execution) of every spectator. I worked on the level of the physical and vocal actions, on the music and the lights, on the characters, stories and events. I upset their obvious relationships, but remained faithful to my shadows so that the performance might resonate diversely in the different world of each spectator.

It is strange to speak about 'dramaturgy of the spectator', and often I have been reproached that this expression is meaningless. I have stubbornly maintained it. It helped me to point out my main effort: to create a performance which could assume a shared sense and at the same time might whisper a different confidence to every spectator. And which appeared diverse every time they watched it. This was valid also for me, the first spectator among others, and was valid for the actors, spectators of themselves and their companions. I wanted performances which could give the actors, the spectators and me the experience of overturning the world we knew.

When the dramaturgies of the actor, the director and the spectator met in a form of life which spoke to an intimate truth of mine, I experienced a change of state and the performance became for me an *empty ritual*. Void is absence, but it is also potentiality. It can be the obscurity of a crevasse. Or the immobility of a deep lake on whose surface ripples appear – signs and shadows of unexpected life.

* * *

I did theatre. I sold shadows. Through these shadows I climbed towards a world different from the one in which it was my lot to live. These shadows were staircases for me, for my actors and for some of our spectators. The stairs of our handicraft and our values were illusory, when seen against the background of that stony sky called 'reality'. To hold myself upright, I gave myself goals: ghosts, illusions, ideals which I superimposed on the raw reality around me, and which I called *superstitions*.

Superstition normally indicates a negative quality, irrationality, fanaticism or deception. Nevertheless, when I invert this term, it shows its literal face: the Latin *super stare* means that which *is above*, something that can crush or attract and elevate.

I have never believed that superstitions should be shared. When this happens, they become a yoke, chains and doctrines. They are roots and shadows which wander in my inner city, in that small and boundless territory enclosed within my skin, my nerves and muscles, in a personal and incommunicable microcosm: *the country of speed*, my body-in-life.

My professional origin is linked to a few theatre men and women of the twentieth century who were not satisfied with the frontiers of their craft. Against these frontiers my theatrical ancestors used determination and extremism, *a hunger for the beyond*. They revitalised their art to such an extent that they ended up clashing with a bitter question: are all our sacrifices, efforts and commitment worthwhile for a result which is ephemeral? Thus they fought against the culture and the conditions of the theatre: an art which cannot have the illusion of not being ephemeral. They conducted their struggle for the *permanence* of the performance in the spectator's senses and memory through the actor's actions, refining their biological nature. *Bios* means 'life': the actor's *bios* which penetrates the spectator's inner world; the performance's *bios* which is confronted with the meaningless *logos* of history; the *bios* of the theatre as rebellion and transcendence, as the embodied presence of individual superstitions, beyond diversion and art.

Dramaturgy is materially constituted by actions interacting on the different levels of organisation of a performance. Can these living actions, which are embedded in fiction, turn themselves into a path towards the origins of life? Towards the origins of the injustices of the world? Towards the origins of our many identities?

Staircases of shadows. Techniques of an ephemeral art against that which is ephemeral. Empty ritual.

FIRST INTERMEZZO

Books are the work of loneliness and the children of silence.
The children of silence have nothing in common with the children of the word.

Marcel Proust

The children of silence

In January 2007 I received a letter from Mirella Schino, a dear Italian friend and a theatre scholar, who expressed a wish:

> Dear Eugenio,
>
> Happy New Year to you under the most splendid sun of Mexico. Here the wind blows and the whole house whistles. I have the impression of being in *Wuthering Heights*. You told me that in 2007 almost all tours by your theatre have been cancelled. I am sure that for you it will be a way to discover new paths. Of course, it is serious, but I like it when you work against the current.
>
> Since I'm in the mood for pious wishes at the dawning of this new year, an insane desire has come over me: to tell you what I would like to read in your future book. (I imagine you under a scorching sun putting in order the bricks which you will then reduce to a joyful chaos.) It is obvious that I am not speaking of what I want you to write, but of what I would like to read between one line and another in the midst of your surfeit of threads. I would like a confrontation between the image of today's Odin, so called 'old' or simply different, and that image of the young or mature Odin that you all still drag behind you (because it is present in your books, in the love the spectators have for you and in your popular image), like a mother cat dragging its placenta behind it. Yes, I know: you have already made a performance about old age. Or rather two. But it is not the same.
>
> I am speaking of a new trace – a new correspondence between theory and practice. Once you told me that young people who know

Odin Teatret only through books, remain a little disconcerted when first they see you and your actors. They don't recognise you. It seems to me, nevertheless, that young people become deeply fascinated by your performances. But I would like to find, in a corner of your book, something about what you are now, and the great effort with which you have arrived there. I'm not talking about age. Is it enough to say that you are old in order to tell what you are and which is the tension pulling you now? Certainly not. Because I hope and I believe that this tension is not the wish to succeed in disappearing with honour.

I will stop here because I realise I am becoming less and less comprehensible. Take this letter for what it is: a declaration of affection.

Mirella

Today, as I swing between ardour and exhaustion, what do I carry with me from my past like a cat dragging its placenta?

There was once a father who was eating bread. His son asked him for some. The father gave him a stone and continued his meal. Then he began to eat a fish. His son asked for some. The father took a snake and handed it to his son. This time the son knew what to do: he killed the snake with the stone. This was the first thing the father taught his hungry son: to kill the snake. The son who had learnt to kill the snake did not thus become less hungry. He saw his father eating an egg. Starving, he did not ask any more: he clutched the stone and rushed at his father, who gave him the egg out of which appeared the poisonous tail of a scorpion. So the son, who had learned to kill, also learned to die and to save his father.

In order not to die as a son, I had to grow, to become a father able to procure what is necessary and yet *incapable* of forgetting the hunger from when I was a son.

More than 50 years ago, when I dreamt of becoming a director, theatre was for me synonymous with revolt. I found it in the theatre of Brecht, in his exhortation to commitment and struggle against injustice and indifference. It took time – the meeting with Grotowski and the association with my actors – for me to cease fooling myself. I understood that the revolt had to be turned against myself, against my idleness and my compromises, against the preconceptions of the culture with which I was impregnated, against that which I had been taught and which I wanted to scrape off my brain as a woman who wants to abort.

Today, my bones hurt, my sight is weakened and it is a lot harder to work 12 hours a day. But the unreasonable fire that I call revolt still keeps my need to do theatre alive. It is the same fire that feeds the scepticism of the father and the hunger of the son which cohabit within me. There exists a black and fleeting face of theatre with which I am in love. It is a path which ramifies and finds itself again, with no destination; a sea that I explore and which is a desert. I love theatre because it makes me feel like an emigrant who returns to his country to live there as a foreigner and without heirs.

I was in love with the black and fleeting face of theatre when I was young, and am still, more consciously, in my old age. It is the same impassioned yearning which has lasted for decades although I express it in different ways. I will try to explain it by telling of my meeting with two brothers who travelled the world, the one as the shadow of the other. They were the children of Silence, two angels with the appearance of hooligans. Their names were Disorder and Error.

I love this word, 'Disorder'. In the last years I have used it more and more when speaking of the theatre craft. I wanted to call this book *The Ritual of Disorder*, well aware of the misunderstandings that this term creates. For me it has two opposite meanings: disorder is the absence of logic and rigour characterising nonsensical and chaotic works; Disorder (with a capital letter) is the logic and rigour which provoke *the experience of bewilderment* in me and in the spectator.

Disorder is the irruption of an energy that confronts us with the unknown.

Today I know that with my performances I have always aimed to arouse Disorder in the mind and the senses of a particular spectator. I wanted to sow doubt, shake up his habits of foreseeing and judging. The spectator about whom I speak is not a stranger, someone to be convinced or conquered. I am speaking about myself. Whoever directs a performance is also its spectator. Disorder (with a capital letter) may be a weapon or a medicine against the disorder that besieges us, both within us and around us.

I know that no method exists to provoke Disorder in the spectator. Nevertheless, I have tried to come close to it through a particular form of self-discipline. This implied a separation, an anonymous and tacit revolt, from the correct and reasonable ways to consider the values, justifications and objectives of our profession. It was not a technique, rather an impulse which nobody could impose on me or teach me.

What can the origin of this impulse be? In 1954, on the outskirts of Accra, the capital of Ghana, then a British colony, Jean Rouch shot *Les Maîtres fous* (The Mad Masters), an ethnographical film which for European theatre of the second half of the twentieth century was like a prediction. This film was the testimony of another rationality, subterranean and subversive. It influenced Jean Genet, who wrote *Les Nègres*, it made an impression on Peter Brook and his production of *Marat-Sade* by Peter Weiss, and it accompanied Grotowski's reflections on the actor. Anecdotes and legends circulated in European theatre milieus concerning the influence of *Les Maîtres fous*. In those years the parallels and distinctions between theatre and ritual were discussed more and more frequently. Some artists were inventing a subtext which today is more than evident: theatre can be a clearing in the heart of a civilised world, a privileged place in which to evoke Disorder.

The ritual filmed by Jean Rouch exposes the mourning of individuals humiliated by the Western civilisation of progress. Its images, raw and deprived of any aesthetic consolation, mix paroxysm, theatrical game and cruelty from which exhales beauty and suffering coloured by a sense of liberty. Rouch forces us to observe Disorder linked to an existential revolt, to resistance against the order of the strongest in an attempt to break the chains.

We all have social, cultural, psychological, religious and sexual chains. I wonder how much, in the struggle against *my* chains, the influence of my ancestors has weighed? I speak of a few theatre reformers whom I recognise as *maîtres fous*, masters of Disorder, possessed by an almost shameless fervour which they expressed in words of fire and through rigorous practices.

When I think about the extremism of their thought, the protagonists of the theatre revolt in the twentieth century from Stanislavski on, become for me *maîtres fous*. In a climate of aesthetic, technical and economic renewal, they raised questions which were so absurd that they were met with indifference and derision. Since the incendiary core of these questions was wrapped in well-formulated theories, they were considered as attacks against the art of the theatre, or 'utopias', which is a harmless way of saying that we do not need to take them seriously. Here are some of these incendiary cores: to look for *life* in a world of papier-mâché; to let the *truth* stream into a world of disguises; to reach *sincerity* through fiction; to transform the training of the actor (an individual who imitates and represents people different from himself) into a path leading towards the *integrity* of a New Human Being.

Let's imagine an artist today applying for a grant from the Ministry of Culture to research the Truth through theatre. Or the director of a theatre school writing in its programme: 'here we teach acting with the aim of creating a New Human Being.' Or perhaps a director who demands from his actors to know how to dance because it mirrors the harmony of the celestial spheres. It would be permissible to consider them crack-pots.

Today it is not difficult to see in their apparent madness a sensible reaction to the strains of an epoch which was jeopardising the survival of the theatre. It is easy, today, to recognise their perspicacity, coherence and cleverness in the *upheaval* that the masters of Disorder brought to the theatre of their time. They rejected its century-old organisation, overturned hierarchies, sabotaged the well-tested communicative conventions between the stage and the audience and cut the umbilical cord with literature and superficial realism. They brutally stripped the theatre down and reduced it to its essence. They gave life to unsurpassed performances which were unimaginable in their radicalism, originality and artistic refinement in order to deny that theatre is *only* art. Each of them, with different words, stressed that the theatre's vocation was to break intimate, professional, ethical, social, religious or cultural chains. They burned entire rooms of the house in which they had grown. Occasionally, they set fire to the roof and the foundations.

We are used to reading the history of modern theatre upside-down. We don't start from the incendiary cores of the questions and obsessions of the masters of Disorder, but from the reasonableness or the poetry of their printed words. Their pages have an authoritative and persuasive tone. But for each of them there must have been nights and years of solitude and fear, suspecting that the windmills they tilted at were invincible giants.

Today we see them portrayed in picturesque photos: intelligent faces, well fed and ironically placid, like Stanislavski; suggestive begging kings, like Artaud; proud and aware of their own intellectual superiority, like Craig; eternally frowning and pugnacious, like Meyerhold. It is impossible to sense in each of these bright spirits the incapacity to forget or to accept their own invisible chains. We are unable to feel that their efficacy derives in part from the strain of tearing themselves away from a condition of impotent silence.

I think about this sort of silence which is not a choice, but a condition suffered as an amputation. This silence generates monsters: self-denigration, violence towards oneself and others, disconsolate sloth and ineffective anger. At times, however, this silence nourishes Disorder.

The experience of Disorder doesn't concern the categories of aesthetics. It happens when a *different reality* prevails over everyday reality: in the universe of plane geometry a solid body falls. As when unexpectedly, like lightning, death strikes a loved one; or when, in a split second, our senses ignite and we are aware of being in love. Or when in Norway, as a recent immigrant, I was contemptuously called 'wop' and a door was slammed in my face.

When Disorder hits us, in life and in art, we suddenly awaken into a world that we no longer recognise, and don't yet know how to adjust to.

Artistic paths are always individual and try to escape prefabricated mechanisms and recipes. These are paths which breathe and remain alive according to a personal need, which is also a mythology and a self-discipline.

For me, self-discipline has never corresponded to a voluntary adhesion to norms invented by others. It has always been the first step towards breaking the chains – one of the premises for Disorder in my mind and in my nervous system as a spectator. Disorder was born out of a clot of silence and had such a particular nature that it remained unknown even to me when I felt the first symptoms. Therefore no method can steer towards Disorder.

However, there existed a method when I came upon the brother of Disorder, Error. I experienced it as a collision between my wish for safety and my longing for an unknown energy which dismantled my psychic and intellectual ramparts.

Generally, when in my work I have tried to lean on safe rules, I was penalised for my naivety. If I resigned myself to the idea of a craft deprived of rules, I paid for this naivety with failures that were just as drastic. What is there, then, between rules and absence of rules? Between law and anarchy? If we think in the abstract, the answer is nothing. But practice has taught me that there *is* something there, simultaneously combining the rule and its negation.

This something is habitually called *error* and it is this that helped me out of the confusion. I used to recognise two types of error: solid and liquid. The *solid error* could be measured, shaped or modified, thus losing its quality of inaccuracy, misunderstanding, insufficiency or absurdity. It could be brought back to the rule and turned into order.

The *liquid error* could not be seized or appraised. It behaved like a spot of damp behind a wall. It signalled something that came from far away. I noticed that a certain scene was 'wrong', or that all my efforts to give birth to a particular performance were mistaken. But I forced myself to be patient and did not make immediate use of my intelligence. I felt that the 'wrong' scene or the mistaken structure of the performance ought not to be corrected, but followed up. Just the fact that they were so *obviously* wrong made me suspect that it was not merely foolish, but indicated a parallel path.

It happened that for months I was convinced that I was preparing a performance on the life of Bertolt Brecht, while my actors noticed blunders and misunderstandings piling up. I persisted in my efforts to pursue this failure until it branched out into a different performance: *The Million*, the story of a contemporary Marco Polo.

The same happened with the material which Iben Nagel Rasmussen presented to me for her new performance. It will be *Oedipus at Colonus*, I declared, and I was ready to explore blindness and vision, old age and the wandering life, loss of one's own city and retrieval of an inner centre. Iben was sceptical and confided her doubts to me. I continued for a long time with the Greek myth until I understood the direction in which the error was taking me. Thus the performance became *Itsi Bitsi*, the autobiography of two young people hungering after freedom.

During the preparation of a performance there could be suggestive scenes that clearly did not fit into the dramaturgical structure. My director's nervous system refused them. I knew that I had to change them radically or cut them out. During the rehearsals of *Mythos*, Julia Varley had created many materials to visualise Daedalus' labyrinth. She had improvised for weeks and found a variety of solutions out of a tangle of threads. Hundreds of metres of golden thread of various thicknesses, rolled up in balls and skeins, decorated her costume, and she unravelled them, forming a cobweb which entrapped the whole space. Her solutions determined routes, positions, rhythms and actions, implying the collaboration of the other actors, single or in groups. Despite the ingenuity of the results, I soon understood that I had to cut the whole lot. Yet I preserved this evident error until a few days before the first night. I let Julia develop her structure as a metastasis, an extraneous body which spread in the organism of the emerging performance, affecting the rhythms and the actions of the other actors. The error was erased: all the threads disappeared, but they had contributed to shape entire scenes with dynamisms and interactions, as well as the way one of the actors used the 700 kilos of gravel that he transformed into paths, a sea, a cemetery and a zen garden.

* * *

The classics say: life is a dream. It is not true. Life is a fairy tale. I discovered this when rehearsing *Andersen's Dream*. A fairy tale is a world of pure anarchy where those who stubbornly try to prevail, struggling along reasonable paths, lose. And those who behave foolishly finally win the princess. This world focuses on the need to break the chains that tie the stories to reality such as it is. That is why it is populated by monsters, shadows endowed with an autonomous life, men and women who are half animal, speaking corpses and objects which think and are alive. It is not the world of myth or imagination. It is one of confusion. It is a world that children love, but which doesn't love children. There they are abandoned and overpowered. They experience naked reality: anxiety and fear interspersed with flashes of unreasonable justice.

Why do I speak of the pure anarchy of fairy tales in connection to my theatre work?

While rehearsing, if confusion took the upper hand, everything became indistinct. The fog prevented me from seeing in any direction. To find my bearings, I forced myself to condense this confusion into solid errors which I might correct and eliminate, reinstating order into the situation. At the same time, I had to know how to detect the liquid errors on which to slide in directions where I had not imagined going, directions that I did not want or believe it possible to go.

If fairy tales can teach us something, then it is that error can be a blessing. The foolishness or the forgetfulness of a protagonist, a person mistaken for another, a prolonged sleep, a dead crow that you put in your pocket – these are the premises and conditions for an unexpected happy ending.

In the confrontation between the old Odin and the young Odin I can clearly perceive an indissoluble bond: the desire to break the chains, the hunger for Disorder, the panic in front of the sphinx – the new performance to prepare – the attraction to obstacles and errors. After more than 40 years, I can say that I have encountered errors that strengthened confusion, and errors which liberated when I had the adroitness to foresee their potential fruitfulness and make use of it. They were signs which detached themselves from the silence. They originated from that part within me which I did not dominate. They contained a message that one ancestor of mine, a master of Disorder, had entrusted me with to help break my chains.

2

ORGANIC DRAMATURGY AS A LEVEL OF ORGANISATION

Shamelessness was in the air.
She had even seen a dog with a bitch.
Clarice Lispector: *Miss Algrave*

The actor's dramaturgy

Over the years I got into the habit of defining the work of the actors as 'actor's dramaturgy'. With this term, I referred both to their individual creative contribution to the growth of a performance, and to an ability to root what they recounted into a structure of organic actions. Let me clarify at once what I mean by 'organic'.

The movement of another person evokes the onlooker's own experience of this same movement. The visual information generates an embodied kinaesthetic commitment in the spectator. Kinaesthesia is the internal sensation of our own movements and tensions, as well as those of others, in our own body. This means that the tensions and modifications in the actor's body provoke an immediate effect in the body of the spectator up to a distance of about 10 metres. If the distance is greater, this effect diminishes and disappears. This was one of the reasons why Odin Teatret's spectators were placed only a few metres from the actors.

The visible and the kinaesthetic are inseparable: what the spectator sees produces a bodily reaction which affects the interpretation of what he sees without his being aware of it. This bond between the actor/dancer's dynamisms and those of the spectator has been defined as 'kinaesthetic empathy'. Thus, by 'organic' I mean the actions that unleash a kinaesthetic commitment and are sensorially convincing for the spectator, whatever the convention and genre used by the actor. In my book *The Paper Canoe*, I described the principles of building a scenic presence from a historical perspective, although I did not use the term 'actor's dramaturgy'. In a performance, it is above all the actor's dramaturgy which has an impact on the nervous system of the spectator.

'A writer may well build castles in the air, but they must rest on foundations of granite.' This declaration by Ibsen about literary composition refers to the dialectics of autonomy and dependence, anarchy and discipline which also characterise the dramaturgy of the actor and the director. A performance must possess a coherence based on the actors' presence – or scenic *bios* – independently from the story which it tells. This coherence convinces at the level of the senses. The granite foundations of the performance are its organic dramaturgy, that is, its ability to engage and persuade the spectators' senses.

When I spoke of the dramaturgy of the actor, I intended to underline the existence of the actor's logic which did not correspond to my intentions as a director, nor to those of the author. The actor drew this logic from her biography, from her personal needs, from her experience and the existential and professional situation, from the text, the character or the tasks received, and from the relationships with the director and with the other colleagues.

The dramaturgy of the actor helped me to consider his contribution not as an interpretation of a text and a character, but as a composition with a value in itself. Thus the three levels of organisation – organic, narrative and evocative – could be developed autonomously and then blended. Without this independent process, to my eyes, an actor was not an actor. He could function in a performance, but was merely functional material in my hands as director. The dramaturgy of the actor was the measure of his autonomy as an individual and as an artist.

The concept of the dramaturgy of the actor implied that my results as director did not derive only from my personal creativity and technical know-how, but was deeply influenced and shaped by my actors' creativity.

It is often claimed that the actors' task consists in digging down within themselves to justify the psychology of the character to be interpreted. This vision is often applied to a theatre whose aim is the *mise-en-scène* of dramatic literature.

The work of the actor appeared to me in quite a different light if I considered the performance as a *living organism which communicates*, and within which different dramaturgies cohabited. The actor's task was no longer to justify a character's psychology, but to develop his own dramaturgy through physical and vocal actions. This dramaturgy should give life to a *scenic presence*, which would set in motion my dramaturgy as director and, subsequently, that of the spectator.

Today I know that organic dramaturgy is the force which keeps the different components of a performance together, turning it into a sensorial experience. The organic dramaturgy is constituted by the orchestration of all the actors' actions which are treated as dynamic and kinaesthetic signals. Its aim is to create a *theatre which dances*. This orchestration produces a flow of physical stimuli, both necessary and unpredictable, which attract or repel the spectator's senses. They are artistic forms and biological signals addressing the reptilian and limbic parts of our brain. Sensuality and sensorial incitements hound the animal nature of the spectator.

The organic dramaturgy is the primary level of organisation of a performance. It is the earth in which I planted the roots of every performance of mine. The living roots of the performance are not a literary text, a story to be told or my intentions as director, but are a particular quality of the actors' physical and vocal actions: presence, scenic *bios*, organic effect, seductive persuasion, body-in-life.

The skill of my actors has been decisive for me. They had achieved, through long years of training and performances, the ability to compose actions, postures and rhythms that they knew how to repeat. The abundance and variations of this organic material allowed me to select and amalgamate different elements in a montage which overturned the spectators' expectations and mental patterns, enmeshing their senses and at the same time awakening thoughts, conjectures and doubts. If I succeeded in this, the performance would probably keep on living in the spectator as reflection and memory.

I have often affirmed that the performance is the *experience of an experience*. The spectator should intuit and grasp the sense of the story or of a succession of actions in a performance. Above all the spectator should live the performance emotionally, recalling it with the same personal implications and the same degree of ambiguity with which they live the usual and dramatic events of daily life. When, in a familiar and predictable situation, something unexpectedly strikes us as being unusual, our perception and awareness are sharpened. Our reactivity in front of a similar scene depends on how much we take for granted.

In order to reach this goal with the actor, I made use of a specific operation: *equivalence*. Tools or interventions are considered equivalent when, although different in shape or nature, they have equal values, produce equal effects or fulfil identical functions. The area of an apartment can be equivalent to the area of a garden or a balcony; helping a beggar can be equivalent to a prayer in the eyes of the gods. Killing a man or accomplishing an act of self-mutilation can both be understood as equivalent proof of devotion and courage; in the ancient exam system in China, knowledge of a particular poetic canon constituted the evidence of an equivalent competence in public administration.

This *principle of equivalence* has often been applied by Etienne Decroux, for example, when he asked for the legs do the 'work' of the arms. According to him, the action of pushing a closed door became clearer and more realistic to the spectator, if the mime made the legs execute the work which, in daily life, was carried out by the arms. In an analogous way, in my performances, I might let a vocal action replace a physical one and a stare be the equivalent of a piece of dialogue. In *Andersen's Dream*, in the fight between the soldier and his shadow, the sudden scream of an actress corresponded to the fist that knocked one of the characters to the ground. In *Brecht's Ashes*,

Kattrin, the mute daughter of Mother Courage, beat the blades of shears against each other accompanied by a surge of inarticulate cries in an attempt to waken the city of Halle from a night-time attack by hostile soldiers. A young Nazi disarmed her with a gaze.

Real actions, improvisation and score

When in the training or during rehearsals I divided any situation (like writing a letter and putting it into an envelope, peeling an apple or picking up a coin from the ground) into smaller and smaller segments, I reached an indivisible point, a barely perceptible atom: a minute dynamic form which nevertheless had consequences for the tone of the whole body. This minute dynamic form was called *a real action* by me and my actors. It could be microscopic, just an impulse, however it radiated within the whole organism and was immediately sensed by the nervous system of the spectator.

At Odin Teatret, the dramaturgy of the actor was not a way of interpreting, but a technique to perform *real actions* in the fiction of the scenic space.

It has been fertile for our work that the actor's actions followed a dynamic logic which was independent from the narrative meaning. This logic often referred to the capacity to display the *equivalent of the energy* (quality of tensions, dynamic design, effort, acceleration, manipulation, etc.) necessary for an action from his score, even when this action was modified. For example, the actor had slapped someone, but the director had changed it into a caress. Although the actor moulded the dynamic design as if to caress, she kept the original tensions of striking a blow. The real dynamic *information* was thus retained, but appeared in a different *form*. The spectator's kinaesthetic sense (or empathy) recognised the dynamisms of striking a blow, but this sensorial information did not correspond to what he was seeing: a caress.

It is undeniable that, in the daily reality as in the extra-daily one of theatre, a *real action*, even if reduced to its impulse, possesses a strength of sensorial persuasion which produces an *organic effect* – that is, one of life and immediateness – on the spectator's nervous system. It suffices to think of the feints in boxing and dribbling in football which are precise impulses of real actions provoking an instant response in the adversary.

Although sport is the practice which allows us to understand best what a real action is, I defined it to myself in a less competitive way: a gentle breath of wind on an ear of corn. The corn is the attention of the spectator. It is not shaken as by a gust in a storm, but that gentle breath is just enough to upset its perpendicularity.

When I indicated the action to an actor, I suggested recognising it by elimination, distinguishing it from a simple 'movement' or 'gesture'. I told him: an action is your smallest perceptible impulse and I identify it by the fact that even if you make a microscopic movement (the tiniest displacement of the hand, for example) the entire tonicity of your body changes. A real action produces a change in the tensions in your whole body, and subsequently a change in the perception of the spectator: then your action is sensed, kinaesthetically, in an analogous way. The action originates in the spinal cord. It is not the wrist which moves the hand, not the shoulder or elbow which moves the arm, but the dynamic impulse is rooted in the torso.

It is obvious that the organic action was not enough. If, in the end, it was not enlivened by an inner dimension, then the action remained mute – *did not communicate* – and the actor appeared to be predetermined by the form of his score.

The character's personality, nature, profession and psychology could be important information and a concrete point of departure for performing real actions. But at Odin Teatret, the actors reached this objective using, above all, various improvisation techniques to create *a score of real actions*.

In general, the term 'improvisation' refers to at least three quite different procedures. Improvisation may be understood as the creation of actor's material. It is a process which gives life to a succession of physical or vocal actions starting out from a text, a theme, images, mental or sensorial associations, a painting, a melody, memories or fantasies.

In the second procedure, improvisation is synonymous with variation. The actor develops a theme or a situation by alternating and combining material which is already incorporated. The elements, previously assimilated, appear 'spontaneously' and assume different meanings according to the options, relationships, succession, rhythm and context. This was the type of improvisation used by European actors from the *commedia dell'arte* until Stanislavski and the reformers of the twentieth century.

The third procedure is far more subtle. Here improvisation means individualisation. Evening after evening the actor infuses life into the character's actions, repeating a score which is often fixed down to the smallest detail. It would appear that everything is established and that possibilities for variations or new choices are excluded. Nevertheless this type of improvisation is the most common in an actor's daily practice. It is the capacity 'to interpret' their scores every evening with different nuances – as a pianist might interpret a composition by Beethoven.

At Odin Teatret, the term *score* referred to:

- the general design of the form in a sequence of actions, and the evolution of each single action (beginning, climax, conclusion);
- the precision of the fixed details of each action as well as of the transitions connecting them (*sats*, changes of direction, different qualities of energy, variations of speed);
- the dynamism and the rhythm: the speed and intensity which regulated the *tempo* (in the musical sense) of a series of actions. This was the metre of the actions with their micro-pauses and decisions, the alternation of

long or short ones, accented or unaccented segments, characterised by vigorous or soft energy;
- the orchestration of the relationships between the different parts of the body (hands, arms, legs, feet, eyes, voice, facial expression).

The creation of a score with the subsequent phases of working out, developing and eliminating or adding details took place according to an exacting process in which I recognised the actor's patience and refusal of easy solutions. This attitude and awareness had been incorporated in the training: the incisiveness of scenic presence depended on the inner justification, on precision and the ability to preserve the smallest details.

A score began to live only after it was fixed and repeated over a long period of time.

The score was the objective demonstration of the subjective world of the actor. It allowed the meeting with the director who *elaborated* it according to shared artisanal criteria. The score was the search for order so as to give space to Disorder.

The term *elaborate* was fundamental in our working jargon and in our practice. This word had multiple meanings implying different and even opposing working procedures, for example, developing and expounding the actor's material resulting from an improvisation or a sequence of actions which he had deliberately structured. But *elaboration* also signified the distillation of this material through radical modifications and cuts. It involved the working out of variations, the polishing and care for details in order to make them stand out, the alteration of the actions' form while preserving their original tensions (their dynamic information). Elaboration encompassed changes in the rhythm and in direction in space, the establishing of micro-pauses between one action and another and an arrangement of the different parts of the body (feet, arms, facial expressions) which differed from the original material.

So when I write that as a director I *elaborated* the actor's material, I mean that I was using one of these technical procedures.

When an actor improvised, he went fishing for material from which later to distil (to elaborate) a score. It would have been foolish to fish with nets with holes through which fish brought to the surface could escape. For me, an improvisation had value only if I was able to utilise its entirety as a fragment of living tissue to be inserted and developed into the overall organism of the performance.

One of my first requests to the actors was that they had to learn to repeat an improvisation. They had to be able to replicate their improvisation in the exact same variety of postures and dynamisms, introverted and extroverted attitudes, temporary halts, hesitations, accelerations and plurality of rhythms. It was easy to improvise, much harder to memorise the improvisation. The actor reconstructed step by step what he had done with the help of fellow actors who had noted down his patterns of gestures and actions, their directions, the increase and decrease of speed, sudden stops and prolonged pauses. It often happened that we recorded the improvisation with a video. Everything was on the screen, in every detail, with the actor's frequent surprise and often dismay because he was unable to believe that he had performed that particular gesture or grimace. It was as if these belonged to somebody else. It took time to take on this behaviour which was felt as extraneous, and make it one's own again through assiduous repetition.

Perseverance, concentration and knowledge of procedures for remembering were necessary to fix an improvisation. I demanded that the actor render perceptible concrete or imagined situations, real or psychic events, the landscapes and epochs that he had crossed in the inner reality of the improvisation. But the flora and fauna of his inner microcosm, which had surfaced during this process, were a friable and fugitive reality like snow ready to melt.

To my eyes, it was a sign of experience and skill to know how to preserve the snow of the improvisation, without letting it melt or become slush. It was this ability to fix an improvisation that characterised the Odin actors. An aspect of their craft consisted in making an inner process perceptible through precise vocal and physical actions.

In the organic dramaturgy, *precision* was for me the essential sensory information which induced a reaction in the spectator. The precision revealed the *need* for a determined action and at the same time its inner coherence.

We used or we invented techniques for remembering that allowed us to reconstruct and recreate the whole variety of impulses, gradations, dynamisms and forms of an improvisation.

A thread guided the actor in finding again the direction of the paths which divided and merged together in his body-mind while improvising. It was a thread made of stimuli, of mental energy and somatic memory, absolute subjectivity and imaginative freedom, permeated by timelessness and biographic episodes.

This thread was the *subscore*. It was what the actor heard, saw and reacted to. In other words, the way he recounted the improvisation to himself through actions. This tale involved rhythms, sounds and tunes, silences and suspensions, fragrances and colours, people and clusters of contrasting images: a stream of stimuli or inner actions which turned into precise dynamic forms.

Subscore

The subscore is a technical element belonging to the particular creative logic of every actor. It is found under various names in all theatrical genres and styles. It is one of those 'recurring principles' which I have described in *The Paper Canoe: A guide to theatre anthropology*, which I have defined as a pragmatic science and a study *about* and *for* the performer. In this book I delved into the distinction between daily and extra-daily body technique, designating the actor's extra-daily technique as a particular use of the body with the aim of achieving a scenic presence. There are some principles which are always to be found at the foundation of the performers' scenic presence in all traditions and genres. Such 'recurring principles' are alteration of balance, emphasis on opposing tensions within the body, equivalence, consistent inconsistency, omission, and also subscore.

The subscore is an inner support, a hidden scaffold which actors sketch for themselves without intending to act it out. The subscore should not be confused with the meaning that the score will assume for the observer. Without a subscore, what the actor presents is not the creation of a subjective stream of reactions, an organic line driven by an inner coherence, but gesticulation, movements and random displacements.

There are many ways of activating a subscore. These depend on the actor's dramaturgy, which is different according to each specific technical tradition. Stanislavski's subtext is a particular form of subscore built up from the actor's personal interpretation of the character's intentions and unexpressed thoughts. According to Brecht's vision, the subscore is a continuous dialogue the actor uses to question the historical truth of the character who, unknowingly, is driven by the author's subjectivity. In codified genres (the various classical Asian theatres and classical ballet) the subscore concerns the sophisticated system of rules belonging to each tradition.

My comparative studies with performers from different traditions clearly showed that it was not important for the subscore to be made up of material which can be appreciated as intelligent, imaginative or original, like a powerful piece of music or a good story. It may be a nursery rhyme or an anecdote which is insignificant for anybody else. The subscore's quality is unimportant from other people's point of view. But from the actor's point of view it has to be extremely significant. It may be something childish, regarded as worthless or nonsense by those on the outside. But it should be one of those pieces of nonsense which has stuck in our mind and been carried with us for years. It must be *our own*, without taking into account how it appears to others.

Odin actors built up their subscores in total freedom. In the beginning I used to set them the theme of an improvisation. Later they chose themselves and got inspired in an autonomous way by points of departure and procedures which varied: situations described by a text or invented by their imagination, associations, memories, photographic images, the subject or the dynamics of a painting, the lyrics of a song, a poem or a story, the postures of a series of statues, a melody, a succession of actions which, after being performed in their natural dimension, were miniaturised.

I have always considered my actors' improvisations as the ability to conduct a dialogue with themselves, dreaming while awake, an active meditation, a personal path on an inner journey which left behind it a wake of perceptible reactions. It was this wake of memorised reactions that I began to elaborate, even changing it radically, until it became for me a coherent sequence of dynamic peripeteias: *bios* (life), scenic presence ready to represent and acquire a meaning by being connected to a text, to the score of another actor, to an object, a melody or a light. During this initial process of elaboration I began to form the first relationships, establishing links which could be logical or analogical, associative or rhythmic. I continued for a long time the elaboration of an actor's score with the intention of shaping dense actions impregnated with conflicting information, a living oxymoron. I composed with care this mosaic of discordant dynamisms and meanings in order to provoke gaps and imbalance in the spectator's perception in relationship to the obvious context of a particular scene.

The elaboration of the score consisted in merging and furbishing forms, dynamisms and rhythms: a process of discipline and precision in which the actor's aim was to render perceptible his own inner process to the spectators. It was a psycho-physical activity through which the actor entered into another state of consciousness, with the probability of becoming incandescent, transparent, bright: a *dilated body*. To dilate did not mean to emphasise, to exceed in vitality and overact. 'Dilation' was a consequence. It resulted from the search for what was essential, from the erasing of superfluous gestures and movements, from the technical ability to know how to preserve the action's energy even though the volume or the pattern of its external form was reduced. The secret of the *dilated body* consisted in safeguarding the dynamic nucleus of the action: the impulse.

The score was a shell that might contain Disorder: a pearl of light.

There are and have always been actors of prodigious effectiveness who have never fixed the pattern of their actions on stage. These have never thought in terms of a score, avoiding every sign of visible precision that might be controlled from outside. Why then did I insist with my actors on the importance of precision in fixing and knowing how to repeat the dynamic pattern of their actions? On the value of their own independence from the intentions of the director and the writer? On the coherence of their score and subscore?

I had noticed that a score was a factor contributing to the actor's *effectiveness in his relationship with the spectator*. The long process of distillation of a score, with its artificiality and awareness in choosing each detail, eliminated all superfluous elements. This formal quintessence presented itself as a compact structure of somatic and vocal dynamisms which were the manifestation of the processes of the actor's subscore and of his specific conditions during that evening's performance. The score reminded me of Aladdin's lamp: a metal oil lamp which, at the actor's will, released a spirit which transfigured it. I was always impressed by the transformation of my actors. It was as if they touched a switch and were suddenly inundated by light. Their immobility, their actions, silences and excesses seemed to spring from a zone of uniqueness. They appeared to be in a different state of awareness, charged with determination, cold blood and suggestive energy. It was not trance. It was the actor's condition after he had broken through the sound barrier: he had overcome his technique, forgotten his score and subscore and was transfigured in what I called a *body-in-life*. But score and subscore continued to operate in spite of him. As a spectator I experienced double vision: I saw a fictive theatrical character and the Disorder of the actor's individual microcosm; the artificiality of the score and the organic process which shook it; the coherence of an external discipline and the dark forces which made it mysterious for me. This double vision contributed to making the performance the experience of an experience.

It was not the simple repetition of actions which brought the actor to this state of consciousness and alertness, radiating particular energies. It was the integration of the score with the multiple levels of the subscore as well as the interaction between inner motivations, their perceptible signs and what was happening all around. Technically, this process took place respecting the dynamisms and rhythms of the score's actions, but in a permanent state of micro-improvisation.

But I also insisted on the score's importance because the autonomous coherence of the actions (independently of the significance they assumed in the performance) bestowed a particular and precious gift on the actor's material: it became *amphibious*, capable of passing from one context to another without withering away, able to mutate without losing the roots which kept it alive and continuing to induce an organic effect in the spectator.

I have often had a particular experience when working with Odin actors and with those of Asian classical traditions who were accustomed to performing the same scores for years and years. I could take a whole score or parts of it, alter it, de-contextualise it, let it undergo innumerable modifications without it losing its associative power and organic effect: its *identity*.

I had the feeling that this autonomy of the score was the consequence of time, as if the years had eroded the bonds keeping the score tied to the situation for which it had been created. Safeguarded by time and repetition, the score had turned into an independent form, animated by an inner improvisation.

I knew what the score was for the actor: a pattern of actions defined in every detail, which may be carried out according to different rhythms, shaped and reshaped, cut and edited. I also knew that, for the actor, every score had an inner lining, a subscore which motivated his actions with a particular quality of energy.

But the score's *identity* depended neither on the external pattern of the actions nor on its subscore. This identity originated from a design which was incorporated to such an extent that it could be changed externally and lose everything except its essential profile, its quality and source: *the permanent improvisation*.

For my actors, it was evident what kept a score alive just after being fixed: it was the search for the original model, the effort to faithfully replicate the first improvisation with all its details. But after having played a performance 40 or 50 times, I noticed that an improvisation emerged from within every score. It was this zone of improvisation which kept it alive and prevented it from becoming mechanical.

Repetition and duration transform a score into a plant producing seeds which may grow in different forms, yet always of the same species.

Inner music was the name given by Stanislavski to the organic quality of the action as the actor perceived it within himself: a tempo-rhythm of the actor's mental and nervous impulses.

I interpreted *inner music* as a fragile and active seed which could not be called *subscore* and which was not a precise structure of actions, but contained the *programme* (coded instructions) for different structures with the same organic quality.

This *programme* comprised three diverse perspectives: form, rhythm and flow. These terms do not indicate different technical principles or aspects of the composition. They designate three facets of the same reality. I distinguished them temporarily when working, well aware that this distinction was a fiction which was useful for research and for the creative process.

An actor and a director may treat a physical score as:

- a form, a dynamic pattern in space and time resulting from an improvisation or a composition;
- a rhythm, a scansion and alternation of *tempi*, accents, speed, acceleration and energy colours and nuances;
- a river bank which controls the energy's organic flow.

In the practical work I swung relentlessly from one to the other of the following perspectives: form, rhythm, colour of the energy and flow (multiple and diverging rhythms). I dissociated them to set up a tension between them. I could stress one of them in order to prevent the supremacy of any of the others. I searched for ways to blend them in densely rich contrapositions. I established an antagonism between them or dissolved their contrast into an indivisible identity.

During the performance, the spectators ought not to distinguish between the action's flow, rhythm and form. In the same way, they should not be able to separate the physical action from the mental, the body from the voice, the words from the intention, the organic effect from the meaning, the performer's pre-expressive level from his expressive effectiveness, nor the actor's dramaturgy from that of a fellow actor or the director.

A theatre which dances

If I moved from the actor's perspective to that of the spectator, I could translate Stanislavski's *inner music* with another metaphor: *colours of energy*.

This was one way to indicate the body-mind, the fusion of score and subscore, the somatic and psychic entirety which is the aim of the actor's dramaturgy.

To me, the actor's score has always had the features of a dance sequence: a non-narrative alternation of tonic leaps of energy, and a simultaneity of tensions and formal patterns which awoke an impression of vulnerability, roughness, exuberance or delicacy, seduction or aggression: a theatre which dances.

This dance takes place through a succession of energy expansions and contractions and is one of the many pieces of information which the performance radiates. Other pieces of information are: the genre (theatre, dance, mime, opera, etc.), the performance's structure, its aesthetics, the story it *wishes* to tell, the story it tells *in spite* of itself, how it tells it, the context in which it has been prepared, the context in which it is performed and the particular value it acquires for each spectator.

I conclude with an observation which throws light on the absolute subjectivity of my choices as director in relationship to the actor's dramaturgy. An action (the smallest change of tonicity in the torso of the actor) had for me a complementary nature. I could model it following contradictory categories: as pure dynamism (dance) or as carrier of a clear meaning for me, yet ambiguous for the spectator. I could turn it into a rhythmic entity or into an 'open' action that the spectator would have filled with his own specific sense. I could treat it as a vague associative sign or as a clear conceptual expression, as a stimulus of energy or as a narrative indication for me and/or for the spectator. It depended on the circumstances and on the web of relationships and references in which I inserted this action.

I carefully appraised the effect of an action in relationship to those preceding and to those following. The action was always integrated in a concatenation and in a simultaneity of other actions, which made it interfere and interact with those of the other actors.

An action was always an interaction. This is not a play on words, the consequences were evident. Its external manifestation interacted with the inner one (the subscore).

As director, I applied myself to exploiting the actions' complementarity and to consolidating their ambiguity by disseminating them into layers of light and darkness.

The ritual of Disorder

Martin Berg, a close Danish friend who offered his help as publisher and writer to Odin Teatret, used to say that at the age of 50 a son should write the biography of his father: the origin of all of our different faces is buried there. He did it. I would not have been able to. I ignore everything about my own father, about his fatherless childhood, what he thought about love, the ideals for which he fought as a volunteer in the Spanish Civil War and in the conquest of Abyssinia, his feelings during his last years when his life and world were crumbling miserably. When I was 50, the people who had known him were dead and I lived among foreigners, 3,000 kilometres and many borders away from his grave.

I remember him vaguely: strong, respected, even feared. Yet he was a death-marked body barely alive who moved around supported by the slender figure of my mother. Fatherly authority emerges from my memory as a 'knot', a dance of embracing opposites: man and woman, grace and disgrace, infirmity and vigour, youth and decrepitude.

My brother and I slept together in the same bed. In the same room, not far from us, my father rested, breathing heavily, alone in a big double bed. My mother was not there, she sat outside on the staircase, staring in front of her. She wore a dressing-gown over her nightdress, a black object in her lap: my father's army gun. Night after night I awoke to the same scene, and I moved closer to my brother without understanding what my mother was doing there, alone on the steps with that weapon.

My father was a fascist officer in command of a legion of black-shirts and had fought with Rommel at El Alamein in North Africa. He had been repatriated through ill health. After World War II, communists in Italy often took the law into their own hands to take revenge against their political enemies. My mother waited for them on the staircase of our house surrounded by the intense fragrance of the climbing jasmine in the courtyard below, and whose flowers she placed on my father's bedside table every evening to perfume his dreams.

My father died two years after the war ended. Most of the time he was bedridden. My mother washed him, patiently cut his beard with nail scissors, helped him to get up, dressed him as you would a child and supported him as she led him to the fishermen's tavern at the corner of our street. Sitting at a table, my father chatted with the customers whom he did not know, but who recognised the ex- fascist general.

I am incapable of putting into words the bond he had with his two sons. He loved us; this is the feeling that remains in the murky depth of my memory. But when my brother and I did not respect the tacit norms of home discipline, he took off his belt, we bent down dropping our trousers and he struck without hesitation.

One evening in June when my brother and I were playing alone at home and my father and mother had gone to dinner with friends, we heard the sound of horses' hooves in our narrow street. From the window we saw strangers lifting our father out of a carriage and carrying him in their arms. He was dying.

My mother busied herself, declining the help of her mother-in-law. She summoned my brother and me, giving each of us tasks. I had to run to the shop where they sold ice. It was needed to stop the haemorrhage. The shop would probably be shut since it was late. I had to shout underneath the window and wake up the owner. Then I should run to the doctor to make him come quickly. I did not have to wait for him. Instead I had to continue to the priest's house and inform him. He already knew. He would come in haste with the holy sacraments. Then I could return home.

My mother insisted that the two sons should witness their father's death. The doctor, an old family friend, tried to dissuade her: the agony would be long and violent and would upset the children. Grandmother Checchina tried with her authority, the priest with reasoned arguments. My mother, stubbornly, did not give in.

Time passed. I looked at the features of the man who only a few hours earlier had resembled my father. Now he was fading away to the sound of death rattles. Reality had lost its dramatic charge and was replaced with tiredness and an ache in my back. I wished the end would come soon. Finally silence fell in the middle of the night, at three o'clock. My mother stopped wiping the sweat from her husband's face and opened the window to let his soul fly out. I was 10 years old.

Seen objectively, that June night was not excruciating. It planted a seed that grew into a sense of absence. The seed began to germinate at the funeral as anger when I felt the pity of others: poor child, he has lost his father. The anger was directed at my brother, who showed his pain and wept. I could not. Later came self-commiseration, pain in observing my mother's loneliness, the constant feeling of absence: the thousand grimaces of an inner suffering. His death was not a climax, only the origin of a bomb with delayed action.

There are nights that last a lifetime.

My mother put us children to bed, then accompanied my grandmother to her room and remained alone with her husband's corpse. She washed him, cut his beard, manicured his nails, dressed him in white pyjamas, long since prepared for the occasion, and joined his hands in prayer. Thus we found him next day, my brother and I, as well as the dozens of relatives, friends, neighbours and unknown visitors: an intermittent procession who stared at him in silence, wept, murmured prayers, made the fascist salute or crossed themselves, embraced the fatherless children and expressed their grief to my mother and my grandmother in compassionate words and gestures.

The whole house was invaded by people who were familiar and others never seen before, seated on chairs along the walls of every room. Some were bashful and taciturn, others told anecdotes about my father, tittering while drying their tears. All warmly greeted the new arrivals who had gravely entered the room where my father lay in the wide double bed beneath an embroidered sheet, his hands folded in prayer and with a white scarf around his head to keep his jaw from falling. He looked as though he had toothache, stern and helpless. Around him sat the people closest to him: my mother, some aunts and uncles, cousins, childhood friends, companions of the same political belief and comrades in war. The new arrivals bade him farewell each in their own way: in silence, in sobs, kneeling, barely touching the dead body, kissing his forehead. Then they turned to the living, hugging my mother and consoling her; at times it was she who comforted them with handshakes and interminable embraces. With soundless footsteps they entered my grandmother's room and a similar scene repeated itself.

Consòli, *'consolations', arrived incessantly, sent by friends, relatives and neighbours: meals for 24 people, cases of refreshments, dozens of* spumoni, cassate *and other sorts of ice cream, huge trays with cups of coffee and marzipan sweetmeats. The family, intent on confronting the sudden grief, was unable to carry out the household chores and feed themselves and their guests. People ate, drank and mumbled while fingering their rosaries, a mother unbuttoned her shirt, bared her breast and thrust it in the mouth of her whimpering child while a group of men stood around smoking and discussing intensely in low tones. My brother and I, like two outsiders, frightened yet curious, went from one room to another in this bustle which recalled an open air café or the people streaming out of church after mass. It was like a performance of* Odin Teatret*.*

There was a scream, confusion and the agitated cries of women. Men raced to my father's room to hold back his brother Aldo who, shouting his name, threw himself on his dead body, shook the bed to wake him and lifted him to make him stand. With great effort, a cluster of men dragged him away, while my mother tried in vain to calm him. At last grandmother Checchina succeeded. Years later I met this same kind of reaction (pain, but above all anger and resentment toward the person who, by dying, abandons us) in a book by Renato Rosaldo, the anthropologist who had studied the state of running amok among the Dayaks in Borneo. He himself had been overpowered by the same frenzy when his wife had died in an accident.

My mother never married again. Her father, an admiral, prohibited her: the widow of an officer who had died defending his country does not seek another husband. Many years later, in one of my visits to her house in Monte Mario in Rome, my mother confided to me that she had assisted at the final agony and washed the dead bodies of five men: her husband, her father, her brother, a cousin and a close family friend. Another time she confessed that one of the most beautiful days in her life had been when she took possession of her house in Monte Mario, all for herself, far away from mother-in-law, father and other family authorities.

I liked to visit my mother in her house in Rome. It was not like returning home (my 'home' was where I had grown up in Gallipoli), but I liked the way she loved and took care of it. To the furnishings and knick-knacks of the past, I watched her add lacquer furniture and Chinese, Japanese, Korean, Afghan curios, but above all books – thousands of books covering wall after wall. These belonged to my brother Ernesto, who deposited them there during pauses from his wandering life in Asia. Sitting in the kitchen, I asked her questions while savouring my favourite dishes from Gallipoli: fried cauliflower with anchovies and capers, aubergine alla fungitiello, peperonata*.*

In this way I came to know why she kept guard with a gun in her lap in Gallipoli, immediately after the war. It was she who told me about my paternal ancestors. About my great-grandfather Emanuele, a republican doctor, follower of Garibaldi and a fighter for the unification of Italy, who conspired against the king of Naples, was condemned to jail and escaped in exile to Florence. And then about my grandfather Ernesto, my father's father, a socialist lawyer, who published the newspaper Spartaco *and who had committed suicide, leaving his wife – my grandmother Checchina – with two children, one aged two years, the other a few months old: my father and my uncle Aldo.*

I asked my mother why my father had become a fascist in this republican family, known for its solidarity with the 'insulted and injured'. She did not know the answer and knew only that my father, lying about his age, had enrolled in the Arditi brigade during World War I at only 16. After the Russian cruiser Aurora *opened fire on the Czar's Palace, the Spartakists in Germany fought in the streets against the* junkers *and the FIAT workers in Turin occupied their factory, my father marched on Rome with Mussolini in the belief that they were defending the values of European civilisation against decadence, corruption and Bolshevism.*

It was strange to get to know one's own father through the tales of his wife. Once I asked her if she loved him when she married him. She did not hesitate to answer affirmatively. 'But I am happy that he is dead,' she said. 'I will be spared the pain of losing him now.'

In 1993, Odin Teatret was performing in the streets of Coyoacan, the neighbourhood of Mexico City where Trotski, Frida Kahlo and Diego Rivera had lived. Judy, my wife, phoned me from Denmark: 'It is not your mother; it is Ernesto.'

My brother had always boasted that he would not live to be more than 60. He had reached this age two weeks before, and I had pulled his leg about his credulous prophecy. They had found him on the floor in the room which he rented in Livorno. He was preparing his suitcase to travel to Algeria as consultant for a hotel under construction. A stroke had surprised him with a pair of socks in his hands. Listening to Judy's words, I did not feel any pain, only amazement: I thought about the shoe in Artaud's hand and of a poem by Ernesto:

What will I become?
A tree in Haiti
A wave in the Pacific
A seagull over the Ionian Sea
A cloud in Japan
A breeze at a regatta
A line in sanskrit
I
Who never change?

With time, my brother's absence, with whom I had shared a night which lasts a lifetime, has changed into a sense of solitude.

My mother was 80 when this happened. She was still vivacious and curious and had taken a degree in psychology at the University of the Third Age, did yoga, and travelled frequently abroad as chairwoman for the association of war widows. After the death of her first-born she decided to forget her pain. It is against nature, it is obscene that the child dies before the mother who has given birth to him. She did not speak to me any more about my brother and only saw her daughter-in-law and her grandchild unwillingly. Her memory began to crumble. Today, while I am writing under this radiant sky of Puerto Morelos, her mind has gone and she doesn't recognise me any more. The nobility, the sense of dignity, that form of anonymous courage I so loved in her have vanished into her slender and debilitated body. A smile appears often on her face; she seems at peace with herself. I kiss her hand as I kissed the hand of the young woman who sustained my father, and who always supported me in the moments of decision, however incomprehensible to her.

> *Thirty-two times I have carried the qualities of my father*
> *I threw almost all of them away on the edge of the road*
> *to have less weight on my shoulders.*
> *With grass in my mouth, I look on in awe.*
> *And the beam I cannot remove from my eyes*
> *begins to bloom in spring with the trees.*
>
> *(Yehuda Amichai)*

I don't know if I am inventing this or whether it is true. When putting me to bed and blessing me on the chaotic day of my father's death, my mother whispered with a kiss: what a day of Disorder, wasn't it?

Sonorous dramaturgy

In Chile, during General Pinochet's dictatorship, the poet Nicanor Parra, brother of the well-known singer Violeta, announced that he would publicly read one of his censured sonnets in a central square of Santiago. He stood up on the platform and remained in silence the time necessary for the reading of 14 lines. He received an ovation.

Silence too is a vocal action. The situation, shared by the Chilean poet and his listeners, made comprehensible and at the same time reversed the sense of his vocal action. The episode explains how much the context contributes to rendering a performance 'political', even if it is simply the public reading of a poem. Shared constraints, both for actors and spectators, allow this kind of communication to be appreciated in all its nuances.

Vocal actions

I have always experienced the voice as a material force which sets things in motion, leads, shapes and calms: an extension of the body. It manifests itself through precise actions provoking an immediate reaction in the person to whom they are directed. The voice is an invisible body which operates in the space.

When in 1966 Odin Teatret moved from Norway to Denmark, becoming a Scandinavian theatre laboratory, its Danish, Norwegian, Swedish and Finnish actors did not share the same language as their spectators. Until then our only performance had been based on a text by a Norwegian author, played by Norwegian actors for Norwegian spectators. I was obliged to devise an arrangement of vocal actions and peripeteias which could enthral the spectators independently of their comprehension of the words. Exclamations and calls, whispers, muttering, shouts, groans, laughter, sudden silence, crystal clear or hoarse tones, phrases modulated as nursery rhymes, psalms or traditional songs, intonations as litanies or animal sounds – bleating, neighing, twittering – were the basis for our sonorous dramaturgy. And, above all, during a dramatic climax, singing replaced words.

Our performances were consciously structured as a flow of vocal stimuli. This sonorous flow acted as music on which the words navigated in a language which often was not understood by the spectators.

In our first three productions (*Ornitofilene*, *Kaspariana* and *Ferai*), which were based on pre-existing texts, the actors spoke in their own Scandinavian languages. In *My Father's House* (1972), however, they did not speak their mother tongues and expressed themselves in an invented Russian. The vocal actions, stripped of the words' meaning, evoked associations and possible significations for the spectators. This experience made me discover the existence of the actor's vocal dramaturgy with an autonomous and coherent life of its own which could be detached from the meaning of the words.

When we speak, two levels of information interact simultaneously: the one is given by the words' meaning (verbal or semantic communication) and the other by the voice's particularities: tone, pitch, timbre, volume, intensity, musicality, dynamism (vocal or sonorous communication). According to experts, communication happens principally through the language's sonority and the physical reactions accompanying it, and only partly through its semantic aspect.

In my practice, dramaturgy was a succession and a simultaneity of events: organic, dynamic, rhythmic, narrative, sonorous, allusive and analogical. The orchestration of the vocal dramaturgy allowed me to build a constant tension between the sonorous communication and the semantic one by opposing, commenting on and unmasking the meaning of the words. I could modulate silence through almost inaudible sounds and enfold the action in music, making it dance.

I had read about this in Meyerhold and seen Grotowski apply it with his actors. But above all I had personally experienced it as an emigrant, forcing myself to find my bearings and decipher a universe of sounds which I was unable to grasp conceptually. When people spoke to me, what were they saying? Was it a threat, a prayer, an order, a compliment?

Odin Teatret's expatriation to Denmark strengthened my personal mythology as a budding director. One of my models was the Russian actress Alicja Koonen, wife of Tairov. I had read the descriptions of her legendary vocal suggestiveness: she did not interpret the text, she warbled it. Another memory did not abandon me. It was an evening in the students' club at the University of Oslo where the East German poet Stephan Hermlin read his poems. I found inexplicable the melodiousness of his native tongue, whose normally guttural sounds I associated with the Nazi barbarity of the recently ended World War II. I had the same amazing experience a couple of years later, listening to Brecht's actors at the Berliner Ensemble. But the strongest influence came from Grotowski, from the *inkantacje* of his actors, who pronounced the text as if it was a magic formula, a mysterious call, a chant or a litany.

Once in Denmark, all these models blended in my attempts to 'inform' the spectator through a sonority imbibed with associations and emotional reverberations. During training, the Odin actors distanced themselves from their 'natural' way of speaking. They worked every day, for years, to rediscover the potential variety which the voice possesses at birth and which wanes as we gradually master our mother tongue.

They trained to create a gamut of intonations, sounds and resonators; they reproduced the 'voice' of animals, objects, extra-terrestrial beings; they listened to records with songs from other cultures and imitated them; they repeated the melodic and rhythmic cadences of unknown languages and dialects. They spoke a text as a musical instrument, as the expression of a medium who tells episodes from a supernatural reality. Or it might be the voice of the

Santa Maria, the caravel which recalled its slow sailing in an endless desert of water, amid storms and dead calm, the sailors' wrath, Columbus's solitude and the screeching comments of seabirds perched in the rigging.

In the same way as we accomplish a physical action (cutting a slice of bread, for example), I made my actors perform the same action with the voice. They had to know the text by heart, and speak it fluently and without premeditation or interpretation, as we do in daily life when we don't act or fix our attention on the words. Speaking the text without the need to remember it, the actor could concentrate on executing *real vocal actions*: climbing a tree, swimming in a swimming pool, threading a needle and sewing on a button, describing a sunset, telling Anna Karenina's story or recreating a painting by Van Gogh. Every vocal action had its roots in the corresponding physical action, and the actor performed it with his whole body, well aware of synchronising the physical impulses with the vocal ones. Without this synchronisation, it was impossible to reach an organic effect.

Working in this way, the vocal dramaturgy became personalised and developed along individual paths. Today, the performances/working demonstrations of the Odin actors present their procedures for overcoming personal blocks, widening the voice range, combating mannerisms and creating vocal scores capable of remaining 'alive' and having an impact upon the spectator in spite of the language being incomprehensible.

Linguistic convention and continuous music

Each language has a specific sonorous nature and occupies a place in the spectator's imagination. The choice of a determined language or dialect provokes immediate reactions and connotations independent of the semantic content.

While rehearsing a production, I concentrated on making the spectators understand the linguistic convention used by the actors.

At times, as in *Kaosmos* or *Mythos*, each actor spoke his own language and the different tongues intertwined in a sort of musical composition, understandable in short fragments only to the spectators who knew them. At others, the actors expressed themselves in an invented tongue, thus building a sonorous homogeneity. This was the case with the Russian in *My Father's House* or the Coptic in *The Gospel according to Oxyrhincus*. Sometimes, their dialogues took place in existing languages, even if not comprehensible to the spectators. In *Come! And the Day will be Ours*, the pioneers spoke English with a foreign accent while the indigenous population spoke Quiché, Quechua, Sioux and Cheyenne.

The choice of the language (or the languages) had consequences also on the semantic level. A large part of my work on a performance consisted in creating a vocal universe with the aim of establishing an emotional dialogue with *each* spectator. However, at times, there were scenes or fragments whose text I wanted to be understood. So I devised stratagems and procedures to let spectators from different countries grasp the dialogue or the monologue in question. During rehearsals I worked on a double vocal dramaturgy: I respected the musical, melodic and rhythmic peculiarity of the language (or languages) in which the actors had created the performance, and at the same time decided the scenes to be translated into the different linguistic contexts. This double vocal dramaturgy threw up new problems of dramaturgical, rhythmic and organic montage.

In certain cases I inserted a simultaneous translation in the narrative dramaturgy of the performance, attaining an added grotesque effect. In *Brecht's Ashes*, for instance, Mack the Knife translated Bertolt Brecht's German into the language of the spectators: 'Mr Brecht affirms that . . .'. I always took into consideration the effect caused by the accent of the actor speaking a foreign language and I knowingly manipulated it to turn these inevitable circumstances into an estranging or meaningful quality.

The actor's vocal dramaturgy represented only a part of the performance's sonorous universe. This was composed by an intertwined plurality of sounds which contributed to determining the performance's flow.

The noises – steps, creaking of doors, objects which were displaced or fell and broke, dripping of water or bubbling of a boiling saucepan – emerged from the actions of the moment. The actor performed them in order to extract a gamut of variations. These were incorporated in the performance's soundtrack which was characterised by auditive associations and a simultaneity of diverging rhythms. The acoustic effects, amalgamated with the actor's vocal actions, composed a *continuous music* which was supposed to conjure up the performance even to a blind spectator.

Obviously, this continuous music was also made up of silences and real music. The latter was present in a mocking, sentimental or dramatic form which had a constant relationship with the other sounds which were not music in the strictest sense. The orchestration of the soundtrack permeated the entire performance cradling it, reining it in or shattering it. At the same time, this orchestration generated a current that transported or obstructed.

Often, in my early productions, I worked in the final phases of rehearsals with my eyes closed or in the next room, reacting as to a concert or a fairy tale told to a child only through acoustic peripeteias.

During the rehearsals of *My Father's House*, some actors learned to play a musical instrument according to a theatrical logic. They treated it as a *voice* which speaks, discusses or makes a speech: a controlled, lyrical, pedantic or sentimental one. For example, the voice of a prophet who seduces with words of fire or that of a conspirator on a dark night.

The actor was not just playing a melody, but theatricalised the action of emitting the sound as well as its result. The musical instrument became a prop, a part of the body, of the *persona*, an artificial or extra limb, an important element in composing the character's behaviour.

In *My Father's House*, the 'voices' of the recorder and the accordion belonged to two servants who spied on their masters. At times they commented ironically on the passions of the rich and the noble; at others, on the contrary, as obedient attendants, they busied themselves creating a romantic, wild or sensual environment for their masters. The voices of the instruments wanted to evoke the wind in the Siberian taiga, the pawing of the horses or the flame in front of an icon above a young woman with her throat slit. The musical instruments contributed to distinguish the characters. The recorder became a long protuberance of the face (the nosy-parker servant) and the actor played it with the movements of a sniffing ant-eater. The accordion, as a dignified and abundant belly, predisposed to the demeanour of a boyar, but it was also a screen behind which to hide and eavesdrop.

That which was visible (i.e. physical) had to become sonorous (reveal its voice), and that which was sonorous (i.e. had a voice) had to become visible (get its presence back).

Historically, music was always *beside* the stage, both in Asian and European theatres. Even when it was not *on* the stage, it nevertheless functioned as a reference point and a hidden guide. Together with singing and dancing, music was a part of the craft's *forma mentis*, its mental habit. It was present during rehearsals; it helped to find the right rhythm, to coordinate the movements and gestures of the actors and characters and, by beating time, provided a web of contacts and invisible partners.

From the very first rehearsal for a new production, music was a tool to sharpen the organic dramaturgy. I shaped time (as duration and as rhythm) by intertwining, in accordance or disaccord, the accents of the music with the actor's *sats* (impulses).

Music was a mine of information for the spectator and had various functions in the performance. It acted as a link and a frame. It suggested a milieu or a particular atmosphere for a situation. It possessed an evocative force, recalled past times and fashions and acquired historical or geographical connotations. It expanded the space and physically filled it, ascended from floor to ceiling if we were in a closed room, and reached up to the sky and clouds when the performance took place in the open air. It accompanied the action as a comment or as a parallel emotion. It became the equivalent of a reaction, as if it materialised the way a scenic action resounded in the spectator's mind and senses.

The musical rhythm emphasised the actor's actions, giving body to their duration and imposing precision. Even while performing a score, in immobility as well as at speed, the actor had to maintain a relationship with the pace of the music. He was transported by it, established a distance to it or created counterpoints. A performance without its 'double' of melodic suggestions was unthinkable to me. I used music as an invisible river on which the actors' presence, their dramaturgy, danced.

Dramaturgy of the space

I have always had the feeling that the scenic space was solid. When an actor displaced himself, this had immediate consequences for the other actors, as though they were linked by iron bonds. As a result, a footstep caused an *equivalent* reaction from all the actors in the scene. Every action, even a small one, provoked a dynamic response: as a spectator, I was part of the mechanism of a biological clock.

A performing space (any place in the open air or indoors deliberately selected to establish a particular actor–spectator relationship) is never neutral. A traditional stage, the courtyard of a castle, a square in front of a church, the threshing area of a farm, the great hall of a university, a piazza or the mess hall in a jail all have a past even if it belongs to our epoch. They are bursting with information and material signs which can be accentuated, opposed or refused, but not omitted.

For me, the effectiveness of a performing space consisted in its capacity to arouse in the spectator a double perception: it was a recognisable space (a theatre, a church, a gym) and, at the same time, a potential space, ready to divest itself of its identity in order to be transformed by the forces of the performance. It was an *emptied* space, not a space with nothing inside, unadorned and mute: it admitted what it was, and at the same time was ready to deny itself. I worked with the various dramaturgies to empty and refill the space, to affirm theatre and negate it, to build conventions, links and separations and to invalidate them.

The space reminded me of the deck of a ship which tilts and pitches and straightens itself again on a sea which is at times agitated by the wind, at times dead calm, at times disturbed by the sudden turbulence of submarine currents: the actors' actions, their dynamisms, their introverted or extroverted characteristics, their way of using the voice – from a whisper to a scream.

I had the feeling that the performing space breathed. Its two lungs constituted a double centre: a fixed geometric centre, which resulted from spatial symmetry and on which the spectators, constantly yet unconsciously, oriented themselves; and a dynamic centre, determined by the actor moving about. At times the geometric centre and the dynamic one coincided, in which case the actor stressed the symmetry of the space. At others the actor, by moving around, created a tension with the geometric centre and shifted the dynamic points and the spectator's attention by transferring them from one side to another of the space. I deliberately used the swing between the geometric and dynamic centres, the alternation of convergence and divergence, of symmetry and asymmetry, of harmonic and discordant relationships, of proximity or distance between the actors, and between the actors and the spectators.

The space was a magic kingdom which I filled and emptied. I interwove real actions, introduced simultaneously several situations independent of each other and shaped a rhythm or a vocal action in a contiguity of images, allusions and tales. But the kingdom opposed resistance, declined to mutate into another dimension and thus transport me and my future spectators into a particular type of perception: *a hallucination which contained a personal truth for each of us*.

The space envelops actors and spectators and, at the same time, separates them. I wanted it to be a kaleidoscope: the actor's least tension had to convert it into new forms and another reality. Pace, intensity and flow (multiplicity of divergent rhythms) were the tools which I used to upset the space, to compress, expand or dissolve it.

I worked on the actors' voice to forge the space, to extend or diminish it, make it sensual, unbreathable, a lifeless desert or a jungle. The vocal actions, from an imperceptible whisper to a shout that hurt one's ears, turned the space upside down, revealing or concealing. The space changed as a result of what was not explicitly expressed, of silence, of that part of the body from which the *sats*, the impulse, the sign sprang. The whole universe was potentially contained there.

Jagat, the thousand things that move: this is the name of the universe for the Hindus.

Jagat was the actors' physical and vocal actions, the flow of their tensions and tonalities. *Jagat* embraced and rejected, offended and appeased. *Jagat* condensed the space and unfolded it, multiplied, fractured, liquefied it, turned it into a castle of perfumes which my senses explored, and into a Leviathan which swallowed me into its guts. I glided from an external to an internal space, to the confinements of a universe and a time which belonged only to me, to my actors and to my spectators.

The space-river

When arranging the space, I aimed at arousing in the spectators a sense of curiosity or perplexity yet avoiding making them feel insecure. I wanted them to feel like children at a funfair, boarding a small harmless boat that the current will drag through a dark tunnel full of witches and vampires. When touring, our spectators did not come to see our performances in traditional theatre venues, with a spacious foyer, a bar, decent toilets and above all the conventional division between stage and audience. Odin Teatret needed any venue big enough to house its 'space-river' with its particular relationship between actors and spectators.

This 'river' had two banks on which the spectators were placed facing each other. Between them flowed the tide of the performance. This was the spatial arrangement I used most frequently. It could take place in a school's gym, a garage, a factory warehouse, a shed, the entrance hall to a museum, a large classroom, a church or the typical black rooms of the alternative theatres – all strongly connoted by their usual functions, but often deprived of comfortable services for the public. The number of our spectators was always limited to between 50 and 180 according to the different productions. The maximum distance between an actor and a spectator was nine metres. Proximity and intimacy were the characterising features.

Entering the performance room, the spectators sat opposite other spectators. They became aware that they were going to look as well as be looked at. Often during the performance the reactions of one or more spectators were such that they attracted the attention of other spectators, thus stealing it from the actors. I succeeded in blending this feeling of known and yet unfamiliar space in *The Gospel according to Oxyrhincus*. A curtain divided the two banks of spectators preventing them from noticing their mutual presence. Behind the curtain, the spectators imagined the performing space with the actors. Suddenly the curtain fell, and the spectators believed they were seeing their own reflection in a mirror. The performance about Antigone and her revolt being buried alive began while they were still a prey to this disconcerting feeling of surprise which turned into smiles and irony.

In my first performance, *Ornitofilene* (1965), I had adopted Grotowski's spatial model and assigned a role to the spectators: they were the participants at an assembly, summoned to take a stand on a political–moral dilemma. An actor, chairman of the meeting, invited them to raise their hands in a vote if they agreed to abolish the right to hunt birds in their town. The actors addressed individual spectators, accusing them of being cruel bird-butchers, and hid themselves amongst them in a pogrom scene. In the following performances I stopped attributing a role to the spectators and arranged a space which compelled them physically to choose by turning towards whatever they wanted to watch.

The typical Odin Teatret performance took place in a straight or oval-shaped corridor that was 10–12 metres long and 4–6 metres wide, between two banks of spectators facing each other and whose visual field could not cover the whole length of the 'river' between them. Their attention sailed on a *tide of actions* which their gaze could not fully encompass. If a spectator concentrated on what was happening on the left, he could not focus on what went on in front of him even if only half a metre away, or at the other end on the right.

The contiguity in the same space of actions and scenes belonging to different situations or stories imposed a process of selection on the spectator who often neglected what the director proposed as the main event. It was my intention that each spectator should decide the hierarchy of events. Equally important scenes happened simultaneously at both ends of the 'river'. Each spectator had to choose and make his own montage, quickly framing first one situation and then the other, or following one of them and ignoring the other. At the same time he was aware that the spectator sitting beside him was looking in a different direction, choosing according to a different logic and therefore receiving different information. Indeterminacy was the all-encircling condition, dependent on the contiguity of various unrelated scenes.

The space-river helped me to strengthen the performance's elusive order, the ambivalence of its sensorial stimuli and the spectator's dramaturgy with her selective perception. This spatial arrangement brought the advantage of discontinuity, although it obliged me to fight against the spectator's possible impression of fragmentation. To counteract this, I deliberately manipulated the elements underlining recurring connections and continuity. These might be stage objects or costumes. In *Andersen's Dream* they were the whiteness of the snow which kept on falling, the white suits that the actors wore at times as a leitmotif, the large sheets of paper – old faded photos – that were burnt or the white tutu of a ballerina. In *Mythos* they were the gravel and the big stones which constantly modified the space's shape and identity: a long narrow path, a beach lapped by the sea, a Zen garden, the graves of a typical church cemetery in the Danish countryside. They could be the characteristics of the text. In *Mythos*, the Danish spectators immediately recognised the particular style of Henrik Nordbrandt's poems. Or it could be a language's sonorous homogeneity, although incomprehensible: the Coptic of *The Gospel according to Oxyrhincus* and the Russian of *My Father's House*. The 'continuous music' – which I have mentioned before – was also an important factor in deterring the tendency to fragmentation, as was, above all, the organic effect produced by the actors' scenic behaviour, their way of acting and speaking.

The stimulation of the spectator's attention did not derive automatically from the space-river. It was up to the director to provoke it. During rehearsals, I moved from one seat to another to check the view that each spectator would have of every scene. According to the quantity of information already received by the spectator, I changed the actors' postures and the directions they faced in order to widen or to restrict their visibility. My changes depended on how long the spectator had observed an actor frontally, in profile or from behind, standing or lying on the floor, close by or far away. If I wanted to make an object in an actor's hands or a facial expression be noticed by all the spectators, the actor had to make a complete turn of 360°.

My careful check on what every spectator saw had consequences for the score of the actors who had also to give the impression of addressing the spectators behind them. The actor could look in one direction, point with his arms in the opposite one and at same time slightly twist his body, as if ready to turn and speak directly to the spectators at his back. He had to vary his position, facing alternatively to the right and to the left, so the spectator saw him sometimes from the front, sometimes from the back. I elaborated the actor's score as if he were a cubist statue whose different parts had to be perceived from any position. This operation on the score applied the principle of equivalence. It was as if I carved the space, reshaping its unity through the organic effect – the sensorial strength and persuasive immediateness of the actors' actions.

In *Ferai*, each spectator made a personal montage during the performance's climax. While the queen committed suicide in the centre of the space-river, at one end could be seen the powerless reactions of the benign king whom she tried to save with her death. A totally different scene took place at the opposite end: the usurper's followers surrendered voluptuously to the power of the new bellicose sovereign. After watching the performance several times, the Swedish sociologist Ingvar Holm analysed the reactions of the spectators in a sociological survey. He discovered that theatre habitués focused on the heroine's suicide, gratified by her tragic pathos, while the spectators less accustomed to theatre conventions were attracted by the usurper's power struggle although disturbed by his viciousness. The two types of spectators saw two different versions of the same performance.

In *Andersen's Dream*, the spectators were introduced into a dimly lit space with a black floor. A few seconds of blackout, and then a shimmering light revealed a garden covered with white snow falling from above.

In *Within the Skeleton of the Whale*, the spectators faced each other seated at two 10-metre-long parallel tables with damask tablecloths, glasses, bottles of wine, bread and olives: a family reunion, a marriage, the Last Supper. The director and one of his assistants poured wine into the glasses of the 50 spectators. The silence was emphasised by the gurgle of the liquid in the glass. Thus began the meaningless waiting of Kafka's protagonist in his short story *Before the Law*.

At first, when placed in a scenic space 'between two banks', the spectators had a tendency to observe the performance as if it were frontal. Soon they found, however, that things were also happening outside their line of vision. From that moment on they started choosing. They realised that they could apply an independent look, one that disarranged the hierarchy between the performance's simultaneous main and secondary scenes. If they came back to see the performance again, they might make other choices, and see a different one. The performance's score was the same, but what the spectator saw was different.

The space 'between two banks' translated into physical terms an ongoing complementarity: the spectator observed both reciprocally contrasting actions being performed and, at the same time, the reactions of the spectators facing them. Since it could not be encompassed in its full length by only one glance, the space-river compelled director, actors and spectators to invalidate the traditional distinction between primary and secondary scenes as well as between central and lateral events. Details and actions which did not seem programmed to attract attention became meaningful sources of information.

The space-river allowed the spectator freedom to make her own decisions and *arrange in her own way* the elusive order embroidered by the director.

Prepare for life and arms

I passed through a large gate, then a vestibule that led into a vast courtyard swarming with boys, some in civil garb, some in uniform. I had just got off the train after a 12-hour journey. I felt small and lonely with my bulky suitcase in my hand. A snail without a shell. Nobody took any notice of me. In the distance, I recognised my brother Ernesto. I put down the suitcase und ran happily to clasp him in an embrace. Pushing me away, he gave me a slap. 'Cappellone, show some respect to a senior!' he hissed. That night, in my bed, in a dormitory full of a hundred snoring boys, Ernesto woke me up: 'It was the only way to protect you. If I had treated you well, the other seniors would have amused themselves at your expense.'

At 14, I went to study at La Nunziatella, a military college in Naples. I found myself under the severe discipline of a barracks which was also an excellent high school where, along with 300 other teenagers, we were subjected to strict rules and heavy doses of patriotic rhetoric. The hierarchy was rigid: the cappelloni *(first-year students) suffered under the prejudices and the whims of the third-year seniors, the* anziani*. At night, the* anziani *raided our dormitories, dragged us out of our beds, beating us, turning our lockers upside down and throwing their contents out of the windows into the courtyard, together with our mattresses. They immobilised us on the ground, brushing our entire bodies with shoe cream or emptying a tube of toothpaste in our anuses.*

The officers treated us as adults, ignoring this wild infantilism. They had fought during World War II in Albania, Africa or Russia. They were all decorated for their bravery: alpini, infantrymen, bersaglieri, grenadiers, the very best soldiers, just as our civilian teachers of Latin, Greek, philosophy, history of art, physics, mathematics, chemistry were the best of their kind.

I had been wrong in presuming I was anonymous. I was overshadowed by the reputation of my brother who, after three years, was a well-known scapocchione *(undisciplined): at night he climbed over the wall and escaped downtown to pursue his vocation as Don Juan. He was reputed to be intelligent, knowledgeable and a poet who had begun to publish under a pseudonym.*

Some anziani *had it in for me. I had to make their beds, polish their shoes and buy them coffee and cakes with the little pocket money which my mother sent me. My brother kept himself at a distance; too much closeness would have worsened my situation. He sent me signs of affection, carefully concealed from the eyes of his companions. At times, during recreation I polished his shoes and then we talked in low voices about our mother, Gallipoli or what we had been doing when off duty.*

My fate was sealed by a misunderstanding. Only a few weeks after my arrival, one Sunday, when off duty, a young man stopped me in the street and gave me a leaflet. I mechanically put it in my pocket. I had neither money nor friends and I used to stroll along Caracciolo Street, enjoying the sight of the sea or sitting on a bench in the park watching the mothers and their children playing. Once, one of them drew near and offered me some chocolate. I was so short in stature that he thought I was a child dressed like a soldier. I felt humiliated, but the chocolate tasted good.

On the day of this misunderstanding, when I got back to my college, the officer on watch asked what I was hiding in my pocket. I had quite forgotten the leaflet: it was an anarchist pamphlet. Furious, the officer sent me to prison: I was smuggling subversive material into the college. I had never before heard of anarchism. Thus I gained, without deserving it, the reputation of being worse than my brother who, amazed, congratulated me. He hadn't imagined that I was endowed with such revolutionary gifts.

From that day on, things went from bad to worse. My least misconduct was considered by my officers as insolence or a rejection of the college's values. It infuriated them that I tore from my uniform the badge I was supposed to wear as a war orphan. Tradition demanded that war orphans be left in peace by the anziani. *I did not want to be set apart by such a privilege. But my gesture was interpreted as though I was ashamed that my father had died for his country. I was rebuked incessantly and often ended up in prison, sometimes in isolation.*

I built a world of my own, ignoring the rules of the external one. I did not get up when reveille sounded. I was always late, slept in class during lessons, did not polish my shoes, wore my cap in an 'unmilitary' fashion, pretended to be ill when there were military marches and exercises and chattered when we were supposed to study in absolute silence. Punishments rained down on me one after the other, and I remained confined to college every Sunday and Thursday when we were given leave to go into town. In three years I went out no more than 10 times, on the national day or for the celebration of the patron saint. I was given a 'solemn reprimand' in front of the whole regiment at arms. The colonel read out the list of my misdeeds entailing expulsion from the college. The chaplain interceded on my part because I was one of the few who served at mass. Moreover I was a war orphan and my family was not well off. My teachers, too, spoke in my defence, pleased with my academic results. Through the bars of my isolation cell, on the top floor, the bay of Naples willed me to escape. On the horizon a soft bluish cloud shimmered – the island of Capri. I took refuge within myself and travelled in countries with no boundaries or customs.

I did not feel like a rebel. I had nothing against my military college and, as far as I was concerned, it could continue as it was. I couldn't care less. It was I who had wanted to come there and I intended to stay until the end of my studies. This was the reason for my diligence for the last two months of the school year. I did not want to risk repeating a year. I lived in that world, but had no wish to belong to it. When I arrived, I had hoped to become an air force pilot. Short-sightedness made this impossible. So I planned to go to the military academy in Modena. Ernesto used convincing arguments to demolish this aspiration: Italy had lost the war, it had no more colonies, no conflict was in sight – therefore there was no chance of visiting exotic countries or making a rapid career. Did I want to become an officer in order to teach recruits to march in a provincial barracks?

At La Nunziatella I developed the capacity to be among people, interacting with them, and at the same time finding shelter in a world of my own. Even when I spent long periods in prison, loneliness turned into a state of freedom. I lived in two separate realities, simultaneously respecting the rules of each of them: the life of daily circumstances and that of an inner reality made up of daydreams and fantasies. Much later, I relived this double condition in very different situations: when I was an emigrant and a sailor, during my years with Grotowski in Poland and when I was at the head of Odin Teatret*.*

I learned to treat military life as a fiction. All this was useful to me when, as a director, I imagined my activity in terms of campaigns, strategies, guerrilla warfare and the occupation of territories. I made a whole street performance, Anabasis*, in which the actors, pretending to be a squad of soldiers lost in hostile territory, advanced with flags and fanfares to occupy a city. They took a stand on roofs and balconies, assembled in compact formation, moved with precaution, suddenly dispersed, sheltering inside front porches, behind monuments, in trees, even in the water of a fountain. I nourished the illusion that during my three years at La Nunziatella I developed the reflex to think like a shrewd general and behave like an impulsive lieutenant.*

When I left, I thought no more about it and I never went back. Yet, still today, I see the faces of my brother and a couple of friends staring into the future. I know that the military college has taught me to live in solitude within a group. For three years it trained me in the art of waiting. It was my first experience of exile. I have not forgotten the words carved above its front door: Prepare for life and arms.

The moment of truth

My method was a craftsman's practice imbibed with rigorous *superstitions* which were kept alive by a specific working milieu – Odin Teatret.

In our working jargon, the scenic materials were all the elements proposed by an actor: sequences of physical and vocal actions, texts, songs, costumes or objects.

With time, my actors had learned to create in an autonomous way their own materials, safeguarding them and keeping them alive. This capacity was the measure of their creative independence, of their actor's dramaturgy. At the same time it guaranteed that every actor spoke in the first person in the performance, with an individualised and a non-transferable presence.

It was almost impossible for an actor to assume materials invented by a companion or imposed by the director without radically transforming them. When an actor left the rehearsals or a performance, her materials also disappeared. If a new actor took over, she had to create her own materials thus modifying the course of rehearsals or the composition of an ongoing performance.

The materials were not a point of arrival for an interpretation, nor did they implement an idea or a goal previously established by the author, the director or the actor. They were the initial surge to start my director's dramaturgy: an assortment of more or less disconnected, obvious or enigmatic fragments and scenes which I had to elaborate and orchestrate into a living organism which communicated.

Once the actors had improvised and flawlessly assimilated their improvisations, then my own improvisation as director began. I did not usually ask my actors for their intentions or motivations. It might happen at the beginning of their apprenticeship, in order to make them aware of their tendency to think 'in general' and of the gap between their intention and the lack of precision in executing it. I never alluded to their subscore nor intervened in it. I considered the subscore an intimate reality, difficult to formulate and belonging exclusively to the actor. The exposure of the subscore would have blocked my associations and flattened the sibylline entanglement of the materials which fuelled my improvisation's motor.

My personal meeting with the actors took place through their fixed improvisations: materials or scores. To me these did not yet reverberate a clear meaning. I experienced them as stimuli: actions, impulses, repeatable dynamic patterns which could awaken disparate associations *or even none*. The simultaneous interlacing and concatenation of actions, élans, stillness and impetuousness constituted the materials' organic flora. They appeared to me as a wealth of signals, obvious or abstruse symptoms, allusive information which had to be protected in order subsequently to be introduced in that work level where I elaborated interactions, connections, clusters of meanings, correspondences, associations: the narrative dramaturgy.

The meeting with the actor was, for me, the moment of truth. Any theatre practitioner knows that such moments occur.

I had in my hand scissors and needle, as my role demanded, but I was cutting and sewing skin and human flesh. I had to know exactly where to put the needle and where the thread should pass, where to join together and where to cut, where to sew fragments torn apart or transplant organs from extraneous bodies. In my hands, the living matter on which I was operating mutated, risking bleeding and dissipating its vital charge.

In the moment of truth, when I interpolated, distorted and amalgamated, the actor risked losing the living roots of her improvisations and materials, seeing them fade into opinions and rationality, feeling expropriated and being left with nothing. Or the actor might feel other roots and wings growing, grafted by a succession of operations resulting from the director's constant interventions and the other actors' interactions.

I observed the commitment with which my actors fulfilled my choices with the utmost loyalty. Even if they didn't understand them, they concentrated on implementing them. It was trust, emotional safety, perhaps also the desire to share a path which had already, on other occasions, led to an unexpected horizon. They knew that I was a surgeon, expert in techniques and different ways of operating. But in the operation's crucial moment, my actors and I were aware that my know-how didn't guarantee the result.

Usually my directorial improvisation started out from a sequence of materials by a single actor. I proposed variations, accelerations and decelerations, modified the directions in space, moulded the volume of the actions (reducing or widening them), reversed the order within a sequence and eliminated fragments of it: the beginning could become the end and a central passage the beginning. I did not worry about the meaning. I wanted only to arrange a dance of sensory stimuli which had an impact on my nervous system. I called this process *the score's elaboration* or *distillation*. I continued sharpening the organic dramaturgy, grafting onto it or extracting from it the first elements of that nebula of associations and meanings referring to the *sources* – the original themes, texts or characters, that which I called the level of organisation of the narrative dramaturgy.

My eyes were no longer detached and they scrutinised the actor who gradually and laboriously fixed and incorporated her improvisation – a process which could last several days. I analysed and appraised every action, every tension and posture. I cleansed the materials of what I considered superfluous (instead of ten footsteps, I might retain only three of them), of redundance (gestures that repeated themselves or movements which to my eyes were not real actions) and of the tendency to 'obesity' (in which case I would cut a part of the action so that it could be sensed although not performed in its entirety). I preserved the nature of dance in the materials and their somewhat eccentric spirit, untamed by an obvious meaning, with hesitations and counter-impulses. Every trajectory of a look, every twist of the torso, an introverted or extroverted gesture, a change of balance or the least immobility had to convince my senses and be approved by my nervous system. If my kinaesthetic sense was not persuaded, I insisted on elaborating day after day, proposing modifications and even radical cuts such as the elimination of most of a sequence.

This first intervention was the premise for a cascade of further changes. Once again I took up the sequence of *organic* peripeteias which I had elaborated: a detailed succession of dynamic events. It was organic dramaturgy, pure presence, a concentration of scenic *bios* (life). I considered it the DNA from which I could develop or extract meanings and allusions through interactions with the scenic DNA of the other actors, with the spoken text, with a prop or a melody. The sequence had lost the immediateness of the improvisation, and I saw the actors' efforts to obey the estranged succession of their own actions which they had learned to repeat coldly.

I made the actors go through their elaborated sequences several times a day, always correcting and chiselling. I noticed that the actors, as they assimilated them little by little, running through them and incorporating my modifications, also reconnected them to the secret life of their own subscores. Maybe they revitalised or altered them. On this subject, I can say only what I have ascertained: during the performance, my actors were able to recreate the symbiosis between subscore and score. It was a matter of imprinting, resulting from the apprenticeship and the demands of their work milieu, from experience and personal needs.

Different scores floated in the same spatial frame. Each actor had his *organic line* (intentions, tensions, rhythms, accelerations and breaks) which had no relationship with the other actors' organic line apart from being *contiguous*, that is, *performed in the same space*.

This contiguity was fundamental in the type of exploration which exploits *serendipity* (the technique of finding that which is not looked for). Just as were the constraints which I had previously imposed on myself and which obliged us to struggle with *real* difficulties. For example, in *The Gospel according to Oxyrhincus* the performing space was reduced to a catwalk a metre and a half wide and ten metres long; in *Mythos* the floor was covered with gravel on which the actors had to walk in their high heels and in absolute silence, using their voices' harmonic overtones; in *Great Cities under the Moon* the actors had to remain seated during the whole performance, standing up only briefly.

It was normal that the contiguity of these contradictory materials unleash a sensorial redundance and an incoherence which confused me. During rehearsals, my first random attempt to build a relationship rarely offered interesting solutions. Discovery through *serendipity* sprang from stubbornness: from the patient elaboration of a long sequence or a detail, from the accuracy in filing down the nuances of tones and rhythms, from rendering some actions more introverted or extroverted, from introducing a new element: a stage object, a costume, total silence, a melody, a dazzling or dim light.

I repeat: in this work's phase, the selected tensions and rhythms, actions and reactions, the dense web of relationships or absence of these did not follow a principle of psychological cause and effect or of narrative justifications. It was the non-conceptual part of my brain which decided. I had the feeling I was choosing these dynamic dialogues as a projection of my animal identity in a dance with the actors in an attempt to attune the performance's nervous system.

Once the level of the organic dramaturgy was established, the moment had come to build up the level of the narrative dramaturgy. I called it the 'level of relationships'.

The level of the organic dramaturgy implied this confusion of contiguous materials. I set out from this confusion to relate the scores of two actors, making a montage of them. I followed the criterion of a dynamic dialogue: action–reaction. An actor *executed* an action from her score, and her companion *answered* with one or more actions from her own score. An actor's *action* provoked the immediate *reaction* of a companion (the space was solid). The *synchronisation* of the action–reactions was decisive for achieving an organic effect thanks to which I saw the first rhythmic, associative and narrative correlations emerge.

The montage of the two scores' actions was structured into a scene which I continued to modify. At the same time I persisted in respecting the criterion of sensorial impact, whilst scrutinising it for images, associations and impressions which related to an episode or one aspect of the performance's *sources* – texts, characters and themes. Despite my wish to achieve a quick result, I tried to be patient in establishing each link and meeting point step by step. The actor needed time to absorb the many changes which came from my ongoing elaboration. I didn't lose heart even if I got stuck. This sort of work on a single scene could last for days, weeks, at times months.

I filed and refined details and rhythms, trying to make out what they might be *saying* to me or adapting them to a narrative episode. I placed the sequence in a larger or narrower space. If the sequence was acted standing up facing me, I made the actor repeat it sitting on a chair or with her back to me. Adjusting the score to the new task, my attention was concentrated on the precision of the actor in 'translating' each action, that is, her capacity to find dynamic equivalents. What is the equivalent to standing on tiptoe in order to see a distant bird to your left, when this score had to be accomplished sitting on a chair and reading a newspaper? This adjustment (physical translation through equivalents) was a true improvisation in which the actor had to respect as far as possible the impulses of her original actions, although these were now executed under different conditions.

This procedure had a double finality: it was a conclusive factor in *estranging the action* and obliged the actor *to negate the action while executing it*. The action was adapted to a new situation which was recognisable, yet it possessed something unusual. The spectator saw a person who sat absorbed in reading. But the tensions which animated this posture did not correspond entirely to those of sitting and reading a newspaper, but to those of another real action: stretching upward and looking to the left, even if the eyes were now directed towards the newspaper. The rhythm of the eyes moving along the lines of print and of turning the pages was the equivalent of the action and rhythm of following the flight of the bird. Thus the actor succeeded, in practice, 'in negating the action while executing it': a good antidote against illustration, emphasis or the vacuity of an action.

In this way, even the simplest action contained a dramatic kernel, a presence of antagonistic forces. In the above example, the drama was at the level of organic tensions: impulses which diverged (seeing the bird and simultaneously reading the newspaper). Yet these contrasting tensions acted on the spectator's nervous system and perception, causing a slightly unfamiliar impression which *brought the actor's action to life* and thus prevented it from being the object of a mechanical hasty look from the spectator.

In fact, I should call my narrative dramaturgy an associative or allusive dramaturgy. It was a way of narrating to myself by zigzag, leaping backwards and forwards in time, full of parentheses and similar to the wanderings of our thoughts or a dialogue with a close person. I inclined to metaphors and paradoxes: the *cangaceiros*, the outlaws of Brazil, were the prophets of the New Messiah and a Zen garden was the image of communism. I favoured the synecdoche: hundreds of wooden hands instead of piles of corpses. I did not linger on the exposition of facts concerning a text or a theme. I liked to make other facts grow out of various simultaneous *sources* in a jungle of events and rhythms which negated each other. All these efforts did not aim to make the performance difficult or incomprehensible. I was driven by the need to plunge the narration into a river of sensory stimuli in a trajectory which facilitated comprehension while at the same time disorientating it.

Technically, the work on the narrative dramaturgy consisted in orchestrating the actors' dramaturgies – their scores – in a structure of *sats*, impulses and counter-impulses which radiated allusions, clear meanings, associations and oxymora. The future spectators would sense the performance as a compact and elusive configuration of dynamisms and descriptions, actions and reactions, causes and effects, emotional and factual information, even if the overall logic might escape them.

For months I was intent on scrutinising the actors' materials, testing them in ever new combinations, gradations and nuances to find interpretative solutions and discover unsuspected possibilities. I knew the materials by heart and I ran through them in my mind, reliving their impulses within me and searching for new correspondences and perspectives. At night, in bed, I ruminated on the sequences' structure in my mental theatre. It was beginning to reveal the features of the approaching performance. I let it run at different speeds, I dismantled and reassembled it in a new succession, mixing and matching it in an innovative way, dwelling on a scene, manipulating and breaking it up into sections.

At times the excitement of this mental montage shook my body and kept me awake. I tried to control myself in order not to wake my wife. It was a moment of exaltation and mystery. Intrigued, I sensed the imminent end of a work which for months seemed inane. The actions, the single cells, had melted together and formed tissues, organs, systems, a living organism which thought with an autonomous will and whispered stories different from those I had intended.

In the rehearsals' final phase I always felt a bewildering sensation. It was the performance which took me by the hand, a creature which followed its own reasons, imposed painful choices and showed the way, demanding the rejection of scenes and situations of which I was particularly fond. Relief and solitude enveloped me. The performance no longer belonged to me; it was in the hands of the actors, my *alter ego*, who set sail towards a continent precluded to me. This is why I have always been so rigorous: in order to provoke this separation, the start of a new exploration. Therefore I insisted that each actor climb his own Annapurna, going to the limits of his capacities and solving the craft's specific task: to recreate every day, at the established time, a living score which we all, actors and spectators, would perform.

SECOND INTERMEZZO

The four cardinal points
are three:
the north and the south.
Vicente Huidobro

What the actors say and the director's reflections

Inspired by my actors' organic dramaturgy, I improvised. That's why I talk of the improvisation of the director. But the actors were the ones who knew how I behaved during this process. I have asked those who have worked at Odin Teatret for a period of more than 30 years to speak about it. But I could not help adding my reflections between their descriptions and comments to illustrate the way in which actor and director live the same situation.

Else Marie Laukvik[1]

From the very first day in Oslo, upon entering the working room, we had to leave our private life outside, in order to protect our work and that of our colleagues. Eugenio didn't allow any comments on it or reactions of any sort, not even a smile. This also applied outside the theatre.

He insisted that we treat the scenic objects and costumes respectfully. He said: 'If you discover the object's soul, it will develop an autonomous life in the performance and behave towards you in the same manner as you have behaved towards it.' He often used the word 'extension'. Not only were costumes and objects an extension of the body, but also the voice. He wanted us to project our voices around us throughout the space.

For the first six or seven years he was just Barba and addressed us formally in the third person. It sounded bizarre to our ears, and must have been a Polish habit. I considered it a form of respect towards us.

Iben Nagel Rasmussen[2]

We rehearse *Ferai* (1968), the scene of King Frode's funeral. The king's corpse, represented by his cloak, lays spread out on the floor. A big wooden egg, painted white, is his head. The peasants moan around the 'corpse'. All, in their affliction, want to be as close as possible to the monarch.

Five actors are the peasants and each of us makes an improvisation for this scene. The theme we have been given has nothing to do with a king or a funeral. Its title is: trees of anguish.

We do the improvisation individually and then fix it in its minutest detail. While each of us is improvising, the other actors note down one action after the other, and all help in reconstructing the succession, the rhythms, the tensions and the directions in space. We repeat this reconstruction several times.

You ask us to perform the score we have worked out, addressing the king's corpse/cloak on the floor. We try one at a time. It takes several days to fix our new scores. At this point, you give us the task not only of performing our score's actions in relation to the corpse/cloak, but also of taking into consideration the other actors.

You let two actors rehearse together and fix the result. Then you add a third actor, a fourth, in the end all five of us. Each actor's action arouses another's reaction. The scene turns into a dance of reactions and corresponds exactly to the original context: the peasants' grief as they crowd around their king. They confront each other, embrace the big wooden egg/head, throw themselves on the cloak, but never touch each other.

The theme 'trees of anguish', with the personal images that it instigated, doesn't correspond to what the spectators see, but to what guides us actors.

Else Marie Laukvik

I was not the only one to feel paralysed during *Ferai*'s rehearsals. Maybe we took the director's indications too literally or perhaps they didn't stimulate us. Many of the improvisations' themes were taken from the Bible.

In my diary is written: 'The burning bush is extinguished.' Juha[3] has to improvise on this theme, but remains immobile for a long time.

Eugenio: 'It is good to think, but do it with your whole body. Four or five minutes of psychic preparation, and then take the plunge. Associations will follow. Don't stop because you are thinking.'

Juha is still immobile.

Eugenio: 'Juha, what's the matter?'

Juha: 'I don't know what to do.'

Eugenio: 'If the actor doesn't know, who else could know?'

The director's comment

Ferai *was Juha's first performance at Odin Teatret after only a few months of training. But exercises are not enough to prepare for the dense dramaturgical structure of a performance. To infuse life into a character implies other ways of using the body-mind. It is necessary to think and transform one's own mental processes – conceptual thoughts, sensations and emotions – in actions that can be controlled, sculpted and related to those of the other actors. Above all they must be repeated with the same quality of life. Juha's previous experiences with theatre had certainly not prepared him for my way of working. As a director, I had not much experience myself. I felt intuitively that the improvisation's theme 'the burning bush is extinguished' left plenty of freedom. But if the actor – then as now – treats such a theme literally, he has difficulty in taking off. The implosion of the theme upon which to improvise, and its conversion into a swarm of associations that goad into action, are the consequence of an apprenticeship and a particular mental process. Who is the bush that burns? God's voice? How many forms does God have? What do they look like? Does each form have its own voice? How do these different voices burn? Against whom? Why is the bush extinguished? How does one perform the different phases of God's (the bush's) extinction? What happens when God's voice fades out? Do the animals die? Which ones die first? How do they die? What can be done? Set fire again to the bush? Or commit suicide, following the example of Chatov, the character in Dostoevsky's* The Possessed*? Break out into a song of pain? Or throw oneself into a dance of happiness because one is freed from His gaze and commandments?*

But the bush can also be the last sapling of a poor peasant from Andalusia: a fire has destroyed his small field. The man cautiously takes the still hot ashes, mixes them with a handful of earth, pours the lot into an empty flask, which he takes on board a galleon to a country over the sea where he has heard there is plenty of land to be cultivated.

Juha was Finnish and expressed himself in Swedish with difficulty. I spoke Norwegian and we were living among Danes. For him it must have been hard to make sense of what I said, the games with words and the paradoxes with which I tried to stimulate the actors' thoughts/actions. In Ferai *the actors were Norwegian, Danish, Finnish, Swedish and Italian.*

Torgeir Wethal[4]

Once the actors' improvisations have been fixed, your director's improvisation undergoes three phases. In the first one, it seems that a dynamic and musical need drives you. You cut and manipulate the actors' materials according to a taste and choices whose criteria are incomprehensible to the observer. In the second phase, you refine those materials containing possible associations, although they don't yet refer to something specific. Finally, in the third phase, you concentrate on linking these materials to a text or a situation, trying to establish or to discover meaningful relationships between them.

You adapt the dynamic and associative materials to a scene which refers to the theme of the performance, giving them justifications, intentions and content. This process totally absorbs you, yet at the same time you try to oppose it.

It depends on the phase in which you find yourself, how long you have been working on the performance and how much you have 'understood' of the new performance which is finding its form. This 'understanding' doesn't follow a coherent line. Some situations are clearer than others to you, some you have just sketched, while you have almost finished other scenes.

In reality you continually jump back and forth among different ways of working. It depends on where the actor is in his work on a character, and in which stage of artistic evolution.

Iben Nagel Rasmussen

Every day we repeat the scene of the king's funeral, over and over again, yet you are not satisfied. You ask one of the actresses to explain each of her actions. 'This gesture means that I am giving some flowers to my father,' she answers with a sob and a trembling lower lip. Thank goodness it is not me – I say to myself, while my colleague bursts into tears.

My turn arrives next day; I have to explain what I am doing with each action. I too start crying. The invisible and secret reasons are exposed to all. Some actions are corrected and made more concrete. It has been the first and last time, since I have been at Odin Teatret, you have asked what lies behind one of my improvisations.

The grief that was the scene's pivot doesn't seep out from the actions, but is expressed by the voice with a hymn in German, *Gott, befrei uns von der Angst* (Lord, free us from anguish), which rises in vehement desolation.

It is the first time that several improvisations are connected in such a tangled mass. I immediately grasp this procedure and am enthusiastic. I have a feeling that this form of montage opens entirely new possibilities: a rhythm that is ours, another way to create meanings.

I think about when I played volleyball at school. Once, my adversary had returned the ball and I had bent down. I would have been able to hit it, but I realised that the person behind me was better placed and had a better chance. The game has its own life, I do my best, I give the maximum. I felt, and still feel today, an inexpressible joy and pride. At times the maximum consists in bending and letting another carry the game forward.

Else Marie Laukvik

Ferai's final scene, in which the queen commits suicide, originated from only one improvisation. I remember it as being very long, half an hour or more. Only Eugenio was present. I would never have succeeded in making a similar improvisation in the presence of my colleagues. Out of their sight, I felt free and audacious. If I did something foolish, I was the only one to know it and the frontiers of the internal and external space expanded. After all, it is a matter of understanding in one's own way and not taking too much account of the director's expectations.

The theme of the improvisation was: 'You contemplate yourself while resting. You are dead and you become one with your corpse.'

For me it was an out-of-body experience; I observed myself from above. It was painful, therefore the beginning was sad. I conversed with my lifeless body and its past. I especially remember how I played with one of the wide sleeves of my costume as if it were a violin. Then I was one with my corpse: my soul penetrated into my body, not with a cry of life, but of death, only the succession was inverted. At the end I woke up to a new life.

Eugenio helped me to reconstruct the improvisation on the basis of the notes he had taken and he condensed it into a scene of about 10 minutes. I had no difficulty: my associations and images came back to me, clear and precise. I already knew Peter Seeberg's text by heart and it was superimposed on the actions.

A state of pre-improvisation exists whose fundamental conditions are silence and concentration in the room. Eugenio promotes it through his way of delivering the theme of an improvisation in a low voice.

Roberta Carreri[5]

I arrived at Odin Teatret in April 1974. It was seven o'clock in the morning when I entered the white room for the first time. Eugenio and the actors sat in silence on one side. Eugenio made a sign to one of them to approach him. He murmured something in his ear. The actor went to the centre of the room and sat immobile for some time, then began to move in the space. It was as if Eugenio had whispered a secret to him. The actor reacted to a precise reality that we could not see.

One after the other the actors moved into the space. Finally Eugenio looked at me. I went up to him and was given the theme for my life's first improvisation: 'You are in the king's garden. You are afraid, but somebody reaches a hand towards you.'

I didn't know what to do; I had never before done an improvisation, but the images to which the actors had given life were still fresh in my memory. I thought of a person: she was beside me and I stretched out my hand to her. I saw her clearly and felt her hand take mine. Then she vanished and I was alone again in the empty white room.

I had only one certainty: I could not stop. I kept on moving in the space and my body gradually decided where to go, when to stop, how to sit down, why run. Was it a dance? Was I still following Eugenio's theme? I was scared, and my body helped me not to be paralysed by panic.

I haven't the least idea how long my first improvisation lasted. I had lost the sense of time.

Torgeir Wethal

When you still don't know in which scene of the performance the material on which you are working will finally end up, or when the content of the different scenes has not yet been decided, I have the impression that above all you follow your dynamic needs. This happens both when you elaborate the improvisations of only one actor, and when you do it with two or more actors. You choose those parts of the improvisations that attract you (or confuse you) and you put them together, often in a different succession. It is as if you were composing music.

You let chance reign. You don't know what you are looking for. You don't search according to a descriptive logic, but a dynamic one. It can be compared to an actor who is preparing Hamlet's monologue in a language you don't understand. You would choose sentences and passages that convince through their sonorous expressivity or because they strike you with their intensity or an intonation you like. You would insert the selected fragments in a succession that follows a musical dynamic fluctuation, not the logic of the text.

Subsequently you subdivide the montage you have been working on. One actor's actions become the elements of a physical dialogue with another actor whose improvisation has been elaborated in a similar way. This actor, too, expresses himself in a language that you don't understand.

This dialogue through actions between two or more actors doesn't contain a narrative development. It may include passages which awaken clear associations, without there necessarily being a relationship between them. You have only made a montage of what you call 'real actions'.

Roberta Carreri

In one of the first rehearsals of *Brecht's Ashes* (1980), Eugenio reminds us that a performance has at least three logics:

- the logic of energy (organic flow)
- the actor's logic (her own ghosts)
- the theatrical logic (the spectators).

He concludes: 'Concepts, notions and symbols shine for a few seconds, then become dim because they don't emanate life. Only you, the actors, can give the breath of life to a performance. Only your temperature can bake the "cake" which the director has mixed.'

Francis[6] shows his proposal for the entrance and speech of Arturo Ui.

Eugenio: 'The scene must radiate threat and danger. You cannot resort to external solutions. You must have precise images to trigger your reactions. What associations do you want to awaken?'

Francis, after a long silence: 'It is difficult for me to think this way.'

Eugenio: 'You must think as an actor, think concretely, adjust your mind's processes, your mental actions in such a way that they influence your behaviour. Let's try an improvisation: "Moses on the threshold of the Promised Land". Moses is aware he will never tread it, yet, despite regret, a sense of injustice and the burden of old age, he burns all his energy to spur his people on.'

Francis improvises.

Eugenio: 'Moses has grown up amid the pomp of the Pharaoh's court and in the refinement of the Egyptian culture. He gives up freedom, comfort and privileges to join what he considers to be his tribe, heading for the Promised Land. Years go by wandering in the desert. He climbs a mountain begging for help and receives other burdens: a heavy stone with the Ten Commandments. He searches the horizon. In the sands and on the stony soil of the Sinai desert, figures from his past dance: the woman he loved and abandoned amongst the dear friends of his childhood. Our birth, the first time we are together with a person we love and our end: these are the three crucial experiences in our life.'

Second improvisation by Francis.

Eugenio: 'It all takes place in your head. Stop trying to be original, don't think too much. No actor does original improvisations. Look for what is simple but precise, the associations which inspire you. Don't be influenced by my suggestions. Go against them.'

Third improvisation by Francis. He repeats it three times in order to fix it. Eugenio advises him to preserve his inner images and forget the external forms.

Torgeir Wethal

You begin to improvise with the actors' scores and to arrange them in space. Your improvisations substantially differ from those of the actors: they constitute the first sketch of a plot or a nucleus of conflicts. You use the rough sketch of the scenes as frames.

You are interested in constructing a labyrinth. Sometimes, these sketches of a plot take form from a task you give and whose result depends on the actor's skill: what happens if you all start to walk on the water?

Roberta Carreri

Once more we rehearse Francis's scene but with all the actors involved in it. Ulrik[7] plays the accordion, I begin my dialogue with Tage[8] and all this takes place at the same time as Francis's scene in which Julia[9] translates into English his German text from *The Resistible Rise of Arturo Ui*.

Step by step Eugenio inserts fragments of Francis's improvisation in the scene, integrating them into the text. Francis has difficulty in repeating the improvisation and forgets his actions as soon as he begins to speak. Eugenio guides him and composes his movements, which confuses him. Then Eugenio makes him go back to the original improvisation, which is repeated several times. Francis constantly alters the rhythm. Then Eugenio makes him count the number of his actions, segmenting them into the smallest details. Francis does this, but the rhythm deflates and loses strength.

Eugenio: 'You will only be able to exploit your improvisation if you succeed in keeping the original *sats*. The scene withers because you don't synchronise the physical actions with the spoken text.'

Francis repeats this several times. In the end, Eugenio asks him to go back to his proposal of three days ago.

For an actor it is depressing to see one's 'creature' being discarded. Three days of work on the same scene and we are back at the beginning again.

The director's comment

Why did I give up? It was simple: both in the 'warm' improvisation (the free one on the theme of Moses) and in the 'cold' one (the work on composition led by me), I didn't glimpse any sign of organicity in the actions. It is not true that all the material created by the actor functions. I cut a lot of material during the rehearsals precisely because it doesn't work at an organic level. It is not easy for an actor to understand this. When an actor has assimilated this way of building characters and performances through physical actions, he believes that any material can be elaborated. But young actors do not have the skill and experience to generate and protect the inner life of their scores. For those with more experience, on the other hand, the materials are often corroded by mannerisms and personal clichés which withstand any attempt to eradicate them.

Even today I could not openly say to actors with whom I have worked for years and years: look, your materials don't offer me any possibility of elaboration and, therefore, of achieving an organic effect for the spectator.

They would understand at once what I'm speaking about if I gave them these lines by Vargas Llosa to read:

> *The story that a novel tells may be incoherent, however the language which shapes it must be coherent in order that this incoherence successfully feigns*

> *being genuine and alive. An example is Molly Bloom's monologue at the end of Joyce's* Ulysses, *a chaotic torrent of memories, feelings, reflections, emotions, whose alluring power is due to the seemingly frayed and shattered prose which preserves, under its entangled and anarchic exterior, a rigorous coherence, a structural conformation that obeys a model, an original system of norms and principles from which literature never strays. Is it an exact description of a conscience in movement? No, it is such a tremendously convincing literary invention that it appears to us to reproduce the wanderings of Molly's conscience when in truth he is inventing it. Literature is pure artifice, however great literature succeeds in dissimulating this, while the mediocre one exhibits it.*
>
> *(*Cartas a un joven novelista, *Planeta 1997, pp 40–47)*

The pure artifice of great literature corresponds to the organic effect. If the actor's actions don't achieve this effect, they become only nauseating artificiality. Unfortunately there are no objective criteria to measure the quality or the efficacity of the organic effect in theatrical actions. The actor must trust the director's reactions. What is inert for me could be alive for another director, and vice versa.

Roberta Carreri

Rehearsals of *Brecht's Ashes* (May 1981). Eugenio keeps on working with Francis and Julia on Arturo Ui's entrance and the translation into English of his speech in German.

Eugenio to Julia: 'Both you and Francis release the tension before the action ends. In the middle of an action, you are already preparing for the next one. The mental influences the physical. If you think, you cannot live in the score. Your rhythm gives the feeling of being accidental. It produces movements, not actions. Each of your postures must have an end which is the *sats*, the impulse, for the next one.'

Eugenio to Francis: 'As soon as I asked you to relate your actions to those of Roberta you started to illustrate them and show their external logic. Before, in your improvisation, you bent your knees in a certain way and then pushed Roberta down; now you simply push her down. The spectator sees something that is obvious; however, ambiguity and the associative radiation have disappeared.'

Eugenio asks Julia which concrete action she is doing while singing. He explains: 'Both you and Francis must perform physical actions while singing. You do actions through the song.'

We repeat the scene. Eugenio to Julia: 'Your actions with the bag have a slowness which is deprived of dramatic nerve. The secret consists in not revealing overtly what you are doing. Do it with your back. If you use only hands and arms, you render your action obvious.'

It is worth mentioning that *Brecht's Ashes* was Francis's and Julia's first performance at Odin Teatret. It is during the creation of a performance that Eugenio trains new actors.

The director's comment

Rehearsals have always been the moment when I formed my actors. I submitted them to a jumble of obstacles in order to develop conditioned reflexes: physical audacity, paradoxical thought and going beyond their limits. Everything was possible. They had to be ready to pursue an invisible unknown prey, marry their own associations and with them engender children with three heads and eleven tails, then turn them into rain, flooding the whole scene with drops – actions. The important thing was to dupe rationality and to think in actions, to assimilate the ability to accumulate density, to secrete complexity, to lay out an inextricable web of sensory stimuli and associations. Here, it was necessary to comply with instinctive anarchic forces and to give oneself over to the rigour of technical principles incorporated during the training.

I didn't always egg the actors on towards an interesting solution or the necessary detail in a scene. There were times when I only wanted to indicate a way of thinking freely, jumping from one subject to another, racing after darting images and ideas, beating our heads against our accountant-like tendency which nails us to obvious reactions.

It often happened, during this type of zigzagging, that I came upon something unexpected. Then I started pursuing it, expecting my unwitting actor to be at my side in this sudden change of direction. My sudden doggedness on a scene also served another purpose: to instil in the actor the reflex to follow me when I broke away from the scene on which we had struggled tirelessly and I chased the traces of a new prey. Or when, incapable of finding interesting stimuli for the actor and for myself, I departed in the opposite direction to the one we had explored until then.

Roberta Carreri

Even working with the most experienced actors requires time. Eugenio tunes each inflection of Torgeir's words for hours.

I write in my diary: 'Eugenio focuses on Torgeir's least action and intonation in Brecht's poem *Jetzt sminke Sie sich*. A long and tiresome dedication by master and pupil which reminds me of the relationship between grandfather and grandson in the film about Kyogen we saw recently.'

The director's comment

Torgeir had founded Odin Teatret with me. He had always been the male protagonist in our performances; was experienced, clever and had introduced all the new actors into our training which he had helped to create. His prestige among companions and spectators was undisputed. But after 10 years, mannerisms –

expressive clichés – were adversaries against which we both fought. Moreover, it was pedagogically important that young actors witness how the skilled actor also underwent the same rigour to which they were submitted. For us all, veterans and beginners alike, it was important to assert the value of each detail as an ongoing initiation ceremony.

From A Story of Love and Darkness *by* Amos Oz*:*

> *I work like a watchmaker or an old-fashioned silversmith: one eye screwed up, the other fitted with a watchmaker's magnifying glass, with fine tweezers between my fingers, with bits of paper rather than cards in front of my desk, on which I have written various words, verbs, adjectives and adverbs, and bits of dismantled sentences, fragments of expressions and descriptions and all kinds of tentative combinations. Every now and again I pick up one of these particles, these molecules of text, carefully with the tweezers, hold it up to the light and examine it carefully, turn it in various directions, lean forward and rub or polish it, hold it up to the light again, rub it again slightly, then bend forward and fit it into the texture of the cloth I am weaving. Then I stare at it from different angles, still not entirely satisfied, and I take it out again and replace it with another word, or try to fit it into another niche in the same sentence, then remove it, file it down a tiny bit more, and try to fit it in again, perhaps at a slightly different angle. Or deploy it differently. Perhaps further down the sentence. Or at the beginning of the next one. Or should I cut it off and make it into a one-word sentence on its own?*
>
> *I stand up. Walk round the room. Return to the desk. Stare at it for a few moments, or longer, cross out the whole sentence, or tear up the whole page. I give up in despair. I curse myself aloud and I curse writing in general and language as a whole, despite which I sit down and start putting the whole thing together all over again.*
>
> *If you write an eighty-thousand-word novel you have to make about a quarter of a million decisions, not just decisions about the outline of the plot, who will live or die, who will fall in love or be unfaithful, who will make a fortune or make a fool of himself, the names and faces of the characters, their habits and occupations, the chapter divisions, the title of the book (these are the simplest, broadest decisions); not just what to narrate and what to gloss over, what comes first and what comes last, what to spell out and what to allude to indirectly (these are also fairly broad decisions) but you have also to take thousands of finer decisions, such as whether to write in the third sentence from the end of that paragraph, 'blue' or 'bluish'. Or should it be 'pale blue'? Or 'sky blue'? Or 'royal blue'? Or should it really be 'blue-grey'? And should this 'greyish blue' be at the beginning of the sentence, or should it only shine out towards the end? Or in the middle? Or should it simply be caught up in the flow of a complex sentence, full of subordinate clauses? Or would it be best just to*

> *write the three words 'the evening light', without trying to colour it in, either 'grey-blue' or 'dusty blue' or whatever?*
>
> *(Chatto and Windus, London, 2004, pp 258–259)*

How many thousands of actions compose a performance, how many thousands of decisions must be taken, what should be disclosed in effortless clarity and what be veiled in laborious enigmas?

Torgeir Wethal

Before rehearsals enter their final phase, I have the impression you scrutinise the actor's work through a particular filter. You are in no hurry to remove or cut away the parts with too many movements, but you bring into relief those actions which can arouse clear images or associations. You shape some actions and their directions in space to emphasise the relationships between the actors.

For example, an actor has made an undulating movement with his hand like a leaf falling gently in a light breeze. You may ask him to repeat the same action more roundly and smaller, moving the hand forward and downward instead of going from above his head towards the floor. To the spectator's eyes, it looks as though the actor wants to caress from a distance and gently stroke the hair of a colleague stretched out on the floor.

You insert new tasks: 'Make a short pause at the end of the undulating action and then quickly move the hand downwards and close it in a fist.' From the outside it looks as though the actor, after affectionately caressing the hair, grabs and pulls it.

You seek connections and contrasts without bothering to put them immediately into contact with the performance's various stories. It is clear, however, that you are hunting, although blindly. You don't know what prey will end in your bag, whether a rabbit or a bird. You try to hit whatever crosses your path.

Roberta Carreri

In March 1984 we began rehearsing a new production which, after a few months, was called *The Gospel according to Oxyrhincus*.

Eugenio:

> You will work one hour a day to create *marble* – the material from which to extract the statue. You must all develop your own ideas about the character you have been given. But these ideas must not colour your marble. Note down what you do, write your character's story as you imagine you will give it life through your materials. In the end, each of you will have an autonomous context of facts and

episodes, the story of *your own* character, and all of them will meet in the performance and influence it.

This is your point of departure. Out of your proposals and materials I must retrieve a thousand possibilities to be cultivated, magnified and distilled.

The process of creating marble takes place in three dimensions: space, time and intensity. Divide and subdivide the results in phases and segments and treat them in different ways: for example, as if they were a gymnastic sequence or you wanted to teach them to another person. I am not interested in your arms and hands, but in how you engage your backbone and displace your weight. Actions are important, but even more so are their transitions, nuances, variations and peculiarities. Don't hurry. Invent new rules to limit your freedom. You have to be in the action that you are performing but at the same time you have to refuse it, as when you hammer a nail: your arm goes back in order to strike a small nail in front of you.

The director's comment

For more than 15 years we had worked with two types of improvisation that we called 'warm' and 'cold'. In the 'warm' improvisations, I gave a theme and let the actor develop it as an intimate and personal dream. They often took place individually, without the presence of the other actors. 'Cold' improvisations were based on composition, on moulding one action after another, concentrating on the design of their form, their details, the rhythm and their capacity of simultaneously suggesting different information to the spectator. For example, the behaviour of an alcoholic: how to show the desire to take a glass of cognac with the action of one hand, and with the other imply shame for one's own weakness; the eyes pretend to look interested in the lamp above; the right leg staggers as if intoxicated, while the left is in sats*, has the impulse to run away from the temptation of alcohol. It was me who introduced the actors to the 'cold' improvisations. For example, I might ask him to raise an arm very slightly as if the middle finger and the index wanted, apprehensively, to touch a spider (and not only with the index finger as in the 'normal' movement); to look up as if thinking, but at the same time counting the stains on the ceiling; to take a step as if the foot was being restrained by a breakable thread attached to the heel. My indications always suggested the execution of real actions.*

Most of the material for the performances originated from 'warm' improvisations. The first two generations of Odin actors received this imprinting and the result was a striking expressiveness that, however, after a few years, showed a tendency to repeat itself. The actor was like a painter who always used the same palette of colours, the same tones, even the same subjects. Therefore, from the third generation of actors, that of Roberta Carreri, I gave priority to 'cold' improvisations or composition. This was also because we had undergone the radical experience of street theatre, with parades and itinerant performances which required an improvisation/composition in response to the street's architectural elements (a lamp-post, a fountain, a balcony, trees) or a sudden adjustment according to the spectators' reactions.

By now I knew that the creative conditions for a new production depended on self-imposed constraints, on circumstances deterring our technical abilities and experience. They could even mock and go against our taboos. For these reasons, in the The Gospel according to Oxyrhincus, *my first step was the 'marble', a purely technical procedure.*

The search for these constraints has become one of the most exhausting aspects in preparing a production. In Talabot *such a constraint, especially for me, was a period of practical work on* commedia dell'arte, *with masks, costumes and rules of improvisation under the guidance of our literary adviser Nando Taviani. We worked day and night, isolated in the village of Fara Sabina, in Italy. I couldn't stand the modern versions of* commedia dell'arte *and had infected my actors with my scepticism. In* Mythos, *the constraint concerned a taboo of my theatrical credo: the score. The actors were free not to fix anything; they could improvise, make alterations, surprise their colleagues during rehearsals and the performance. The only rule to be respected was the* møtepunkt, *the meeting point, the dynamics of speaking–answering, acting–reacting. In other words: no pauses.*

Torgeir Wethal

You shape the actors' actions to fit your logic. Let's take the example of the action that is reminiscent of a falling leaf and is transformed into a caress and then pulling of the hair. It may happen that this action is no longer logical for you. You cut it out, but you store it waiting to insert it in another context.

The actors react in different ways in these situations. Some gradually change their own logic making it parallel to the character and the performance which is emerging. Others hold on to the logic of their original improvisation.

Once, rehearsing a performance that we had not performed for months, you said to one actor: 'You have modified the fragment where you accompany the text by a strangling with the hands.' I intervened to help the colleague to remember the changes you had made in that fragment. 'Ah, there where I hold a bunch of flowers with two hands and show it,' exclaimed the colleague.

Your only change had been to ask him to hold his hands more apart, making the circle between them bigger, and at the same time pressing slightly with the fingers. For us onlookers, the image appeared radically changed. But in his imagination the actor had continued 'to show a bunch of flowers'.

Else Marie Laukvik

In *The Gospel according to Oxyrhincus*, the actors received 'homework'. Once we had to prepare a scene in which a child was killed. I at once had a stream of associations about the newborn babies slaughtered by Herod at the birth of Jesus. Later I understood that Eugenio was thinking of the revolution that devours its own children.

It may be hard to believe, but I forgot to prepare the scene. The day I had to present it, I ran to my dressing room, opened the cupboard and took out what I found there: old newspapers, a pair of scissors and the contents of my sewing basket – reels of cotton, buttons, needles, pins and a couple of thimbles.

When my turn came, I wrapped these objects in a newspaper, made an oblong package reminiscent of a baby and struck it with the scissors, puncturing it in several parts from where the reels of cotton unravelled in threads of different colours.

In this way, through sheer accident, my character became a tailor. Eugenio proposed to exchange the newspaper with the brown paper used by tailors for making patterns. He gave me a Jewish prayer shawl that I hid among two sheets of brown paper which I glued together. I added a Yiddish song *Bin ich mir ein Schneider* (I am a tailor), humming it while I cut the large sheets of paper in the form of a human figure. I slashed it and extracted the shawl in which I wrapped myself, protecting myself in prayer.

I could be childish and mild in the role of Zusha Malak, the patient and pious Jew who was waiting for the Messiah 'in a world of truths gone mad'.

The director's comment

It was certainly sheer accident, but a basic attitude already existed too: to question the errors and dissect them, investigating their nature. It was one of the first rules I taught the actors: to structure an error. During the performance, this procedure consisted in committing the same error again. What seemed to be a mistake or an inaccuracy, when repeated, acquired a deliberate character. If the error happened during an improvisation, it was fixed as an integral part of the score. As I have already said, I distinguished between solid *errors, which could be found and corrected, and* liquid *errors, which were ambiguous and indefinable, inducing deviations and encouraging their development to the point of suddenly becoming their opposite: a landscape of unsuspected perspectives.*

Roberta Carreri

Eugenio:

> It is true, I explain, comment, describe and analyse. I have no intention, however, of imposing a common logic. You must translate what I say into a language which is familiar to you and yet stimulating. Every living thing struggles against the law of gravity. This applies also to my words: you must give life to them. Anything I say, the contrary is equally true. But if I keep telling you this all the time, I will confuse you even more. If you don't feel stimulated, you will not be stimulating.
>
> What can we do to preserve and bring to fruition the many lives within you? It is essential that you build divergent perspectives and points of opposition in respect to what I work out with you. Over and over again I keep saying: negate the action while executing it. Now the performance is consolidating into a story. In order for me to negate this story, your actions must not correspond to what we are narrating. You have to develop a medley of references which is yours alone. They constitute the invisible yet sensory perceivable foundations from which *your stories* seep into the performance, eroding its certainties.
>
> Rehearsals are now at a critical phase. The performance is gathering strength and is in the process of developing a brain and nerves. We must oppose this process. Neither I nor you must be too sure at this stage what the performance will be about and how it will behave. This uncertainty is exciting for me, but perhaps a nightmare for you. If you don't fight it with proposals, ideas and solutions which counterattack, you will be crushed by the growth of the performance.

Long, complicated and wearing work on a performance with six protagonists. The process is painful, and it changes the people.

The director's comment

In the past, I had an image of what it was to prepare a production: climbing a mountain. I was not alone. I had some companions with me and we were tied together by a rope. Each one of us had his own rhythm, yet if one hesitated, all had to slow down, and all speeded up if the guide managed to find a better trail permitting faster progress. Sometimes the director pulled the actors, at others the actors towed the director. Each choice was made to avert jeopardising the entire group. Each step, each stop, each tiny individual action entailed consequences for everybody.

During this ascent, it could happen that we had to turn back. It seemed as if we were moving farther away from the summit, but it was only a detour in order to discover a more solid point on the mountain face, a safer foothold, a better grip for our hands to climb even higher. We were aware where the peak was; it was hidden, but it was there, in the haze.

Over the years the image of the mountain faded. At the outset of a production, I didn't see the slopes of a mountain to be climbed, but a peak with a windy black abyss: the crater of a volcano. And I plunged into it. After me my actors too plunged and sank into the darkness and I didn't know if I would succeed in saving them, if we would escape together.

Still today, after almost 50 years, I am spellbound by my work, by the silence and the concentration of the rehearsals, by the meticulousness of the process and the tiny sparks which spring from it. Yet, at the idea of launching a new production, I almost feel repugnance. It is as if I have lost the sense of the summit, and I detect only the presence of the void, of a black bottomless crater.

I have always thought about this reaction of both fascination and repugnance in female terms. I feel like a woman who wants a child, but opposes the body's deformation, the long waiting and the nausea.

The first hours, the first days, the first weeks of rehearsals are unbearable. The many plots and stories I long to materialise flash through my brain: images, texts or simple words are only marks on the paper, suggestive ideas or abstract thoughts. I torment myself over how *to transform them into flesh and blood, into a living body with a nervous system, a skeleton, a skin, which reacts with laughter, compassion and fear. I take pains to extract from the story its hidden ramifications and events, turning them around in my head and wondering, in anguish, how to convert generalised situations into clusters of actions and detailed reactions.*

Flesh is tender, it decomposes. In our craft, the aggregation of the cells is not a natural law. In theatre, the force which reigns is not cohesion, but a centrifugal exhaustion which pulverises our energies.

Else Marie Laukvik

While rehearsing *The Gospel according to Oxyrhincus*, Eugenio asked me to improvise on my character's grandfather, who was also a tailor. I used a small tape-recorder to record what I was doing in the improvisation which I recounted and commented upon loudly to myself. Eugenio let me carry on. Listening to the tape, it was easy to reconstruct the actions and their succession, the length of the silences and the vocal intonations.

I also used this technique of memorising an improvisation with the help of the tape-recorder in *Memoria*, my next performance (1990) together with Frans.[10]

We rehearsed *Memoria* in the blue room, which is small and intimate. With the years it was normal to use different spaces. I prepared the initial scene and a few songs at home in my kitchen. One weekend, the heating in the blue room didn't function and Eugenio moved the rehearsals to his office. I got ill with influenza one week before the opening night. Eugenio came to my home; he had retouched the final text and made me try it. In this way I recovered.

Torgeir Wethal

You improvise with the actors' materials in hundreds of different ways. But from the very beginning two things are important for you: care for the detail and a search for the dynamic musicality of the actions.

We all know that the scene will be elaborated again and again. Yet you concentrate at once on the refinement of the details, both in the technical solutions (for example, how your hand is placed while unbuttoning your jacket) and in the actors' initial material, when they may not yet have found their logic.

At times you develop a scene exploiting a technical problem in order to find a double solution, thus welding together two images which fascinate you. For example, how to make a grave become a path of gravel without the spectator being immediately aware of it.

Julia Varley

Working with Eugenio, I noticed that he concentrates, almost automatically, on creating another story in addition to the one narrated by the words and actions in a scene. For example, in a dialogue from Shakespeare's *Othello*, during which Iago (me) plants the seeds of jealousy in Othello (Tage Larsen), Eugenio asked me to focus above all on my eyes, peering and glancing at the surroundings with suspicion so as to give the impression we were being spied on from the outside. On the contrary, my actions and intonations had to signal a deep-felt friendship between the two characters. In following these indications, I understood that as an actress I could let the words tell one story, while I was focusing on how to reveal a different one.

Iben Nagel Rasmussen

For many years, at Odin Teatret, improvisation has given the actors the possibility to define their own mental space, related to personal fantasies and dreams or to a specific dramatic figure. Today we actors are much more independent and we know how to compose, improvise and fix scenes. The director can elaborate, cut and combine them with the proposals of the other actors. But they can also be manipulated to such an extent that they lose their incandescent core. Thus the actor's inner space risks being flattened.

A fertile collaboration, as I see it, consists in an alternation between doing one's own thing and being led by the director. There are situations in which the director should resolutely elaborate the material of the actor who has something important to say.

Julia Varley

Often I am asked how I react to the fact of being manipulated by the director who cuts, mixes and edits my improvisations and materials. Whoever observes this process sees the director who models my actions as a sculptor sculpts stone. The same person, however, doesn't perceive the opportunity offered to me by the obligation to refuse banality, dig deeper to face other limits and to constantly give the maximum of myself.

The collaboration with a trusted director who takes responsibility for the result vis-à-vis the spectators gives great freedom. I can concentrate on the work without worrying about the final result and the intentions ascribed to it by the spectators. I don't need to look at myself and judge myself from the outside. I can focus on the muddled threads of my interests and needs and let my actions say what I cannot myself explain.

Roberta Carreri

The performance *Salt* was born from the material assembled during five years by Jan Ferslev and me. In April 2000, Eugenio decides to make a performance, in Italian only, inspired by Antonio Tabucchi's novel *Si sta facendo sempre più tardi* (It is getting later and later).

Eugenio starts by letting me improvise. He wants some materials with a different density to those I have proposed. The themes of the improvisations are drawn from Tabucchi's text. For example, 'a few grains of sand and a shell', or 'a strip of white foam'.

Eugenio works with me on the text. He wants vocal actions. He points out four phases through which I can escape the conditioned reflexes of my speech and avoid 'recitation':

- I have to translate all my Italian texts into English and learn them by heart.
- Do an improvisation on a theme given by Eugenio and fix it.
- Overlay the English text on the fixed improvisation, adapting and synchronising the physical impulses to the vocal ones.
- Use the resulting rhythms, intonations and melody for my Italian text.

Eugenio:

> I miss variations. The precision of your physical actions is spoiled when you speak. Only your motivation's inflexibility makes your actions logical, and therefore plausible. When you bite your hand I

must intuit the reasons, even if I'm unable to explain them. You bite your hand because:

- you want to suffocate a scream?
- you want to hurt yourself?
- you would like to bite someone else?
- you remember someone who bit you until it hurt?

I now see a woman who bites her hands but I don't receive any additional information – logical, emotional, sonorous, sensual or political.

The director's comment

With the years, it had become more and more difficult to challenge my actors' strong identities, the skill they had acquired in order to capture the spectators' attention. However, this identity, or personal manner, also created a boomerang: mannerisms. How can the director shatter the clichés of an actor who possesses intuition, experience, a capacity to guide herself and is partially aware of her mannerisms? When the actress was young, she accepted all my indications. With time, when she didn't agree that I change or cut part of her score, she proposed other materials. In recent years, some of the actors have a tendency to discuss, explain and justify. But I could see their mannerisms and felt obliged to protect the spectator from the déjà-vu. *On the other hand, I was incapable of saying directly: you have already served up what you are showing me, in a different sauce, in such and such performances. I strove to give stimulating tasks, but after years and years of work in common my proposals were not always effective. Then I became impatient and irritated. Later I was always unhappy, as if I had slapped a defenceless person.*

Julia Varley

As an actress, I see three main capacities in Eugenio: he is an 'animal' director; he carries a vast baggage of reading and knowledge; he is able to identify symptoms and themes emerging from the individuals' and the group's needs.

By 'animal' director I mean that he knows how to recognise the appropriateness of a physical impulse and to attune it to other impulses in the space; he intuits the potentiality of music and sounds to be treated as theatrical actions; he knows how to develop the logic of a text's intonation; he contrives to extract a dramatic essence from the dynamic relationships between the actors.

I believe that his incorporated 'library' springs from his curiosity, speed in reading and memory.

I suppose that the identification of symptoms and themes derives from his habit of thinking in associations and facing a problem by imagining what another person, director or historical character would do. This has given him the habit of wandering along the paths of imagination, but always tied to what happens around him. He has a lot of practice in switching relentlessly from the story he is telling to history, and from history back to the story.

I am an actress turned director. As I imagine is the case for other directors reading this book, a couple of questions ring in my head: when Eugenio elaborates the actors' materials, *how does he manage* to swing between his need for organicity and one of the many threads in his skein of 'narrations'? *How does he manage*, in the moment he unravels a new thread, *not* to modify the whole performance, letting coherences which are reciprocally incompatible coexist side by side?

These questions were in my mind while rehearsing *Andersen's Dream*, when Eugenio got stuck on the scene prepared by Roberta from Andersen's fairy tale, *The Tinderbox*. He made us repeat it again and again, introducing every day new changes and ideas, the obvious fruit of his moods and circumstances. He took up again discarded situations that we had almost forgotten; the space became a narrow street in Naples with lines of clothes hanging out to dry; then he turned it into a grill party, a typical gathering in a Danish garden with a barbecue spreading a greasy smell of singed frankfurters and beer. We improvised a long text and learned it by heart. Eugenio shortened it bit by bit as the *Tinderbox* characters and plot melted away. The first to be eliminated were the three magic dogs which had showered the soldier with money and gold, and then the imposing mobile towers we had built for them. Then the witch and the soldier who had killed her faded away, and another soldier who had nothing to do with the fairy tale made his entrance. It was Augusto Omolú,[11] our Afro-Brazilian actor, carrying on his back a stuffed Alsatian dog in a black sack. Eugenio called him 'Tage's shadow', but we no longer knew what character Tage had become in this amateurish party, which clashed with the rest of the previously prepared scenes. Suddenly, one day, Eugenio emptied the space and, with the whole scene covered only in white snow, he installed a black swing that hung from above.

Much later, when the performance was ready, I asked Eugenio how he managed to conclude the scene coherently. He answered: the solution came with the swing. But why did he think of a swing? And what was the essential change provoked by the introduction of this object? For me, the qualitative narrative leap had come about before, when he had interlaced Andersen's two fairy tales, *The Tinderbox* and *The Shadow,* with the scene between the 'white' Tage and the 'black' Augusto. Why had the swing been so conclusive?

The director's comment

Roberta had prepared a scene with all the actors in a couple of days, telling the whole fairy tale in half an hour. For me these materials needed to be compacted, perforated, explored in depth. The exploration had to happen at a geological level, not a geographical one. Therefore the landscape changed. What was bucolic became wild, and the external signs (the anecdotes) which helped us to understand, and which could be linked to the fairy tale, were eradicated while other signs emerged, although none of us was yet able to decipher them. These new signs engendered a sensation of chaos and turbulence, but they were fermenting, waiting for us to discover their analogical, rhythmic, associative, narrative correspondences. For me too the scene had acquired a narrative density when I succeeded in establishing the bond with the theme of the Shadow in the fairy tale of the same title. The Shadow takes the upper hand over its owner who is hanged in its place. It is exactly the contrary of The Tinderbox, *in which the soldier who is to be hanged is saved by the three magic dogs. I had furnished enough information to the spectators to mislead them into believing that the scene was inspired by* The Tinderbox. *And we 'negate this action while doing it' by laterally telling the fairy tale about the Shadow.*

This density and the continuous interpolations worked on an intellectual level and for the narrative thread. However the 'animal' director was unhappy. I was obsessed by a problem: how to shake up the spectators' nervous system, make them live the equivalent of the Shadow's threat through their senses and confront them with the bewilderment of a reality which suddenly went to pieces. I faced this problem with a question: what is the reality of a fairy tale? What makes it different from the reality of a novel, a play, a myth? My answer was that the fairy tale is based on the necessity to break the chains which tie its reality to that of the world as it is. What happens, then, if I break the chains of physical laws and, for example, don't respect the law of gravity? We could fly. Here I uncovered a narrative link with The Tinderbox *in which the princess flies at night, riding on a dog. I had to turn upside down the given conditions and make the whole scene fly, not just the dog and the princess. I told the actors: this scene should be like a Chagall painting. But how do I make people levitate, without anticipating and spoiling the surprise of the flying dog and princess? The swing!*

It looked as though it was the swing which moved, but I was soon struck by the sensation that it was the space which was swinging, projecting the Shadow and its master through the air, one lying on top of the other, bringing them alternatively close to and far from the spectators with the impetus of a battering ram, at first only a few centimetres from their faces and seconds later a few meters away. The swing unhinged the space, causing precariousness, menace, amazement, doubling its effect in the sky of mirrors that encapsulated actors and spectators. Simultaneously it evoked a hierarchy: 'the black, the shadow' (Augusto) above the 'white, its body' (Tage). The swing rhythmically and analogically related to the following scene: the space became once again immobile and stable and the princess carved a path through it, flying on the back of the dog towards the Shadow. Their union in the air was reflected in the trembling waters of a pond: the mirrors on the ceiling.

The swing permitted the 'animal' director to create, in the language of the reptilian and limbic brain, the equivalent of what the director 'narrator' had achieved by weaving different fairy tales through synapses in the cortex.

Roberta Carreri

Through the years, the themes for the improvisations given by Eugenio have always been suggestive and open to any interpretation. At times they awoke personal memories in me, at others reminiscences of a 'me' I didn't know. At other times they plummet to the ground with a thud, leaving a heavy silence. In these cases I have tried to translate the theme into images that could guide me. I have never refused a theme. I have always had the feeling that if I hadn't taken the first step, I would not have been able to delve into it.

At times Eugenio's words are rational and at times irrational, they help, surprise, clarify, confuse, hurt and mystify. They often express the opposite of what he had said yesterday. Looking back, I can see that he confuses us on purpose to make us come out of our cocoon. Sometimes he succeeds, but not always.

There are words that Eugenio uses in the context of training and seminars, and there are words which he adopts during the creation of a performance. Often, especially at the beginning, one is tempted to interpret in the same way the same words said in different contexts. It is a simplification due to our need to believe that we have understood. We may have understood with the head. But the process of turning this understanding into experience and knowledge assimilated by the body is longer and more laborious. Re-reading my diaries, I have the impression that Eugenio has repeated and contradicted the same words many times. The situation in which they were said and to whom they were addressed was decisive.

During the rehearsals of *Salt*, Eugenio's words often caused a great confusion in my head. I didn't succeed in doing what he asked me, but at least I succeeded in *not doing* what I did before.

Torgeir Wethal

With caution and without haste, you select those sequences of actions which have for you – or that you shape in order to acquire – a logical or emotional sense within the dramaturgical structure which is growing.

The logic or the images which you discern in some of the actors' actions make you see a fragment or a whole scene in a different light. You begin to follow this trail to see where it leads. Maybe it takes you to a new episode of the story or discloses a side of this same story that you had not thought of.

Maybe it ends in a cul-de-sac that may contain an interesting story, but extraneous to the theme of the performance. Although we have worked for a long time, a whole long scene is amputated and thrown away. It is a decision that hurts the actors and – I believe – you too.

The director's comment

At times my actors seemed to glide back to their animal nature, to previous incarnations. They struck my senses as an animal would: a cockroach, a cat, a horse.

A particular way of moving, lifting the head, looking, staying still, keeping silent or whispering gave the impression of coming from a remote inner space, a familiar yet mysterious common universe. They were not symbolic, conceptual or abstract signs; they were biological signals which had an impact on my nervous system, imperceptibly or with a shock. Inexplicably, they seduced or repulsed me, intruded beneath my skin evoking metamorphosis, internal changes, other bodies in which I had lived.

The actor's organic actions struck the reptilian part of my brain, the one which I share with other animals. But I modified their actions also to make my cortex react, to reflect on myself, to fly back and forth in time, to imagine and relate facts and distant people, even non-existent ones. I looked at my actors with tenderness and trepidation: after so many years I knew them so well, yet they always succeeded, even if only for a few seconds, to make me shiver. Half human and half animal: my actors were centaurs.

I was fond of them because, with their fantasy and laboriousness, they upset what I had in mind, like a strong breeze. Their materials pointed in unexpected directions, they cast to the winds my propensities and convictions. Thanks to them, I also became a centaur. My dilated senses, like those of a horse, dragged me beyond my certainties.

In what did my work as director with my actors consist if not in following half-erased traces and in deciphering, consciously or blindly, the signs scattered by the dark forces which accompany us?

3

NARRATIVE DRAMATURGY AS A LEVEL OF ORGANISATION

> Enfin, mon oncle me tirant par le collet, j'arrivai près de la boule.
> 'Regarde, me dit-il, et regarde bien! Il faut prendre des leçons d'abîme.'
>
> Jules Verne: *Journey to the Centre of the Earth*

Creative thought

Who can guarantee us results? What, in theatre, is a result? The ability to aim at and strike the heart and mind of every single spectator? We are speaking of an unusual archer's technique.

In 1700, in Russia, a recruiting officer enters a village in Volhynia. On many trees on the outskirts can be seen the results of an extraordinary archer: dozens of arrows piercing the centre of a small circle drawn on the trunks. Who is this great talent? It is Misha, they reply, the village simpleton. First he shoots an arrow and when it hits the tree he draws a circle around it.

In his book dedicated to 'the history of the changes in man's vision of the universe' (*The Sleepwalkers*, New York, Macmillan, 1959), Arthur Koestler demonstrates how every creative act – in science, in art or in religion – is accomplished through a preliminary regression to a more primitive level: *reculer pour mieux sauter*. It is a process of negation or disintegration which prepares the leap towards the result. Koestler calls this moment a creative 'precondition'.

To burn the house.

It is a moment which seems to negate all that which characterises the search for results. It does not determine a new orientation, but is rather a voluntary disorientation which demands that all the energy of the researcher be set in motion, sharpening his senses, like when one advances in the dark. This dilation of our potentialities has a high price: we lose control of the meaning of our own actions. It is a negation which has not yet discovered the new entity which it affirms.

In Volterra, during a session of the International School of Theatre Anthropology (ISTA) in 1981, I worked on Edward Bond's play *Narrow*

Road to the Deep North, surrounded by a group of young directors. For explanatory purposes I separated the two ways of thinking. The first phase took place at the table: cutting, interpolating and restructuring the text since the characters were ten and I had only five actors. The second one was a sketched *mise-en-scène*. It was hard for the young directors (and also for myself) to understand why the practical work entailed an unending tussle with the options and ideas I had opened up at the table.

A thought is a force in motion, an action, energy which changes: it travels from one point to reach another, following paths which abruptly change direction. Just as there is a lazy, predictable and characterless way of moving, there is also a lazy, predictable and characterless way of thinking. The flow of thought can be burdened and blocked by stereotypes, judgements and ready-made objections. Creative thought is distinguished by the fact that it proceeds by leaps, by means of sudden disorientations which oblige it to reorganise itself in new ways, abandoning its protective shell and perforating anything inert with which it is confronted when we imagine, reflect or act.

Creative thought is *not* linear, *not* univocal, *not* foreseeable. It is the subject of a labyrinthine science.

I speak of labyrinthine science to define the exploration which starts from the foreseeable to clash with the unforeseeable. It is not pure *chance* which ignites unexpected meanings and unintended connections. Nor is it the unprogrammed links, meetings and combinations which give us the opportunity to question ourselves on the meaning of what we are narrating.

In the creative process we must forge our own chance, just as the Romans used to say that we are the forgers of our own good or bad fortune. Here Pasteur's words are appropriate: 'Chance only favours minds which are prepared.'

Sometimes I had the impression that it was not me who led the working process. The only thing I could do was to silence the prejudices which restrained the thought-in-life as it danced.

At first, this was a vexing sensation, like being on board a ship in a tempest. Before it became a feeling of freedom and opened new dimensions, I experienced it as a conflict between what I knew, had decided or aspired to and, on the other hand, the *thought-in-life*.

When I succeeded in establishing this creative 'precondition', I felt as if I was being battered by a storm, as though I was possessed or in a state of *ex-stasis*, taken out of myself. But this feeling remained always anchored to the solid *terra firma* of craftsmanship.

Being master of my own craft signified, above all, knowing how to prepare the storm which threatened me. In other words, I had to contrive how to resist without resorting to easy or familiar solutions.

In bygone days, when their sailing ships were in the midst of storms, the sailors had to perform the most difficult operations with absolute precision and competence, each at his place, without too many words, groans, curses and invocations. At the same time, the thoughts of each of them flew to the image of his patron saint or protecting demon.

When I was in the throes of the storm which I myself had deliberately chased and which threatened the result of my efforts, I often had a mute thought which sought the protective image of Picasso.

In the summer of 1955 Pablo Picasso accepted, contrary to all expectations, to make a film showing how he painted. It was Georges Clouzot, the French director, who had convinced him. For a whole month Picasso had risen early in the morning to go to the film studio in Nice. He agreed to submit to all the technical demands of the film-maker. He took a white canvas and began to paint in the presence of many 'spectators': lighting and sound technicians, electricians, photographers, production staff, director, all the numerous members of a film team.

Several times, when the painting seemed finished, he stopped and announced that now it could really begin. The surrounding crowd expressed amazement and incomprehension. Meanwhile he disarranged everything he had done up to that moment. He drew other scenes and figures which he interwove or superimposed on the preceding ones, cancelling them out. Finally, he seized a new canvas and on it painted the picture which he had mentally extracted from the difficulties with which he was confronted while painting the previous canvas.

Every time I have watched the film *Le Mystère Picasso* to deduce something which might be of interest from the professional point of view, I have not allowed myself to be dazzled by his extraordinary creativity. His exceptional qualities disclosed the humble procedures on which his artistic work was based, whatever the level of the results.

* * *

In the first years I strove to capture and make theatrically perceptible the story's kernel, the evident or potential conflicts of a situation, the tensions and contrasts between the characters. This pragmatism helped me to lay the dramatic foundations of the actors' presence and actions. Above all, it was useful when the text was too literary or included scenes which I planned to change and when the number of actors didn't correspond to that of the characters. I struggled to resolve these problems. In time, I acquired a certain skill in this field. Then it became crucial *to invent problems*, to impose constraints and obstacles on myself which would unleash the storm during rehearsals. By *storm* I meant the construction of a system of relationships which could not be explored in a single glance. It was a composite order in which many forces acted simultaneously.

During rehearsals, every element which entered the space – text, costume, object, song, sequence of actions, sudden pause and, above all, *errors and misunderstandings* – became a precious collaborator, in addition to being an obstacle to take into account. Obstacles were enigmas offered by chance.

I loved to decipher these enigmas that, in theatre, are not solved with words, but by action. I couldn't expect an explicit answer from them; I had to snatch it, lay traps and devise stratagems. They were androgynous enigmas: for one actor they assumed one form, for another a different one.

It is natural to use words, costumes and objects for what they are. But they are also autonomous entities, with a will of their own and a temperament. They have a spine and a voice. We must discover their typical conduct, their dynamic features, their sonorous traits, their desire to be independent from the ways they are usually treated.

> A certain overcoat lived at our house for a long time.
> It was made of good wool
> a finely-combed wool
> a many-times-made-over overcoat
> well-worn, a thousand times turned inside out.
> It wore the outline of our father
> his very figure, whether worried or happy.
> Hanging on a hook or on the coat rack
> it took on a defeated air:
> through that ancient overcoat
> I came to know my father's secrets
> sharing his life, in the shadows.
>
> (Alda Merini)

Only when I was absentminded did I believe that objects and costumes were lifeless. They have a will of their own and recount. They are accomplices and lovers. I had only to listen and fulfil what they wanted me to do and express. I tried not to forget they were generous gifts from the gods, carriers of veiled messages.

For me, it was impossible to collaborate with the storm – with its system of relationships that cannot be dominated – without having at my disposal a vast variety of materials and *sources*, and without straying simultaneously in several directions. This profusion of fragments produced confusion.

Confusion, when it is sought after and practised as an *end* in itself, is the art of deception. When it is deliberate and used as a *means* in a creative activity, it is one of the factors in a fertile organic process.

The tension between the various divergent forces could end in disaster. But if I was able to restrain these forces, discovering the kind of relationships which could hold them together and make them cohabit in a dialogue, I neared the threshold of complexity instead of disaster.

A working process is not true, authentic or sincere, but only functional and usable in relation to a given person. The use of knowledge or of an image is always determined by the system of thought and the superstitions of the person who chooses them for the benefit of his own interpretation.

The intricate lines of my exploration did not mean that the exploration aimed at intricacy or progressed towards the solution. The accumulation of heterogeneous elements and the collision of conflicting lines aimed to mark out unthought-of perspectives and to cast a new light on my *sources*, my points of departures. According to the criteria of economy and saving, this was a paradoxical way of proceeding.

But there is no creative work without waste. And there is no waste if that which is discarded is not of a high quality. The proportion between that which is produced and that which is finally used should correspond to the disproportion of the seeds which are dispersed in nature in order that a single fertilised cell may succeed in engendering a new individual in the animal or plant world. This attitude illustrates the difference between the organic character of art and the organisation of daily tasks which are all the better for having the *easy* extracted from the difficult.

Extracting the difficult from the difficult is the attitude that defines artistic practice. This personal attitude decides the incisiveness and the dense nature of the result as well as the moments of obscurity, exhaustion, intuition, disorientation and sudden reorientation which make up the process.

It is easy to read *creative precondition* and *collaboration with chance, storm* and *meticulousness, confusion* and *complexity, accumulation* and *waste* as formulas for extracting the difficult from the difficult. It is also easy to imagine how, in the repetitive daily reality, they are experienced as doubt, discomfort, sense of loss and sometimes despair.

During rehearsals, when the result of a long-lasting commitment was treated as a point of departure, some of the actors lost heart. It was always a critical moment for actors and director alike. The irritation of each against the others prevailed as a destructive virus. Yet we continued, with clenched teeth, because it was part of the craft.

Working does not only tire, sometimes it hurts. But sadism and masochism have no place here. If they surface in the web of relationships which make up a group aiming at a performance, the consequence is immediate and bitter dissolution.

The creation of a performance is necessarily a collective yet deeply solitary process, projected towards a horizon which eludes us. It is an intimate and incommunicable path which unites the people submitting to it. And as always with complicity, in the case of failure it separates them.

An entry in Anton Chekhov's notebook: 'In Montecarlo, a man goes to the Casino, wins a million, goes back home and commits suicide.'

From glance to vision

Thousand and One Nights, Freud's psychoanalysis, Jung's analytical psychology and cultural anthropology all show how narration – *mythos* in Greek – may help to save the life of the individual and a society. Men and women, children and adults, all need stories to orient themselves in the world. We understand people, things, concepts, numbers or gods only if narrated, put into a story. Even mathematics consists of stories about numbers, and about journeys and peripeteias which take place between the two extremes of a formula.

Tell me a story . . . the rest is silence.

A European medieval theologian would have asserted that our craving for stories is typical of human imperfection. In the Beyond – the theologian would have reassured us – instead of stories, vision will be enough, and we will grasp human and divine things, penetrating them with our gaze and *seeing within them* (*intuere* in Latin, from which 'intuition').

Telling a story involved the mental activity which I projected in my work. In the end, I could hide my story or contrive to make it unrecognisable for the spectator. But I could not expel narration from all the phases of the rehearsals.

For me, the work on the narrative level didn't aim to set up a plot which the spectator would understand during the performance: only one story for all the spectators. I had a tendency to create conditions in which every single spectator could read his own personal story into the performance. My narrative dramaturgy differed from what is meant by 'narrative dramaturgy' in the theatre which starts out from a text. Or also in the theatre which, although not starting out from a text, aims to develop only one narrative thread, equal for every spectator. In this kind of theatre, the margin of liberty left to the spectator concerns the story's literary, social, political and ethical connotations. But the story is presumed to be the same for every spectator.

In my way of working, I did not have a text in the usual sense of the term as a point of departure, and there was not only one story at the point of arrival. What I call narrative dramaturgy was only my particular way to narrate. It didn't refer to the interpretation of a pre-existing text or to the more or less coherent intertwining or collage of various writings. It was a *narration-through-actions*. Or more precisely, my narrative dramaturgy was *the constellation of meanings and orientations which I knowingly concealed or revealed behind-actions*. I repeat again, strange as it may sound: when I started work on the performance, there was not *one* play or *one* adaptation of a novel as a point of departure, nor only *one* story at the point of arrival. I started out from *sources*, references, orientations, strong stimuli which had an impact on me and were often texts of various types: articles, poems, fables, legends or tales that I invented around the various themes dealt with in the performance. But not necessarily. For example, one of the *sources* of *Mythos* was a song, the 'Internationale', and the story of its murder.

There are directors who mould the performance with their will and originality knowing in advance which paths will fulfil their intentions. And there are midwife-directors who help the performance to come into the world, accepting images and actions whose sense they don't dominate completely, but which they trust as signs of an underground presence of life. I belonged to this second kind, who ignores the fruit of the process and observes it with the critical and curious eyes of the first spectator, a little sceptical and a little astonished.

My first three performances (*Ornitofilene*, *Kaspariana* and *Ferai*) told only one story, the one proposed by the author. With each new production, I reached a broader understanding of the ways to stimulate the actor, to guide the spectator's attention, to interlace the threads of the plot, to narrate through associations and allude through analogies and antithesis, to find interpretative solutions and discover what I didn't know or thought I didn't know. I contrived different ways to launch a performance, also in order to avoid repeating myself. The 'narrative' motivation, which in the first years was an author's text, materialised in *My Father's House* as a tangle of heterogeneous stimuli which I imagined as the performance's *sources*. Since then, disparate sources induced me to narrate-through-actions.

In order to start work, I felt the need for different and contradictory motives which fell within the preoccupations of that period of my life or simply made me curious. In my activity as director the *sources* have been of various types: a play (*Ornitofilene* by Jens Bjørneboe, *Ferai* by Peter Seeberg), a long poem (*Kaspariana* by Ole Sarvig), 22 books of poetry by Henrik Nordbrandt for *Mythos*, a novel (*It is getting later and later* by AntonioTabucchi for *Salt*), scenes extrapolated from a play (*The Three Sisters* by Chekhov for *Kaspariana*), fragments of religious texts (gnostic ones for *The Gospel according to Oxyrhincus*, biblical ones for *Judith*), a news story (for *Mythos*, the descriptions of the celebrations for the year 2000 and the question: would the myth of revolution survive in the new millennium?), a proverb, an aphorism, a paradox or a known quotation ('a ghost wanders through Europe, the ghost of communism' for *Kaosmos*), the biography of a historical figure (Joseph Stalin, for *The Gospel according to Oxyrhincus*) or a literary one (Dostoevsky for *My Father's House*, Brecht for *Brecht's Ashes*) or an unknown Brazilian soldier for *Mythos*, a memory, a picture, a photo, an anthropological essay, a metaphor (the revolt which was buried alive, for *The Gospel according to Oxyrhincus*). The *source* could be the pleasure derived from confronting a technical issue. For *The Gospel according to Oxyrhincus*, I wondered if the actor is the theatre's demiurge, how can she always be present even when invisible?

The performance's organic level can be organised by working with the actors in a precise way. My way is personal, and as such it can be shared or not. But it is objectively verifiable, and as such it can be explained or, at least, described.

But on the narrative level, I could only arrange the conditions. In order for the performance to open a plurality of possible stories, I needed some 'taps', even if with little water, which were the sources of what would become the performance's river with all of its tributaries.

It was not easy to find themes which moved my imagination or motivated me to throw myself into the work. They were not accidental pretexts or arbitrary choices. They could seem abstruse and meaningless in the eyes of others, but I had to be pestered by them. Sometimes I too felt uneasy in their company; I weighed them up with scepticism and discussed them in an indirect way with trusted friends. I was reticent to expose them in their fragile simplicity and extravagance. I waited for a long time, until the decisive meeting with the actors: the first rehearsal. Then I let these *sources* flow untamed in an oral improvisation with all the appropriate, inadequate and disrespectful associations which galloped through my head.

The *sources* constituted for me the equivalent of what the subtext was for the actor: an intimate reference allowing the scene to acquire a depth and to be fed, as well as contradicted, by a remote echo. During rehearsals, the waters of the initial sources could blend, even sink and disappear inside rivers and lakes which they unexpectedly met on their course. The meeting of new sources (themes, situations, texts, technical challenges, questions) caused unprogrammed turns and fluctuations: a new orientation. Without the original sources or those which appeared while rehearsing, the performance lost its echo. The performance could be interesting, suggestive and entertaining, but it was just theatre.

When the moment of orchestrating the narrative level arrived, I proceeded with caution, careful not to confine the materials of the actors in a univocal pre-arranged sense. I used the actions which aroused thoughts, impressions, rhythms or images as traces to be followed towards regions far from the sources. Then the situation lost its clarity and I plunged into the mists of confusion. I had to sharpen all my senses to discern the direction of the next step.

I paid for this 'method' in terms of time. The true midwife knows the child will come into the world after nine months and an early delivery is risky. But the midwife-director must understand each time what kind of birth it is going to be, when it could be premature and when late, always according to an uncertain criterion: some performances require the gestation time of mice, others of elephants. I was never able to guess in advance.

A performance doesn't limit itself to narrating, and its effectiveness and value do not reside *only* in the narrative aspects. But the narration technique remains a major component of the theatrical craft and of the impact on the spectator. It is a technique that above all influences that part of the perception which belongs to the glance.

Normally, in theatre, actors recount a story through a system of more or less univocal meanings which capture the spectators' glance and unify it. It could be said that they limit it to facilitate clarity.

When I tried to overturn this relationship between narrative dramaturgy and perception, I discovered that the technique of narrating can be a valid tool *to dilate the director's glance* during rehearsals and, subsequently, *the spectator's glance* during the performance.

In the concreteness of the work, *to dilate the glance* means to open the spectator's perception to the awareness of a personal meaning.

My aim was to turn glance into vision.

The path leading from glance to vision passed through different fields of experience: *foreseeing, not seeing, continuing not to see, seeing anew*.

The human brain is programmed to foresee, to prefigure the carrying out of an action, anticipating its trajectory and its ending. Seeing the beginning of a gesture, the brain jumps to a conclusion. If I get up from a chair, an onlooker realises, by the way I perform this action, whether I will remain standing or move into the space. The onlooker guesses which direction I will take and often even what is my intention. This prediction is due to our kinaesthetic sense: the sensation by which bodily positions, muscle tensions and movements are perceived. It is the awareness every human being has of his own body and of that of any other living being. It is the kinaesthetic sense which allows me to touch the point of my nose with my finger without the least hesitation or to join my hands behind my back without looking and consciously directing this action. It is the kinaesthetic sense which, by recognising the impulses, responds to an embrace or avoids bumping into the people coming out of an elevator. The kinaesthetic sense was the secret weapon I employed to achieve an organic effect in our performances. It was this exceptional prerogative that my actors and I exploited to manipulate the spectator's perception.

The kinaesthetic sense deciphers the *sats*, the characteristics (the information) of an action's impulses and tensions, predicting its further development. If the actor reaches out to take a heavy dictionary on a table and at the last moment picks up the pen instead which is nearby, the consequence is an infinitesimal, subliminal disconcertion in the perception of the spectators. These, on the basis of the initial *sats* – the actor's impulse of the arm, and position and tension of the fingers – had forecast and therefore imagined a different intention: to lift the dictionary.

I applied this fundamental principle of perception when I composed a narration-behind-actions. The actors' actions, with their detailed and precise tensions, provoked mental patterns in the spectator, produced predictability, comprehensibility, connections and dynamics of cause and effect. I paid attention that the actors *negated the action while executing it*, performing it with the tonicity corresponding to another action. Sometimes this different action was part of the subscore, concealed yet generating contrasting tensions in the visible action.

The aim was to deceive the kinaesthetic expectation. I wanted the spectators to project a justification on the actions of a scene which, in the end, would have a value and a sense other than the ones shown by the actions. Through this sensorial oxymoron the spectators could live the experience of an experience, of a slippery and turbulent reality, one which refused to be dominated at first sight and demanded to be scrutinised and reflected upon. An actress bends down with caution as if carrying a heavy weight in her hands and drops a daisy; Joan of Arc burns on the pyre with a smile; 'I am free' – Scheherezade (a puppet) exults while she breaks in two; Brecht vivisects a fish expressing the need for a rational and scientific approach to reality, and in front of him Walter Benjamin hangs himself; in a Berlin freed from Nazism, Mackie Messer breaks into a wild tango with Kattrin, Mother Courage's mute daughter, and suffocates her by stuffing *Pravda* in her mouth ('The Truth', the official newspaper of the Russian Communist Party); in *Talabot* the earth's globe burns like a heap of garbage and Kirsten Hastrup, the protagonist, watches it happily in love with a bunch of flowers in her hands; in the same performance the Trickster dances, joyfully humming a litany of wars, massacres and historical misfortunes; in *Kaosmos*, the grave is closed and wheat sprouts from it; Daedalos, in *Mythos*, flies, galloping like a horse.

Obstructing the mechanism of pre-vision is the premise to acquiring *vision*. In fact, vision is always an unforeseeable experience.

My narration-behind-actions followed the sensorial rules of a labyrinthine science. This consisted in submitting the spectator's perception to elusive sequences of detours and ramifications. Every action, also the most insignificant, was a dynamic peripeteia. The action started arousing in the spectator the sensation of foreseeing its progress. But it altered its tonic quality (its dynamism and intention), provoking a stinging effect on the spectator's attention. But there was always the risk of arbitrariness and lack of precision, which resulted in a confusion of stimuli.

This stinging effect which captured the spectator's attention was the experience of *not seeing*.

My arrangement of deviations and tiny distortions, resulting in ambiguity and indeterminacy, aimed at sharpening theatrical reality, both for those who looked as well as for those who acted. It was *estrangement*, but also an experience of *uneasiness*.

As a director, I had a credo: in order to have in impact on my 'glance' while rehearsing, and on that of the spectators during the performance, a story had to be put to the test. Its components had to be separated and modified, as in a process of distillation in a retort. Confronted with a story or a situation, I immediately thought of how to dissolve it into its many incompatible details, how to split its ingredients, how to render them reciprocally autonomous and let them sail alongside each other in a sea of contiguity, favouring unpredictable interactions and combinations. The *storm* which I had unleashed made me *sink into a state of not-seeing* in order to find a way of *seeing anew*.

Every action becomes a story when something prevents it from racing towards its conclusion. Whatever the point of departure and that of arrival, any story is made up of peripeteias – turning points – which make it *deviate* from a straight course. Many have explained and repeated it convincingly. It has become a commonplace. Its intelligent, humorous or provocative opposite were the two-line tragedies invented by the futurists (The curtain goes up. He: 'I love you.' She: 'I don't.' He and she, in unison: 'Goodbye.' The curtain falls). Without incidents and hindrances, a story is not reduced to its essential, but to a stunted dwarf, just a beginning and an ending. It is no longer a story, but a headlong rush.

I looked for the *essential*, and for me the essential emerged from maceration. It consisted in coalescing the stories which appeared from behind a labyrinth of organic actions.

Who made me what I am?

The landscapes, the villages and the cities of Europe exhibited the traces of World War II. After passing the frontier, people no longer spoke a comprehensible language and their food had no taste. 'Abroad' was the kingdom of the irrational. Everything needed to be understood anew, catalogued ex novo, *inserted in categories yet to be discovered. I felt myself to be half fool and half impostor. I was a stranger, a foreigner, a person without features, history and bonds. Here my mother's love or my good marks in Greek and Latin were of no help. With very little money, sleeping in the open air, with an enormous military rucksack that my brother had got from the American Boy Scouts by writing to them that he was consumptive, I protected myself behind an innocent expression, hitchhiking towards a mythical Sweden, the heaven of free love. It was June 1953; I was 16 years old.*

Torrential rain had drenched me and the rucksack at my feet. The cars disappeared rapidly in a halo of spray, indifferent to my arm begging a lift. I had been waiting for ages on the motorway between Stuttgart and Nuremberg, frozen stiff in my wet clothes. Then the unthinkable happened: a miracle. A fat Mercedes stopped, a well-dressed young man lifted my rucksack onto the back seat and made me a sign to sit next to him. A litany repeated itself in my head: this is generosity, this is empathy, this is altruism, goodness, breeding, class, magnanimity. The gentleman handed me his scarf to dry my face and neck. I felt shame, as if I had urinated on myself, thinking about the water which was dripping from the rucksack on the back seat.

Each time I was picked up by a car, the conversation followed the usual course. The same questions: where I came from, where I was going, what I did. And the same answers: I was Italian, a student, going to Scandinavia. I hitchhiked because I didn't have much money and it gave me the opportunity to meet interesting people. With this formula I was halfway there, as far as being accepted was concerned. At times there was even a meal or an ice cream to boot. The driver of the Mercedes asked if I had thought of visiting Bergen. I didn't know what it was and he explained that it was a Norwegian town. He added: it was the first target I bombed. He described his first raid as a pilot during the war, then other similar situations. I hardly understood any German, mostly names of towns. I have learned much of my geography like this, travelling in Germany, where the drivers told me of their wartime experiences. In France, Holland, Denmark and Norway, on the other hand, I learned the names of other places in Europe, those of the concentration and extermination camps. The driver of the Mercedes gave me hospitality in his house in Nuremberg. His wife dried my clothes and the following morning, when her husband had already gone to his office, she accompanied me to the motorway in her Volkswagen.

The less we know of a nation or a culture, the more they seem to us to be endowed with a collective identity. The cultural identity, the genius loci, *the soul of a place or a country, the spirit of an epoch or of a civilisation are products of distance. They acquire consistency in books, anecdotes, memories and generalisations. As soon as we approach them, they fade away like a mirage. Looking from afar, while keeping our distance, allows us to generalise effectively and put order into our mental schemes. But this harmless 'objective' procedure, which ought to organise, becomes a tool of chaos if we have the illusion that these generalisations are founded on reality. The same is true if we ask questions such as: what is the identity of an Italian or a German, of a European or an African? What do we have to do to embody and develop our identity? What threatens to pollute it?*

In Norway I discovered the many faces of generosity and hospitality. I lived out my immigrant condition in the warmth and the affection of Fridtjov and Sonja Lehne. They adopted me in their house like a younger brother. There were not many foreigners around and, in the eyes of the Norwegians, my inadequacies and awkward reactions were exotic, arousing the desire to help. Eigil Winnje was the owner of the sheet metal workshop in which I worked in Oslo. His example taught me the daily discipline of a manual activity, the respect for tools, the satisfaction in keeping a workplace tidy, the pride in a job well done. He was always at his workers' side sharing their tasks with them. With rigour and patience, he introduced me to the art of welding. When passing from the practical example to words, he assumed an attitude of earnestness and at the same time a slight irony. I had the impression of grasping, behind his advice, a teasing attitude, as if in the moment in which he tried to make me understand, he was also saying that I would not understand. His words seemed to be direct instructions, almost simple recipes, but instead were intended to be preserved for a more or less distant future. They were 'word-appointments' to be saved for the day when they could be put into practice and be actively misunderstood. I had the same feeling some years later with many of the expressions in the books of the theatre reformers.

My first year as an immigrant was like a privileged adventure, an unfolding of unimaginable horizons and epiphanies and the gratification of earning my living with my hands. I sat as a model for Willi Midelfart, a painter who had lived in Paris in the 1920s and in Berlin and Moscow in the early 1930s. He was my guide in the universe of the arts, advising me in my reading and showing me the many ways to perceive a painting.

There is a time for illumination and a time for humiliation. The moment arrived in which I experienced rejection as a foreigner. How do you behave when you become the object of injustice? When others consider it normal to treat you with contempt, call you insulting names and expect you to submit in silence?

I had a dream: to visit Ramakrishna's house in Calcutta and, following his example, descend the steps of the ghat to the waters of the Ganges at first light. At that time, the only way of materialising such a dream was to embark as a sailor on a Norwegian cargo boat going to Asia. Many sailors welcomed me with tacit solidarity, aware that we were sharing the same condition; others, fascinated by the demon of racism, treated me with contempt. Rejecting their attitude meant conflict, and I have suffered violence, and at times I have had to resort to it.

At nightfall, the streets are strident
with neon signs, a black
dance of ideograms; a blond-haired Dutch girl
shows clammy breasts to Japanese tourists
in a smoky cellar; a Filipina girl does the same
for beer-happy Yankee sailors
while a bulldog British businessman is daintily escorted
by a tongue-tied little Hongkongese.

This poem by Kenneth White describes my first intercultural experiences. Violence is concealed behind exotic and attractive faces. Nothing is more instructive for a young man discovering the world than the company of a woman of another culture.

In 1956, in Singapore, a woman called to me from the threshold of a house. Her hospitality didn't cost a lot. Or would I prefer to be entertained by her daughter, a little girl of about 10? I had been brought up with sound principles. I refused indignantly and joined my ship's crew in a bar near the harbour. Sailors of all languages, ages and colours – the internationals of the sea – bought tokens from the cashier, allowing them to dance with reasonably priced girls as a prologue to a more cosy situation. That evening I didn't ask: who made that woman who tried to sell her (presumed) daughter what she is? I didn't think: who made me what I am? It was another mother who asked me this question, three years later.

It happened when I travelled through Israel. I slept for weeks on the desert beach of Eilat, among taciturn characters, similar to those that Avner had described in Memories of a Terrorist *five years before. It was 1960. Israel was a small country, very different from that of today: two-thirds of the population were fugitives who had escaped from the Nazi hell and a Europe gone mad. Seven years were to pass before the Six Day War in June 1967 and the permanent occupation of territories of other states.*

In a moshav, an agricultural cooperative village, I worked with Alex, a Romanian with blond hair and blue eyes. He explained that in Romania, Jews were recognised by these traits. They were the descendants of the Khazars, a tribe from the steppes who converted to Judaism and built an empire that lasted three centuries. The inhabitants of the Jewish shetls of Eastern Europe had their origins among the different tribes of the Khazar Empire. In the night, I was woken by cries and weeping. Alex calmed my fears: they were the Dutch who had lived through the extermination camps. In the dark, memories haunted them.

I visited the kibbutz Lohamei HaGetahot, 'Fighters of the ghetto', founded by the survivors of the Warsaw uprising against the Germans in April 1943. It was similar to the other kibbutz in which I had worked. 'The space of memory' was a hut: three rooms with photos and a few objects – gruesome documents that seemed inconceivable to me. 'Who made the Germans what they are?' A woman of about 40, my guide, quietly asked this question as if she didn't expect an answer. 'Their fathers? Their docile and caring mothers? Their efficient schools? The despair of the economic crisis? A single man called Adolf?'

She had participated in the ghetto uprising, was captured by the Germans and sent with her little child to Treblinka in a cattle truck.

With her child clutched to her breast, she succeeded in escaping by slipping through a hole in the floor of the moving truck, and left her son at the door of a farm with a short explanatory note. Then she joined the resistance. At the end of the war, she found her child with the Polish family who had taken care of him, crossed half of Europe to embark in Trieste and clandestinely disembarked in Palestine. Her child must have been the same age as me. I asked if he lived with her. No, he didn't want to have anything to do with his mother or the other kibbutz members. He had turned into a sabra, the nickname given to the Jews born in Israel. It means 'cactus leaf', thorny on the outside, tender and sweet within. Sabras are rough, dynamic, ready to defend themselves and counterattack. Her son was incapable of understanding how the European Jews had allowed themselves to be taken to the slaughterhouse without taking up weapons. He refused to be identified with them. But you did fight, I retorted. The woman repeated in a low voice: That's what I told him, too.

I recognised this tension boiling inside me. I had felt it many times before, like a transfusion of black blood enflaming my veins. In front of that mother, and just as helpless, once more my anger hurled me against the fickle collective will that we call nation, civilisation, family: the idols of the tribe which legitimate outrage. The spirit of the time sneered in my face, and I didn't know with which weapons I could oppose it.

After six months in Israel I made myself a promise. To whoever asked me about my religion, I would answer: I am Jewish.

Was this also a way to burn my *house?*

Knots

The organic dramaturgy can live without a narrative dramaturgy, but no narrative dramaturgy can live without the organic one. It suffices to think about a dance performance which does not always claim to tell a story.

For me, to narrate-through-actions or behind-actions implied, first of all, the exploration of the relationship between these two levels of organisation: the non-obvious way to establish bonds between the organic level and the narrative one.

On the organic level, the logic embraced precision, oppositions, rhythm, colours of energy (soft or vigorous), the organic effect of each action, the quality of their form, introvert or extrovert features, the dynamic action–reaction, the accelerations and pauses, simultaneous and divergent rhythms of actions: their flow.

On the narrative level the logic aimed to build relationships, associations, allusive paths, images or clusters of actions which guided the spectators towards a personal sense in the scene they were watching. Often, what functioned at the organic level of rhythm and variety of actions risked protracting the narration, thus weakening it.

In the reality of the performance, the narrative dramaturgy engraved itself on the organic one and the two were inseparable. But during rehearsals I could *practically and conceptually* separate them in two adjoining roads. Thus these two paths were simultaneously present each with its own logic, and started to collaborate in an unplanned way, combining precision (necessity) and chance (unpredictability).

The collaboration between these two paths forced me to follow simultaneously dissimilar orientations, opposite traces, disconnected associations and contradictions. During rehearsals, this provoked the growth of a multitude of disparate fragments and allusions which cast a long-lasting shadow on the narrative clarity.

When I narrated-behind-actions, I didn't lean on the organic dramaturgy in order to expose a story, but I used it to *entangle* the threads of the narrative dramaturgy.

In this type of work, the true difficulty resided in safeguarding the organic integrity of the performance and in avoiding shattering and debasing the actors' materials. During most of the rehearsals, the performance's growth was dictated not by the story's meanings, but by the efficiency of the organic dramaturgy: the actors' actions and interactions.

I succeeded more or less in following and explaining to myself an actor's actions because they had an evident meaning or were able to arouse associations in me. Suddenly these actions no longer advanced in the direction in which they seemed to point, but they twined around one another becoming a dynamic firework whose multicoloured filaments exploded above, behind, before me. It was a situation of confusion and turbulence, typical of the rehearsals.

At times, very rarely, this indecipherable criss-crossing of actions was set on fire. In our jargon we deferentially called it a 'knot'.

A 'knot' seemed to spring accidentally from simultaneous actions which negate each other, giving life to a *powerful and irrational image*. It was the consequence of a montage which detonated in a unique and privileged moment: the opposites melted, each accentuating its own identity. Then it became for me, as well as for the spectator, a physical and intellectual koan, historical and timeless, merciless and compassionate.

When I composed a scene, I strove for a synthesis of contradictory information in a convincing sensory form. These antithetical elements originated both from the organic/dynamic and the narrative level: physical and vocal actions, ways of using objects, costumes, words, meanings, iconographical motives, sounds, melodies, lights. I stubbornly wanted to unfold and simultaneously structure the innumerable complementary facets of the internal and the material reality.

A 'knot' was a tangle of conflicting information which, instead of creating confusion, resulted in a paradoxical effectiveness.

In *Ferai*, the young libertarian king (Torgeir Wethal) never let go of his sceptre: a recorder which was at the same time the handle of a knife and a whip.

In *The Gospel according to Oxyrhincus*, The Great Inquisitor (Tage Larsen) tried to erase Antigone's shadow with a bunch of flowers whose stems ended in a dagger.

In *Brecht's Ashes*, Arthur Ui (Francis Pardeilhan) raped the mute daughter of Mother Courage (Iben Nagel Rasmussen), setting a basin full of water between her thighs and sinking his face into it for a long time, until he lifted it, purple and gasping for breath.

The 'knot' put a piece of reality under a magnifying glass, overturning it. It was a troubling ambiguity.

When I think about the 'knots', I have a tendency to use expressions such as: technique which has no technique, skill-less skill, distilled experience, existential truth. I have a feeling that the director and the actor were not conscious craftsmen, but the first unintentional witnesses of a more consistent and deeper reality than the historical or imaginary situation that their theatrical fiction tried to evoke. A probability had materialised, chance had guided our steps. The scene was a gift of grace: the Mother had smiled at us.

Yet, when I reflect on the rare scenes which capsized in 'knots', I notice that I have respected certain technical conditions which were always the same.

Once more: the actor's actions had to be real (which doesn't mean realistic). I started from the opposite: I developed the action, the image or the idea contrary to the explicit ones in the situation on which we were working.

I strove for density: a multiplicity of suggestions which dilated and imploded the univocal fixity of the form of each action. I thought in paradoxical ways, often giving a material reality to idiomatic expressions such as: 'to die with laughter', 'to run with the hare and hunt with the hounds', 'to pull someone's leg'.

Real actions, oppositions, density, paradoxical thinking: these were the premises to collaborate with chance and escape from my mental inclinations.

In 1988, while rehearsing *Talabot*, Iben Nagel Rasmussen presented, among her materials, a doll-child she had made. Suddenly she pulled a thread and the sand inside the body of the doll-child streamed out.

I asked Iben if she could feed the doll with sand. She found the solution with a false breast. We added a birth scene. We had wound a sequence of actions into a 'knot', which became a part of the performance's final scene: the androgynous Trickster gave birth to a child and nursed it with sand flowing from her breast. She lifted the newborn baby as if in play, but the child disintegrated as the sand poured out from its body. In the end, what was once a child was reduced to a rag. We believe we nurture, and yet we are destroying. We imagine we are protecting the future in our arms, but it is just a handful of sand.

This complementary way of thinking and proceeding was also the means to orchestrate a whole scene. In *Come! And the Day will be Ours*, the new laws were posted on the fences delimiting the huge estates on the American continent. The victorious pioneers (Else Marie Laukvik, Torgeir Wethal and Tage Larsen) humbly knelt in front of the shaman of the defeated tribe (Iben Nagel Rasmussen). They gently placed a Bible – their compass and talisman – on a wooden plank on the ground. Torgeir lifted the axe with which they had cut a path through threatening landscapes, and using it as a hammer, nailed the Book to the plank. The Bible was crucified. Every stroke of the hammer piercing the flesh of the sacred pages echoed with the agonising song of the shaman.

In *Kaosmos*, in the final scene, the actors stripped themselves of their traditional costumes and buried them in a grave: the Door of the Law which lay wide open on the ground. They put on modern clothes while singing of the imminent arrival of the Deluge. The tomb changed into a corn field and a maenad stamped on it in an ecstatic dance.

In directing the actress, I thought about the Uru women of the Titicaca Lake who give birth standing up and swaying to the rhythm of their labour pains. They dance the perpetual flow of life which they carry and which is detaching itself from them.

Simultaneity: narrating according to the laws of space

I say 'narrate', and the first thing that comes to my mind is a tale through words. It is not possible to pronounce two or three words at the same time, one on top of the other or one inside the other. In phonetic writing, which we are accustomed to, it is impossible to write two or three words one within the other.

In ideograms, on the other hand, the logic of writing does not take into consideration the logic of the spoken language. While the latter presents the words in a linear way, one sound after another, ideograms proceed in a synthetic way, joining and simultaneously weaving images. They don't represent the sounds of the spoken word, but the things being spoken about, their relationships.

Man, in Japanese, is written with two different signs: *tambo*, 'rice field', and *chikara*, 'strength'. Together they are read *otoko*: 'man is the field's strength'. Whoever knows the ideogram understands the concept, but at the same time sees two different symbolic images, and how something different from the simple sum of rice and strength is born from their composition.

For Ezra Pound and Sergei Eisenstein ideograms were the essence of the art of montage, of the construction of meaning through the conjunction and clash of distant concepts. Drawn from daily life and not from aesthetic practices with their apparent 'complications', ideograms were the example of how adjoining and interlacing dissimilar elements can interact, creating a new reality of thought and perception.

In theatre, even the simplest action can be elaborated as an ideogram in which sensory and intellectual elements, physiological signals and symbolic signs, are amalgamated. The action can be thought and realised as a *simultaneous montage* of different components which, by interacting, provoke unforeseeable and diverse feelings and meanings *for each spectator*.

The actor can reach the synthetic effect of an ideogram by working on the physical score separately from the sonorous and semantic aspect of the vocal score. In the next phase the resulting score of his first montage is simultaneously connected with the scores of other actors, thus producing unexpected concordant or discordant links.

This was Meyerhold's extraordinary discovery way back in 1905: 'a plastic which doesn't correspond to words'. Postures, movements and gestures don't illustrate the text, but *say* what words conceal. In this process, the synchronisation of the voice's impulses with those of the physical actions is decisive. This synchronisation is the condition for a rhythm-in-life which the spectator perceives as an organic flow: multiplicity and variety of rhythms.

Simultaneity concerns not only the actor, but also the story and its peripeteias. The great difference between a story-through-words and a story-through-actions can be likened to the difference between the logic of time and that of space.

A story-through-words, both written and oral, must necessarily organise events one after another, following the vector of time. A story which takes shape in theatre can on the contrary show two or more different events *at the same time and in the same space*.

In a story made up of words it is also possible to describe two different situations at the same time, jumping from one to the other and using the type of montage which, in film, is called a Griffith. But it is one thing *to narrate* simultaneity, and another *to implement* it as director, and still another *to experience* it as a spectator. It is one thing *to tell* that *while* his right hand caresses, the left is searching for the knife hidden under the chair on which his lover sits. It is another thing *to see* it. It is one thing *to explain* that *at the same time* as Oedipus defeats the Sphinx, the gods plot his blindness. It is something else *to see in the same instant* Oedipus's perspicacity and his groping in the dark.

When I made different events simultaneous, I composed *a story which was articulated according to the rules of space instead of those of time*. I could relate independent events and situations when their only bond was to be contained within the same space. It was *simultaneity* which connected the different events.

Different lines of actions proceeded in parallel. At times I deliberately placed one of them in the foreground and the others in the background. At other times I let the spectator choose which line to follow and which one to disregard.

The alternation between a pre-arranged hierarchy and a free hierarchy, between main actions and secondary actions, was one of the rhythms on which I concentrated in every scene. It was a dance in which at times the author of the montage – the director – was intent on guiding the spectator's attention. At other times the spectator was free to decide the montage according to the rhythms of his own choices.

'Caesar defeated the Gauls. Did he not even have a cook with him?' This line from Brecht's poem, 'Questions from a worker who reads', was the inspiration for her character – a cook – by an actress (Silvia Ricciardelli[1]) in *Brecht's Ashes* (1980). The narrative context was the biography of the German writer, but also the characters and the plots of his plays, novels and poems. During rehearsals, I placed the actress among the spectators, where she did her cooking while watching the events of history and of Brecht's life from the sidelines. She mingled only occasionally with the other actors. I believe that Meyerhold would have called this solution 'grotesque', Brecht would have spoken of *Verfremdung* and Grotowski of a 'dialectic of apotheosis and derision'.

The actress unravelled a detailed line of actions that ran contiguously to Brecht's vicissitudes.

During the whole performance she prepared food. She peeled potatoes, washed vegetables, grated carrots, crushed cloves of garlic, chopped celery and parsley, fried onions and bacon and poured the whole lot into a huge pan which boiled on the hissing flame of a primus. Soon the aroma of a minestrone tickled the spectators' nostrils.

The cook had no direct relationship with Brecht's world, she constituted a self-sufficient context, absorbed in the preparation and tasting of the food. Her actions composed a symphony of images and sounds, a *continuous music* according to a rhythm which didn't connect her to the narrative logic of the performance's scenes.

One could say that her actions were the background to the main actions. It was the contiguity which influenced the spectator's nervous system, producing, subliminally or consciously, links and interpretations. The spectator supposed that the cook followed what happened around her, that she cut up a chicken with vigorous strokes of her knife to illustrate the cruelty of the Nazis or to relieve her sense of injustice. Or else they imagined refusal, indifference or resignation seeing her carving two pieces of wood in the form of a cross.

At times, an unsuspected associative short circuit exploded. A Jew (Toni Cots[2]) attempted to run away from the deadly hold of the Nazis. He ran desperately around the room, just a few centimetres from the spectators, but he couldn't find a way out and frantically he accelerated his pace. With a dignified gait Arturo Ui (Francis Pardeilhan) came forward and, lifting his arm in a blessing, stopped him dead. In that instant the cook poured chopped onions and bacon into a frying pan of hot oil. The onions sizzled as might burning flesh and fragrant smoke filled the room.

In *The Gospel according to Oxyrhincus* (1985), a Jewish Hasidic tailor (Else Marie Laukvik) searched for his messiah among the builders of the New Society who were applying the precepts of Stalin, their messiah. The tailor didn't take any notice of what simultaneously happened around him and, reciprocally, the builders of the New Society took no notice of him.

Here, too, contiguity presented situations and actions in the same space. From the narrative point of view, these flowed independently of each other, the one acting as a 'background' for the other. However these two different stories were connected on the level of the dynamic dramaturgy through rhythm, quality of energy and associations which they arouse. The spectator was aware that no relationships of cause and effect existed between the Jewish tailor's actions and those of the builders of the New Society. Yet simultaneity linked the different scores in unusual effects of sight, sound and smell.

One of the builders of the New Society, whose *nom de guerre* was Joan of Arc (Julia Varley), testified to her faith re-enacting her ascent on the stake and martyrdom among the flames. At the dramatic peak of the monologue, the Jewish tailor blew on an old coal-heated smoothing iron, freeing a swarm of sparks. He ironed a jacket in a cloud of vapour and smell of burnt cloth.

After *The Gospel according to Oxyrhincus*, an unknown character who didn't belong to the obvious narrative context strayed into almost all my performances. It was not an anecdotal apparition, but a real and ambiguous presence repeatedly intersecting the orbits of the other characters. The spectator perceived this presence as a character thanks to the persuasive strength of the actor's organic dramaturgy. The estranging yet enticing effect of such a figure was not a consequence of the explicit narrative events: it was the contiguity which engendered unexpected meeting points and interferences. In the director's mind, this 'character' belonged to a secret story which, in an elliptic and fragmentary way, surfaced in the interstices of the known one. In the mind of the spectators, however, other meanings were projected on this figure.

I'm thinking about the Trickster (Iben Nagel Rasmussen) in *Talabot*, half human and half animal, who shadowed the other characters, mimicking their passions and sufferings; or about Doña Musica (Julia Varley), in *Kaosmos*, the Law of Life – the invisible Death – dancing around the characters of Kafka's short story. In *Salt*, an indefinable character (Jan Ferslev) sitting outside the clearly delimited scenic space, acted independently of the evident protagonist (Roberta Carreri). He looked like her prompter or her shadow, yet his music, songs and humming as well as his actions didn't correspond to those of the protagonist in the centre of the space.

I exploited the possibilities of simultaneity and contiguity to its extreme in *Within the Skeleton of the Whale*. The performance originated from *Kaosmos*, created four years previously, but the new version had been stripped of anything recalling the narrative dramaturgy and all reference points of this earlier performance: story, language, costumes, colours, objects, accessories, narrative references. Only *Kaosmos*'s organic dramaturgy remained, the designs of all the actors' actions and songs, without the objects which had been manipulated and justified by those actions.

Onto this dynamic dramaturgy I grafted the texts of *The Gospel according to Oxyrhincus*. In that performance they were said in Coptic, *koiné* Greek and Yiddish. Here, on the contrary, the texts were comprehensible, interpreting blasphemously the words of the Holy Book.

Out of the nine actors in *Kaosmos*, only seven participated in *Within the Skeleton of the Whale*. At times, respecting the score of the original performance, they turned to an invisible partner – one of their colleagues who had left. The proximity with the other actors gave the impression that they turned to one of them. But their actions didn't fit at the narrative level, only at the organic one.

An eighth actor, who had not participated in *Kaosmos* (Tage Larsen), acted in *Within the Skeleton of the Whale* just a few centimetres from the other actors. He was physically in the centre, yet extraneous, never interacting with the actions of the others, as if they didn't concern him or were far away. He reacted in relationship to a 'partner', a thick wood tablet used in a hundred different ways: as a lectern, a book, a stool, a comb, the bow of a violin, a spade, a staircase, nail scissors, a fork, binoculars, a fan, a skateboard. The contiguity provoked grotesque, puzzling and cruel effects. The spectators had the suspicion that the actions of this solitary actor moving among the others were an intentional comment on what was going on around him. At times they wondered if the resonance was purely accidental, at others they remarked a deliberate effect of counterpoint. Only in the final scene did the secret sense of his presence emerge.

Within the Skeleton of the Whale is undoubtedly an example of all *one should not do* in theatre. It is therefore worth emphasising that it was not the result of a preliminary project of mine or of the actors. In defiance of common sense and our expectations, circumstances made us ascertain that the scores of previous performances maintained a mysterious effectiveness and a capacity to produce meanings, even in the absence of all that which usually creates a bridge between the actors and the spectators. When we glimpsed this opportunity, we decided to explore it.

A performance which is based on the simultaneity of situations which have nothing to do with each other can easily fall into meaninglessness and boredom resulting from arbitrariness. It must prove that it is able *to live in the spectator* in spite of its deliberate unintelligibility.

Success depends on the living roots which the scenic materials have developed in the body-mind of the single actors. Whatever the refined interlacing of stories and evident or secret narrative sources, if such roots don't produce actions whose organic effect resounds in the spectator's emotional and associative universe, the performance literally goes to pieces. It fades away like a ghost at the dawning of the day.

Exú: swimming in a lasting presence

Action is any change, however minute, which consciously or subliminally affects the spectators' attention, their understanding, sensibility and kinaesthetic sense. In a theatre performance, actions (that is, everything that has to do with dramaturgy) are not only what the actors say and do, but also sounds and lights as well as modifications of space and costumes. The ways of manipulating the props are also actions. It is not so important to define the number of actions in a performance. What matters is to be aware that actions become theatrically effective only when they are interlaced and woven together, thus becoming a fabric (texture): a performance text. This interlacing and weaving can unfold according to two modalities.

The first is accomplished through the development of actions in time by means of a *concatenation*, a linking of cause and effect; but also through an alternation of actions which carry forward two parallel developments.

The second occurs by means of *simultaneity*, the contiguous presence of several actions.

Concatenation and *simultaneity* are the two dimensions which trigger the interlacing of the actions or, in other words, the weaving of the plot. They are the two poles whose tension and dialectics spark the *bios* of the performance: the actions at work, the dramaturgy.

In the Brazilian candomblé, it is said about one of the Orixá divinities: Exú throws the stone today with which he killed the jaguar yesterday. A performance, too, can give the experience of a space-time in which the 'after' can precede the 'before'.

A conditioned reflex makes us associate the connections between a 'before' and an 'after' with those of cause and effect. The fact that one event follows another doesn't mean that the latter is the result of the former. When in my work I stressed the links based on simultaneity, I tried to oppose the spectators' tendency and need to recognise the relationships of cause and effect in the evident concatenation of the actions in time.

I felt the need to deal with my narrative materials as if they were fragments of a myth or limbs of an archetype. From a technical point of view, what gives myth a power which is valid in different epochs and speaks to each one of us is its use of time. Myths are told as unfolding stories whose episodes follow one upon another. Yet all the episodes are *simultaneously present* in the awareness of the reader or the spectator. It is a story which proceeds in a circle and, looping back on itself, induces a renewed insight.

In the narration-through-actions or behind-actions, I mingled the present with the past in the box of the performing space which enclosed actors and spectators. The temporal dimension was not regulated by the reasons which preside over language and the tense of the verbs, clearly distinguishing the present from the past and future. It was no longer the tense of the verbs which imposed its order, but a concatenation of actions which was a continuous presence of past and present in which everything floated.

Then time retrieved its freedom and could glide forwards or backwards.

When we remember, our thought proceeds by leaps, connecting the past with the fantasies about the future and blending planes and dimensions which don't respect a chronological or logical succession.

A performance can reproduce in a spatial dimension the specific nature of thought: its capacity to jump forwards and backwards in time, to establish connections between distant facts and to simultaneously follow two or more adjoining logics. The narration-behind-actions grafts the analytical dimension onto that of the historical time: it distinguishes the potentially narrative elements, weighs them, considers them in the light of possible alternatives, sorts them out in concordances or divergences and disarranges them to escape from known categories.

Different images, one after another, already make up a story. Many psychological tests are based on this simple principle. There are paintings or frescoes in which the episodes of a story or a biography are depicted in different parts of the same landscape. In this case, the different scenes are not concatenated. The onlooker's gaze can wander in the painting, always connecting the many episodes in a different succession. From the content of only one frame, various stories are born.

In *Judith* (1988) the story was the frame which compressed the many scenes, preventing them from fragmenting into disconnected images. In the first scene the actress (Roberta Carreri) told the biblical episode about Holofernes' murder by Judith. Subsequently, the performance became an orchestration of variations on already known facts.

The actress's actions didn't interpret the story, but questioned it through a succession of perspectives, moods, motives and memories which negated one another reciprocally. In its labyrinthine unfolding, the performance advanced and receded in time, developed a detail into an autonomous episode, presenting events which *might* have happened and constantly proposing the same climax: Judith's voluptuous pleasure in severing Holofernes' head.

A performance could also grow according to a narrative dramaturgy like a bunch of grapes or a *kippu*, the Inca bundle of knotted threads. In *The Castle of Holstebro* (1991) Julia Varley wove scenes and characters together from her different performances. Among them, as a leitmotif, was Mr Peanut, the character whose head was a skull.

The actress's story switched between irony and poetic fantasies. The actress and her double – both herself and her character – showed the meeting between a young woman and a venerable old man. The two characters, played by the same actress, confronted youth and death, juxtaposing vulnerability and cynicism. In the end, the initial splitting into two figures underwent one more mutation. Seated on the floor, the actress nursed Mr Peanut, cradling him in her lap, like a baby, a grandfather-infant, or the newborn Death.

The origin of the Odin Road

Two roads diverged in a yellow wood,
And sorry I could not travel both
And be one traveler, long I stood
And looked down one as far as I could
To where it bent in the undergrowth;
Then took the other, as just as fair,
And having perhaps the better claim,
Because it was grassy and wanted wear,
Though as for that the passing there
Had worn them really about the same,
And both that morning equally lay
In leaves no step had trodden black.
Oh, I kept the first for another day!
Yet knowing how way leads on to way,
I doubted if I should ever come back.
I shall be telling this with a sigh
Some where ages and ages hence:
two roads diverged in a wood, and I –
I took the one less traveled by,
And that has made all the difference.
(Robert Frost: *The Road not Taken*)

The true professional origin, the one which makes us choose our road, often does not coincide with our first steps in theatre. For me and Odin Teatret, founded in Norway by Norwegian would-be actors, the expatriation to Denmark implied the upheaval of our way of imagining and doing theatre. Our emigration became the initial impulse to exploit our technical vulnerability and human resources in enterprising ways in a country unknown to us. We had lost our language and the natural advantage of sharing it with our spectators. We stammered and were forced to invent our own scenic language of vocal and physical actions.

The instinct for survival, combined with a knowledge of theatre history, made me bold. A foreigner is often not inhibited by the norms and customs of the country which hosts him. The enterprising attitude of the new arrivals and the urgency to find a solution to the conditions which were crushing us influenced our style and our way of thinking: our professional identity.

In Oslo, when we were a small anonymous amateur group with no venue, no money, no performance and no spectators, a friend asked me: 'Are you just doing theatre for yourselves?' It was easy to answer: 'If I do theatre, it is obvious that I want to show the results, in the hope that many spectators will appreciate them.' I remarked to him that, on the other hand, nobody had ever asked me to become an artist or expressed the wish to see my performances. Maybe my friend was trying to discover something else with his question: what did my decision to do theatre mean to me? What were the origins and the purpose of my resolution?

I had not chosen theatre as an artistic vocation. As an Italian immigrant in Norway, I looked for a solution to justify my difference. I was not interested in imposing this difference as an identity with a specific value. I wanted to use it like a Trojan horse, welcomed by the inhabitants who would demolish their walls of defence. My actions, words and behaviour would be judged differently if I was a theatre artist instead of a simple foreign worker. Criticism and bias would deal with artistic, aesthetic or political categories, without being coloured by racial or cultural preconceptions.

I didn't intend the theatre-Trojan horse (this beautiful image by Julian Beck) as an expression of my personality, rather as an escape from the personality in which others confined me. It is no accident that in my first theatrical stammerings, I spoke of a theatre reflecting the conflicts of society. I was influenced by Brecht and by what I had read about his performances at the Berliner Ensemble. The theatre became a way of taking a stand in a period of hateful 'cold war' where class struggle belonged to my daily reality. I was finishing university, and in a few months I would no longer need to earn my living as a welder. My education had prepared me for the life of a high school teacher. Instead of complying with the challenges and gratifications of this foreseeable future, my impulsiveness blew the small world which I had built to smithereens. The explosive at my disposition, which I had to learn to dominate, was the theatre.

My friend in Oslo was fond of me. He was sorry to see me running after a theatre chimera together with four young people rejected by the national theatre school. To him I was just a man with no theatre experience and a head full of the eccentric ideas of a young Polish director totally unknown at that time – Jerzy Grotowski. No wonder the professional milieu and the cultural authorities took no notice of me. This happened at a time when theatre buildings and playwrights' texts shaped the profile of our profession.

After a year in Oslo, we finished the performance Ornitofilene, *based on the play by Jens Bjørneboe. We also showed it in Sweden, Finland and Denmark. Then, after a few months, an amazing proposal arrived from Holstebro. This Danish municipality offered us the chance to leave Norway and the language which was the affective and communicative bond with friends who meant so much to me. We had to leave the known world of the Norwegian capital and our first spectators and move to a town of 18,000 inhabitants, in a peripheral region of Denmark noted for its religious pietism and with no theatre traditions. In exchange, we would receive an abandoned farm on the outskirts and a derisive subsidy.*

I had lived in Norway for many years and seen my Italian way of thinking radically transformed. I had adjusted to my condition as a worker and reached a personal autonomy. I was deeply bound to a few people who had influenced my political and intellectual development and I felt at ease in the company of my friends, accepted and loved by them. I left this milieu which I had conquered person by person and moved to a small town in Jutland to create a 'theatre-laboratory' –

whatever that was. I was accompanied by four 20-year-old Norwegians who left their families, friends and native tongue. What were the motives for my decision? And what were my young actors' reasons for following me? Each of us could give many and contradictory answers. I have a feeling that any reflection on our own origin cannot be separated from a hunger for vertigo and adventure, a longing for risk and a challenging life. It is the same hunger which, for fun and with solemnity, urges us to set our house on fire and enjoy the crackling flames with incredulity and trepidation.

Courage, perhaps, is not to surrender totally to the fears which restrain us.

My first emigration from Italy to Norway had been a voluntary diaspora from the world I knew and recognised, from the certainties and the alibis of my culture, my family, teachers and officers of the military college. The separation from my culture was the first step towards the conquest of my difference during years of manual work and continuous wanderings in Europe and Asia.

When this way of living became a habit, I decided to cast anchor. I chained myself to the theatrical craft, and let my roots grow into it. I emphasised my idiosyncrasies and delved into myself to reach a country which was mine alone. My emigration and chaining to the theatrical craft enabled vital superstitions to blossom. All my efforts in creating the reality of fiction have been made in order to be elsewhere. The theatre is the art of ubiquity: it has helped me to take a stand in the circumstances of my personal history, and has granted me an uncertain sanctuary in the brutality of history. I have used my craft with patience and without cynicism, following a discipline which has transformed a feeling of absence into a search for presence.

Therefore I like the word 'transition'. I tell myself that being in transition means to persevere in escaping. From what? From the tangle of my origins and from the subsequent changes and small stabilisations; from what I am to what I dream of being; from what I know to what lies in wait. I have left what I knew and moved towards a horizon which today is coloured by traces of return. I am like a foreigner who gets off the train, doesn't recognise anything and says: this is home.

I love the theatre because, by its nature, it is foreign whether it wants it or not, whether it knows it or refuses to acknowledge it. History tells me this. Those who practised the theatrical craft, in Europe as in Asia, always lived the condition of foreigners, as if they were in transit. The actors' troupes were composed of people coming from different regions and social classes. Theatre was foreign in the world in which it lived and among the spectators who made it live, above all because it contradicted the limitations and the hierarchies which maintained order in the surrounding society. For this reason theatre often constituted a separate micro-society, discriminated and despised. And therefore it was, at times, an island of freedom.

When in the twentieth century theatre seemed destined to perish because it appeared inadequate for the demands of modernity with its urban structure, economy and new types of performances, theatre people practised a double strategy, rather through force of circumstance than as a conscious plan. On the one hand they induced the surrounding society to recognise the stage profession as a cultural good to be protected, releasing it from the chains of commerce. Our profession is art, they claimed, and managed to get it subsidised and safeguarded as a valuable national legacy. On the other, while this change of mentality was taking place, a few men and women established archipelagos of small autonomous theatrical islands. Each of these small islands lived, and still lives, as a foreigner in its own cultural environment. It is a negligible minority, capable nevertheless of opening its own path into new territories and escaping the customary enclosures of commercial theatre and traditional artistic performances.

I have personally experienced the theatre's foreign nature also from another perspective when Odin Teatret toured abroad. We were foreign, not because we came from a different part of the world and spoke different languages, but because the roles were reversed. We, the foreigners, became the hosts in the small space of our performance and welcomed the spectators who, for an hour or so, became 'foreigners' on a visit. They were confronted with something which originated from another history and geography: the manifestation of 'otherness'. They entered, took their seats, observed, at times like simple tourists, curious, open-minded or animated by an arrogant superiority complex.

This also happens, to a greater or lesser degree, when the majority of the spectators consider the theatre which is hosting them as a local theatre. The feeling of distance is more explicit and noticeable when a theatre comes from a far away country. But it is always the same relationship between 'foreigners' that comes into play, here dissimulated, there disclosed.

It is undeniable that I have integrated my private experiences in the artistic work. By turning them into theatrical fiction, today I can affirm that the intensity of this process of transformation has transformed me into another person. Theatrical experiences are not of the same quality as religious ones, yet they belong to the same species. Like the ecstasy which certain mathematicians and physicists have felt in a few moments of their research. Or 'the cosmic harmony' which pervaded Poincaré when he worked out a mathematical formula which was aesthetically enthralling.

I have experimented with various ways to use illusions without allowing illusions to use me. Making theatre means to live enchantments, to create archipelagos of magic islands – tragic or grotesque – to invent mirrors of the world as we know it, or of worlds as dissimilar from reality as a fantastic delirium. But each evening, after every enchantment and labyrinth where nothing was certain, I broke the magic wand. I always returned to history after the last scene. I let our performance grow into a sacred tree and then I felled it. Sometimes, dark seeds were scattered from the branches and sank into the depths of a single spectator where they germinated, leaving him or her mute and motionless.

This too was the theatre for me: a clearing populated by the presence of living and imaginary spectators. I was in the centre of the jungle, in the feverish heart of my epoch and society, surrounded by people who were motivated to become acquainted with my work, to share their questions and study with me. I had an ongoing dialogue with many living people who were strangers to me, and with a few dead ones whom I loved. I protected my vulnerability behind the prestige of an antiquated ceremony called theatre, honoured as art.

Thus, the past lives in the present and by now, adult and wiser, I can still be the child who daydreamed at the foot of a grave. I am still nourished by those zones of silence which the abandonment of my culture has unlocked in me. I act, speak and write without pause, anchored to the immediateness of the theatrical craft. I am waiting. Waiting is the present of the future. In this landscape to come, theatre is a path which makes me worthy of returning to my childhood and progressing into time with the illusion that I will disappear in a legend.

Not text, but narrative context

With the years, the enmeshed heterogeneity that during the rehearsals derived from the variety of the actors' materials, from the different narrative sources and the unfolding of simultaneous scenes, had become an effective tool to sever the branch of the certainties on which I sat. It satisfied my need to escape from my inclinations and habits and to discover unexpected paths in a jungle of probable targets. But this process also satisfied my desire to go again through an experience which I had lived as a trauma during *My Father's House*, my fourth performance.

The *sources* of my first three performances – *Ornitofilene* (1965), *Kaspariana* (1967) and *Ferai* (1969) – were texts by the Norwegian Jens Bjørneboe and the Danish Ole Sarvig and Peter Seeberg respectively. However, I was forced to interfere radically in the script because of objective circumstances. Jens Bjørneboe's text had 15 characters and about 20 scenes happening in different places and lasting two hours. I had only four actors who performed among the spectators for one hour. *Ferai* had five characters and numerous changes of scene. I had eight actors and the various dramatic situations unfolded in a bare space. *Kaspariana* was a long poem with no characters and subdivisions. I extracted some characters from the text, and invented the others corresponding to the number of actors at my disposal. These constraints taught me to intervene in a text for pragmatic reasons and not for creative originality. Therefore, during the rehearsals, I added new wordless scenes or fragments taken from other books by the same author.

The characteristics of the texts, which didn't correspond to the material conditions at my disposal, taught me to guide the actors without starting from characters rooted in a written narrative structure. Moreover, I felt the need to translate the long monologues into theatrically visible solutions. In *Ornitofilene*'s original text, the protagonist told how he had been tortured by the Germans during World War II. I set up a realistic scene of violence interspersed with an authentic letter from a young Norwegian partisan shot by the Nazis. In *Ferai*, a messenger described in a long speech the struggle of the pretenders to the throne. I cut the whole monologue and replaced it with an acrobatic combat.

I beat my head against the wall to discover theatrical solutions for situations which were effective only on paper. How could my six actors become the equivalent of a crowd in a huge square, gathered around Kaspar Hauser? How could I inform the spectators, with a synthetic and pregnant image, about the living conditions of this crowd? I imagined a floor covered with bread that was trampled on with indifference: an opulent society drowning in the superfluous.

In *Ornitofilene*, the executioner flagellated himself, and his victim leapt into the air, falling heavily to the ground with shrieks of pleasure. In *Ferai*, the young democratic king preached his ideals of equality kneeling on the back of his defeated adversary. I could suddenly interrupt the rectilinear narration, intertwining two or more simultaneous contrasting actions. But the anecdotal structure and the existential vision of the text – and therefore of the author – were important to me. The text was like a wind blowing in one direction. The performance sailed against the wind. But although proceeding in the opposite direction, it was thanks to the wind's strength that the performance found its bearings and route.

In *My Father's House* (1972) another road revealed itself to me. Once more, certain constrictions had placed me with my back to the wall. We had waited for months for a new text by Peter Seeberg, but when he delivered it, it recalled *Ferai*'s plot. We could not wait for a new proposal. With the acceptance of the actors, I decided to adapt the biography of the young Dostoevsky which I had just read in a book by Alain Besançon. I felt naked: it was the first time that I threw myself into a performance without the safe thread of events described in a text. Now it was up to me to devise a plot, to choose, among thousands, the salient episodes, to condense them and shape dialogues, conceiving an intelligent dramatic ending. I began with an improvisation: Dostoevsky's father's house. His serfs enter their owner's house at night and kill him while he is sleeping in his bed. Then they crush his testicles. It was their revenge towards the patriarch who abused their young daughters.

This first improvisation, which later gave the title to the performance, was followed by many others inspired by historical and literary facts from the period of the Russian author, as well as by episodes from the actors' and my contemporary history. I reacted with reluctance and fear to the impressions provoked by the actors' improvisations. Their materials were impregnated with eroticism, vehemence and vulnerability. Like acid, they acted upon my sensibility and dissolved the thematic constellation (Dostoevsky's biography and novels) into a *living context* which left me uncertain and confused. Without characters and without a previous succession of scenes and dialogues which guaranteed the progress of the narration, the actors' actions scattered like sparks in all directions, leaving me in darkness. The more I worked out their improvisations, the more I moved away from the theme of departure. I was swallowed up and lost in a giant body.

This has been, perhaps, the most troubling experience and the most illuminating revelation in my professional life: my work as director was not guided by meanings, but by the actors' real actions and the synchronisation of their relationships – *their organic dramaturgy*. My reason was put to a test for two years, the time it took to prepare the performance.

This unthinkable process opened my senses: I discovered nuances, folds and tones previously never noticed in the actors' materials. I became conscious of my new awareness, however, only in the performances that followed.

Towards the end of rehearsals I was in doubt whether to show *My Father's*

House to the spectators. The performance touched me, awaking many incomprehensible resonances within me. But it had nothing to do with Dostoevsky's life and novels. At the most I could admit that it was inspired by them. I was unable to explain what the performance *was saying*. It had no evident narrative thread and was deprived of the most elementary references which usually help the spectators to follow the plot. Moreover, the actors spoke an invented Russian.

We were in 1972, a period of strong political tensions and socially committed performances in Europe. In my perplexity, I invited all the schoolchildren in Holstebro to Odin Teatret. Instead of paying for a ticket, they had to write about their reactions.

Children from primary schools who knew nothing about theatre as well as self-confident teenagers from high school came with their comments. A child, who had never been to the theatre, wrote of his surprise on arriving in his classroom only to be put on a bus and ending up in a dark room among adults who raced all around him or lay on the floor at his feet, while yelling at the top of their voices. He had enjoyed being free from school, but theatre was scary. A girl remarked that in the performance's darkness it was as if she had slid back into her mother's uterus. Another pupil described his emotional upheaval and apologised for having considered us parasites. Many wrote, irritated or with amazement, that they had understood nothing, yet had been moved by the performance. It had not bored them, but they could not explain why.

These comments made me aware of the indefinable ways with which a performance lives in the spectator's interiority. They pointed out for me an invisible and rather unknown dimension of the theatrical experience: a performance is a concrete yet immaterial reality which escapes its authors, and which radiates an emotional logic which is different for every single spectator. It is the performance's *temperature* which entices, even when it is inexplicable and threatening.

This evocative dimension doesn't spring from the narrative dramaturgy, but from the actors' organic dramaturgy and from the dramaturgy of the spectators. A performance is a Leviathan haunted by ghosts released from the belly and the head of those who have been swallowed up. It was also my task, as director, to help give birth to the Leviathan which will swallow the spectator.

I have preserved the tradition of inviting Holstebro schoolchildren in the final phase of a performance's rehearsals. Children cannot be seduced by metaphors, original interpretations, symbolic images, known quotations, abstractions and texts of famous authors. They take note of what literally occurs in front of them, not of what this represents. To their eyes, two vagabonds waiting for a certain Mr Godot are not the symbol of the human existential condition, but two adults who chat for two boring hours. Still today, schoolchildren are my first spectators. Their reactions are precious to me: they signal to me whether my work on the different levels of dramaturgy has bolstered or lulled the Leviathan.

After *My Father's House*, I was aware that a performance does not recount only *one* subject which I had interpreted, denied or grafted onto personal or historical experiences. The spectators, too, didn't filter an identical story through the actions of the same performance. Slowly an axiom began to coagulate in my mind: the narrative dramaturgy must be thought in the plural – more subjects, more perspectives, more stories.

The actors' improvisations assumed more and more importance. The organic materials which sprang out of them were not programmed as illustration, comment or interpretation of the text or a theme in the performance. The resulting scores constituted a hailstorm of sensory stimuli which precipitated me into a turbulence, unfathomable or incoherent according to the normal narrative criteria, but with an astonishing potentiality of meanings.

During the improvisations, I did not focus on the thread of a comprehensible story, but on distinguishing actions and reactions, *sats* (impulses), directions in space, introverted and extroverted postures, soft or vigorous tensions. The improvisations were registered by my senses as a dense flow of single actions whose rhythm, dynamism, tonicity and illustrative character constantly contradicted themselves forcing upon me the questions: what is all this about? What do they say?

It was evident that I could unfold this flow according to two contrasting dimensions: simultaneity and concatenation. But the hailstorm of actions didn't clarify my ideas. I had difficulties in connecting it to one of the themes of departure or in detecting an immediate narrative nucleus. It often aroused inconceivable and inadmissible associations which pulled me elsewhere from the territory delimited by the initial sources.

During the rehearsals of *My Father's House* I had discovered that Dostoevsky's biographical circumstances and the various episodes of his novels helped to validate my choices on the organic level of the performance. Cutting, combining and integrating the actors' materials, I primarily followed their scenic *bios*, their organic faculty to convince and goad my senses. I justified my choices in relationship to one or more of the sources of departure, or to the new ones that emerged during the rehearsals. I dramatised the actions in micro-stories, amalgamating them, in a wider narrative frame which had a sense for me.

By now I knew that the theme for the following performance would contain the doors through which I could slip into a realm of questions. *Come! And the Day will be Ours* (1976) did not take its start from an author's text. Its initial source was the Spanish conquistadores' greed for gold in the New World. I was drawn by the wild energy of these men who challenged an ocean on ships 20 metres long and marched through an unknown and threatening continent, overcoming mountains, forests, deserts and keeping intact their passion for their deity: a yellowish metal. They had loved and raped native women, massacred entire populations, given life to new races, unperturbed by the violent death of those who had preceded them.

During the rehearsals which, with some interruptions, lasted more than two years, I inserted another theme: the unfortunate and persecuted mass of Europeans who set sail for the Americas to escape their destiny of poverty, longing for emancipation and a dignified life. The new *source* was an entanglement of historical facts which I summarised to myself in one sentence: the meeting between the European pioneers and the native populations of the New World. But this vast frame offered thousands of detailed contexts: the alacrity of the puritanical immigrants and the lavish potlatch of the natives; the stakes of the puritans and the visions of Crazy Horse, the Cheyenne warrior/shaman; the massacres perpetrated by General Custer to the tones of Irish tunes and the rape of myriad cultures as an act of birth of a nation which welcomed the disinherited from all over the world. At first sight, I had only the difficulty of choosing among a multitude of historical episodes in this merciless clash between unequal forces. But I was fascinated more and more by the paradoxical aspects of my actors' improvisations, by their impetuousness, sensuality and lack of restraints.

The process of creation, understood as a journey into our own microcosm and as a meeting with our 'other', became the equivalent of the emigrant's journey in an unknown geography. I was astonished watching an identity disintegrate or come together in front of my eyes. The sensible pioneers appropriated the Indians' garments, frantically dressing up in them as trophies or like a new skin to conceal the wretchedness of their history as an excluded people. My disconcertion in front of this behaviour was overcome by the conduct of the natives who, in European garb, strove to ape the fury of the conquerors.

I could not withstand a feeling of empathy for the emigrants who had left country, family and language. They had crossed the sea, crowded like beasts, toward a dream of liberty: a piece of land to cultivate. And in front of them, like a shadow, I saw the indelible image of the defrauded indigenous population. What I would never have imagined or programmed was the idea of building the *presence* of these pioneers – desiring only to earn their bread honestly with the sweat of their brow – out of the unbridled vitality of my actors' improvisations.

Taken by surprise, I learned something about my identity as an emigrant and 'Westerner'.

During the rehearsals, neither the actors nor I thought in terms of characters. The preparation of *My Father's House*, as well as *Kaspariana* and *Ferai*, had determined a particular way to connect us to this aspect of the creative process. The so-called 'building of the character' consisted in composing a kaleidoscope of structured actions in order to orient or disorient the spectator. The performances grew through improvisations. The personal motivations of the actors (usually working without written texts) constituted the solid roots producing a harvest of actions which the director moulded into 'characters' as perceived by the spectators.

In the performance's programme, the characters of *Come! And the Day will be Ours* didn't have a name, but they were presented in this way: with the banjo – Roberta Carreri; with the white dress – Else Marie Laukvik; with the drum – Iben Nagel Rasmussen; with the guitar – Tom Fjordefalk; with the violin – Tage Larsen; with the book – Torgeir Wethal. This did not mean that the actors didn't have an inner thread that justified and coherently held their actions and scenes. However this thread – or subscore – was personal, not shared with the director and above all it was a point of arrival. It didn't derive from the interpretation of a pre-existing character.

By now I was convinced that the narrative dramaturgy of a performance was made up of a plurality of stories. I believed that a performance was made up of several performances, each with its own story recounted in a distinct way. At times, these stories were evident to the spectators. At others, I kept one or several of them hidden, letting them surface in a discontinuous way, in short fragments or through hints. It was usually in the final scene that I revealed the meaning of the 'invisible' story which was disseminated in minute doses throughout the performance. The work on several stories allowed me to apply different systems of causality and opposing narrative logics. The essential elements of the various stories had a multiple function and I used these in different ways in each of the performance's stories. The meeting points of the essential elements in the many stories were the foundation of my narrative dramaturgy.

It was obvious that the contiguity of several actors' scores and narrative episodes in the same space enhanced the simultaneous weaving of different stories. *The Gospel according to Oxyrhincus* allowed me to explore these possibilities in 1985.

When the rehearsals ended, I maintained that *The Gospel according to Oxyrhincus* was Stalin's biography. I also wrote this in the programme. But I had started out from a short story by Borges, *A Dead Man*, which took place among criminal gauchos in Uruguay. I had worked on it for a few weeks in order to select the actors who would participate in the next performance. Later, I didn't begin the rehearsals with the usual improvisations. Instead I gave the actors the task of creating 'marble': a succession of real actions built coldly and without any personal motivation. When these scores were fixed, I began to elaborate them. I created relationships among the actors, sketched scenes which had a sense or were rooted in rhythm and organic effectiveness.

I didn't have a theme or a constellation of texts around which the performance might grow. Only a phrase: 'lions gone mad in the desert'. Gradually I added Hasidic sayings and fragments of Gnostic gospels excavated in the Hellenistic city of Oxyrhincus, today Behnesa in Egypt. I amused myself writing parables and sacrilegious dialogues. I let the actors translate all these texts into Coptic. This dead tongue, which was spoken by the first Christians, was the equivalent, for me, of today's dead language of politics, of collective mirages and faith which blinds.

The revolt buried alive: this other phrase imposed itself during the rehearsals, pursuing me. I saw the men and women of the Revolt, saints and nihilists, climbing Calvary to gather at the feet of the cross: Buddha and Francis of Assisi, Mohammed and Teresa of Avila, Jacob Frank and Zarathustra, Captain Achab and Mirabai. When did I associate the revolt buried alive with Antigone? And when did I start to weave the story of the *cangaçeiros*, the Brazilian outlaws accompanying a false Messiah, while a Hasidic tailor sang and danced around waiting for his Messiah? Was it when I thought about the lions gone mad in the desert? Or when I imagined that these criminals believed themselves to be exterminating angels of religious mythologies, who had come down to earth to give life to an era of justice? Or was it just the continuation and development of Borges' short story, *A Dead Man*? And when did I decide to permeate every scene with the immaterial presence of Sosso Djugashvili, known as Joseph Stalin, whose reassuring fatherly smile exuded blood?

It is difficult for me to answer. The biography of the Russian dictator became the box which contained and justified in my eyes the different caskets and boxes with stories, associations and emotional needs which had been secreted and elaborated during the rehearsals.

While rehearsing, I sailed for a long time without a rudder or a route, in a state of uncertainty, even despair. I was exhausted by the double effort of fighting against my doubts, and behaving with confidence in front of my actors. I tried to utilise their materials in order to recount several stories at the same time. I wanted to involve the spectators in a liturgy. Together with the actors, they had to read some texts from the programme in a choir: paraphrases of parables and apocryphal evangelical sayings. I imagined the performance's rhythm according to the heart's contraction and expansion: the spectators were drawn into the theatrical illusion with faint candlelight, then suddenly the electric lights came on, the theatrical time-space was shattered and spectators and actors read together loudly a text as a litany. I dreamt of a mass infused with hate, a remedy to exorcise my pain over General Jaruzelski's coup d'état in Poland and Grotowski's exile. I maintained this dialogic structure until the performances for the schools in Holstebro. From one day to another, I cancelled it. I started elaborating a new structure, searching for a performance which was not a mental construction, but which *lived*.

Unlike with *Come! And the Day will be Ours*, I had given specific characters to the actors at the very beginning, asking them to develop their biographies and write them down. In this way, we had six stories plus mine. The seven different narrative paths, or contexts, had to flow within one performance.

The characters were: Sabbatai Zevi, the Jew who in the seventeenth century claimed to be the Messiah and abjured his faith, converting to Islam (Torgeir Wethal); Antigone and her brother Polinice (Roberta Carreri and Francis Pardeilhan), Joan of Arc (Julia Varley), the Great Inquisitor from *The Brothers Karamazov* (Tage Larsen) and a pious Hasidic Jew (Else Marie Laukvik). I extracted the seventh story, mine, from Borges's *A Dead Man* and added, as its shadow, the character of the Golem (Christoph Falke[3]).

The working process on the actors' characters and stories ended with a literary text and a performance on the manifestations of faith in our time. But this experience revealed an unexpected technical perspective: the narrative context had not been the performance's starting point, as had been the case in previous productions, but was the point of arrival.

How could I tell a story which I didn't know, while telling another one? This question synthesises the technical challenges in my narrative dramaturgy of recent years. *The Gospel according to Oxyrhincus* was crucial in mapping the many ways to work out a *constellation* of references, interactions and connections among a performance's different sources, both the evident and the hidden ones. At the same time the work showed that it was possible to compact this constellation in a unitary organism impregnated by manifold senses. *For me this constellation was the narrative context.* To tell-behind-the-actions had become the technique of merging dissimilar and distant narrative elements in order to discover an unprogrammed context, giving it life.

I have paid for this knowledge with uncertainty and doubts. These states of mind have never abandoned my directorial work. Searching for a narrative context, my actors and I were similar to a pack of hounds pursuing a prey which may or may not be ahead of us. They proceeded together, dispersed, got in each other's way, rushed into thickets and ravines which tested their abilities and energies and, discouraged at having lost the trail, ran around in circles. But sometimes the disbanded dogs joined up again and the reassembled pack tracked down the prey and discovered the context.

It was not certain that this *context* to be discovered was there waiting for me, ready to be pursued. It was a pure potentiality. I didn't know what it involved, nor how it could be used. Sometimes, it all came to nothing. At other times, an unsuspected track lured me onto unknown ground. During the work I might become aware that another performance was holding my hand and I was just following it, oblivious of where it would lead me.

I had the habit of watching each and every Odin performance. I saw them again and again, evening after evening. But *The Gospel according to Oxyrhincus* was an exception. I was unable to watch it more than two or three times consecutively. It forced me to take a break and stay away for a few days. The performance aroused hate, destructive memories and the pain I felt for people dear to me, crushed by the Moloch of politics. I let my group tour for long periods without me.

Watching the performance, the director is just one of the spectators. For me too, every evening the performance told distinct stories. I discovered the truth or the truths which the performance told me only after I had finished it and had seen it several times. I had not forced it to tell only one thing. I had woven a web of possible destinies. I had liberated it, and the performance – an empty ritual – spoke with a voice which was not the echo of my director's voice.

Centre of the book

Only relationships count. They are fragile and deceptive threads, tempered by the years or the intensity of a meeting. They form a country which no geographical map can depict. We live in solitude in a geography made up of bonds and knots: affections, books, memories, passions, unions lasting a lifetime. Here only the action belongs to us, not its fruit. It is the path towards the origin: our centre and our aim. Following this path can be the purpose of theatre which knows that it is pretending and does not pretend to know.

What is the centre? I would like to race like the wind and I go back in time to a scene I have read and can imagine in every detail. I say to myself: it explains everything. Yet I am unable to say why.

The Emperor is the centre.

We are in the Forbidden City, a morning in March 1601. Li Madou wakes up long before dawn. He has to get ready for the meeting with Him who is the centre of the Celestial Empire, beyond all the seas which a European has to cross to reach Him. A long and meticulous preparation precedes the imperial audience. The result of his mission will depend on this encounter. He has to learn to bow and pronounce the customary formalities. This morning, his long journey will find its sense.

Li Madou is the Chinese pronunciation for Ricci Matteo, the renowned Jesuit and great mathematician from Italy. This missionary has been dreaming of converting the Chinese Emperor and all his subjects and has spent years of his life in small Chinese provincial towns, learning their dialects. He has studied the Confucian vision of the world in order to discuss with mandarins and simple people, always hoping to enter the gates of Peking, a city out of bounds to foreigners. For almost 20 years he has longed for this moment.

The huge square in front of the Emperor's palace is full of soldiers, eunuchs and dignitaries. Ten thousand people, perhaps twice as many or even more. Li Madou realises that he will not be allowed to talk to the Emperor. But at least he will see him and be able to get an impression of him in order to orient himself, like the sailors who look at the pole star in the sky. It is said that the buildings of the Forbidden City represent the map of the constellations around the polar star. The throne on top of the stairway is ready to welcome the imperial star.

In a long procession, the bystanders start to perform the formalities of the ritual. Now it is Li Madou's turn. He advances towards the throne, kneels and bends down, touching the earth with his forehead. For a second he lifts his eyes: the throne is still empty. He has been unlucky. The emperor will appear to the bows of the others. But not one of the ten, twenty, thirty thousand people who are led to the throne is more fortunate than him. In perfect order, all are driven towards the exit. The square returns to its vast loneliness. The ritual is as precise as a mathematical formula: an empty throne – the centre.

For almost 20 years – Matteo Ricci writes to his parents – I have been waiting for this moment. For this empty throne I have burnt my house, I have eaten and drunk with foreigners, I have known their wisdom and their distrust.

Working *for* the text and working *with* the text

The narrative context of a performance can be given by a written text and there are infinite ways of dealing with it in theatre. But they can all be grouped within two tendencies: working *for* the text and working *with* the text.

Working *for* the text means to consider the literary work as the principal value of the performance. The actors, the director, the organisation of the space, the musical accompaniment and the lighting design are all striving to emphasise the quality and complexity of the text, its allusions, its connections with the original as well as the current context, and its capacity to radiate out into different directions and dimensions. I do not believe for a moment that it is characteristic of old-style theatre. It can be the height of what is *new*. The theatre that works *for* the text transmutes literature into an experience of the senses and the mind. The written words become flesh and thought-in-action. I love the theatre which follows this path to the bitter end, but have rarely practised it.

Working *with* the text means choosing one or more literary scripts and – instead of placing oneself at their service – extracting a substance which must nourish a new organism: the performance. The literary text is used as one of the components in the real life of the theatrical fiction.

The literary text was originally an autonomous and complete organism. Now it is *material ready to change*, plunged into a process of choices and visions which are foreign to it. It gradually becomes eroded by the experiences and the ideas of the actors and the director, put to the test, dismantled and reassembled in something that is unrecognisable.

It could be said that this is not *with*, but *against*. I don't think so; I believe it is a complementary way of thinking.

I talk of text as an artisan, using the term in its etymological sense: text as texture, weaving, from the Latin *texere*. I refer to a literary product with a high level of craftsmanship and complete in itself. It may be prose or poetry; it may have been conceived specifically for the stage or for some other purpose: a comedy, a tragedy, a short story, a novel, a collection of poems or even an essay.

A text may be taken apart and reorganised in a form far removed from the original. This process is similar to breaking down, decontextualising and recomposing the materials of the actors' dramaturgy, or to a film director's editing when she intertwines two separate sequences of images and makes them interact. This is sheer theatre directing technique and implies a way of detecting and weaving together – through actions – paths of thought.

My relationship with the text was similar to that with an actor. I treated it as a living organism, confronting it with its secret and possible destinies.

From a dramaturgical point of view, to tell a story – which already exists or is invented during rehearsals – means to infuse life into it. This life should not be confused with vitality. It is something which acquires a personal sense for the spectator. To infuse life or revitalise the sense are metaphors concerning the process of tearing a story from its original context and projecting it into another one, arousing unexpected and unthinkable thoughts and associations, starting with the actors and the director.

Literary works of art are characterised by the fact that *life* pervades every level of their organisation, every part, every cell. Not only the entire organism of a play or a poem, but also the small knots of words, images and sounds all bear the trace of the skilled hand and mind which have woven them together and given them their density. This means that a dialogue, a short story or a poem may be subdivided into small 'verbal actions', clusters of words, images and sonority which, however, are not reduced to impoverished fragments.

For the thousandth time: the range of details and intonations in the actor's physical and vocal actions make the behaviour of a character convincing and alluring for the spectator. In the same way, the language of a poem becomes suggestive for whoever reads or listens to it, because it is made up of 'vocal actions', meaningful, sonorous and rhythmic dynamisms which are more dense and astonishing than those of daily language. By density I mean a form containing a variety of information.

For me, working *with* the text implied the capacity to split it into its verbal actions and rearrange them in order to discover new sonorous and mental associations to be juxtaposed to the physical actions. I treated any text, even the most prosaic, as if it were poetry.

I repeat: there exists a *life* which pervades the text/woven fabric. This determines the complex simplicity which integrates its diverse components in a way which is not obvious. Compared with daily forms of speech, poetry in particular makes use of *deformation*: unusual combinations of words; sonorous, rhythmical and semantic tensions; leaps from one level of reality to another; interferences between logics which in 'normal' thought are mutually incompatible; surreal conglomerations, oxymora and synaesthesia. These procedures are labelled in the terminology of literary technique as metaphor, synecdoche, allegory, metrics and symbolism. But this literary technique shows us a way of interweaving the 'paths of thought' – hence my predilection for poetry as the substance of the dialogues and monologues in my performances.

Therefore, Charles Dullin indicated Japanese prints and the poetry of Poe, Baudelaire and Mallarmé as models for the actors in his Atelier. They were not intended as models to be imitated, but for training the mind. Artaud, one of Dullin's actors, spoke of the art of the actor as consisting literally of 'poetry in space'.

For *Kaspariana* (1967) Ole Sarvig didn't give us a play, but a poem of about 10 pages inspired by the figure of Kaspar Hauser. Also for *Brecht's Ashes*, in 1980, I avoided Brecht's plays and I focused on his poems. In these, as in many other similar cases, I abided by my director's craft: the montage of the actions.

Something similar happened in the case of *Mythos* (1998). Two years previously I had read Thomas Bredsdorff's book *Med Andre Ord* (In Other Words) devoted to Henrik Norbrandt's 'poetic language'. I decided that the characters of my next production would express themselves through the words of this well-known contemporary Danish poet.

Henrik Norbrandt does not live in Denmark. He has set up house in Greece, Turkey, Spain and Sweden. He is certainly not an 'easy' person. When I suggested he wrote something for us, he replied that he found it difficult to collaborate with anybody. For Odin Teatret, too, collaboration with an author is far from easy. We agreed that we were made for each other, and could use his published poems in whatever way we wanted. We made one condition: that he should first see one of our performances. He came to Holstebro and saw *Kaosmos*. The next day he signed the contract. That was at the end of 1996, and since then he has visited us only once, three years later. Collaboration, like the performing arts and the language of poetry, can also be paradoxical

We had at our disposition Norbrandt's 22 books of poetry. If I relied on my tastes as a reader, I would never have dared to touch his poems. It was my task as a director that determined their metamorphosis. It was the need to integrate them into the new organism which was beginning to take form through the actors' actions.

Poems about love and travel to far-off places, existential reflections which were both mocking and despairing, atrocious yet luminous personal visions became the words of Oedipus and Cassandra, Odysseus and Medea, Daedalus and Orpheus, and of a Brazilian soldier from the 'Prestes column' who rebelled against his government at the beginning of the twentieth century.

In many cases I kept the original form of the poet's compositions. Sometimes I adapted them by changing the tense of a verb, by moving from the first to the second person, or else a proper name might be added or taken out.

The most interesting examples were when the transmutation was profound and the life which permeated every single cell of Norbrandt's poetry showed its full force. Fragments of different poems could melt into a monologue, or a single poem could be distilled in a dialogue between several characters, as in the case of *Hvis du kunde se dig selv* (If you could see yourself):

> If you could see yourself // in my dreams // you would run away screaming. // You would scratch your face till it bled, // cover yourself with petrol // and shout for a flame. // Through my childhood's evenings // its autumns, its rain // you now drag yourself off // like a ghost from the future, // weighed down by a burden // greater than you thought // you could bear: // the chains you drag // are twice as heavy as you, // twice as long as // your time // and the ghosts of those I have killed // night after night in anger // frighten you: the

terrifying ghosts // of my relations, my school friends, // my first love. // From all the doors // stream bones and hair. // From the trees, which time // has not yet felled, // hang the dead, scorched by the sun. // Nails grow out of the ground. // What you are treading on is cartilage. // I shout your name // would call you back from the dead // but you do not hear me, do not know // that I walk by your side // and that only you can wake me // even with the lightest touch, // the caress of your eyelashes.

In the performance this poem became a dialogue:

Daedalus:	Medea, if you could see yourself in my dreams, you would run away screaming. You would scratch your face till it bled, cover yourself with petrol and shout for a flame.
Cassandra:	From all the doors, stream bones and hair.
Medea:	Orpheus, I call out to my dead children, but they do not hear me.
Orpheus:	At your side walk the ghosts of all those you have killed night after night.

Sometimes it was as though the poem had undergone a process of evaporation. A few drops of it remained in suspension and joined together as if in a new solitary constellation of stars. Of the first six lines of *Ud til havet* (To the sea):

Finally we have reached the sea! // It stretches out in front of us // ten miles deep and full of secrets. // But from the flat beach where we stand // we can only see the surface. // It shimmers in the light of the July sun, but that is not all

only a sort of haiku remained, the leitmotif of the choir in the performance:

The sea in front of us,
deep, secret.
The surface shimmers.
That is not all.

On other occasions, fragments which came from various compositions were brought together, losing their original logic and creating another. In the same way, the scores of the different actors, each of which was elaborated independently from the others, could detach themselves from the original intentions and, merging together, produced new meanings. For example, these lines from the poem *Gobi*:

> Seven steps from spring the questions become answers. // Your face from the dark is dusted by violets. // Nine nights from the mountains. // Thirteen mouths from madness. // God masturbates us with his sickening mathematics. // The Gobi desert counts its cells by grains of sand, // we by tears, when we look into the spring sky.

And from *Barberblade* (Razor blades):

> The spring has arrived and has split my life apart // like a packet of razor blades // which I dare not keep and dare not throw away // fine, small blades // which reflect the light like Asian lakes. // The thought that they will rust // without being used torments me just as much // as the thought of using them. // And when I try now and then to forget them // in offices or bars // they come back to me from places with exotic names // where I have never set foot. // Where on earth shall I put my feet // with so many razor blades around // without cutting myself and without breaking them? // They are so beautiful, they are so small. // It is because it is spring and the sky is blue. // And I stand here and call and call, // stiff as an icicle, with eyes closed until I fall.

And from *Om foråret bygger de et hospital* (In spring they build a hospital):

> In spring they build a hospital around me // so that I can have a blue room in which to shout. // I do not know who they are. I do not know what I shout. // I only know the answers, answers, answers.

Fused in Cassandra's vision:

> Seven steps from spring the questions become answers // and the face of darkness is dusted by violets. // Nine nights from the mountains // and thirteen mouths from madness // you wake in the labyrinth and the sky is blue. // You do not know what you shout, stiff as an icicle, // with eyes closed until you fall.

I am well aware of the risks involved in providing such examples. Selecting only a few cases out of a hundred might make it appear to be mere mechanical *bricolage*. But what was essential was a sort of *state of necessity* which emerged in the course of the work and which sprang from the precise framework of the actors' actions; their relationships with the other characters in the particular scene; the position of the scene within the overall dramaturgical structure; the actions immediately preceding and succeeding it. This *state of necessity* cannot be exemplified. Transposed onto paper, the physical process in which the texts were treated as the actions of the actors risks resembling a literary game which would not only be disrespectful, but also meaningless and arbitrary.

The setting up of a performance's verbal structure (words which were spoken or sung) could start from an opposite direction: not from a 'poetic language' but from a specialised or anecdotal prose. One of the sources for the text of *Talabot* (1988) was a long article in a scientific magazine written by the Danish anthropologist Kirsten Hastrup. The author confessed that, during her fieldwork in Iceland, she had been 'seduced' by a man from the *skjulte folk*, the 'hidden people' of the Icelandic legends. For me, this article's fascination sprang from the evident contrast between the scientific discourse and the experience of seduction, perceived as reality by the senses of the anthropologist and with scepticism by her intellect.

Also her condition of anthropologist was for me another inspiring source. It was the example of a type of person who had chosen of her own will to leave her country of birth and unfold an activity among foreigners, as for instance the explorer, the revolutionary, the doctor, the missionary and many theatre people.

The actors and I met Kirsten Hastrup and bombarded her with questions. We still didn't know what to do with this woman who had generously consented to be the protagonist of our next theatrical adventure. I proposed she should write a hundred autobiographic episodes, each no longer than a page. They would constitute part of the verbal fabric of the performance, in addition to offering inspiration for scenes. Other sources of *Talabot* were *la commedia dell'arte* (which I could not stand, but was one of the constraints I imposed on myself), and a poem by the Danish B.S. Ingeman, which has become a moving psalm. Moreover, I had the story of Minik, an Inuit child from Greenland who, with his father, followed a group of American anthropologists to New York in order to be 'studied'. Soon his father died and the anthropologists organised a mock funeral in the presence of the child. In reality they anatomised the corpse and exhibited the skeleton in a museum.

Many of the episodes written by Kirsten Hastrup circled around the relationship with her father, her studies, the difficulty in combining her career and family life after giving birth to four children, her fieldwork in Iceland and her divorce. Each of the actors chose three episodes and directed them with their fellow actors, deciding the texts to be said or sung. At the same time, they prepared materials and 'knots' relating to their characters – among whom the most significant were Che Guevara, Antonin Artaud and the polar explorer Knud Rasmussen – and selected texts from their books and letters.

The final text of *Talabot* – its dialogues, monologues and songs – originated from these heterogeneous sources, all in prose and without much poetic density. It was the interlacement between the daily style and the actors' vocal and organic dramaturgy that evoked *the Unreal*, which, according to Kirsten Hastrup, became empirical through her personal experience of the fieldwork.

Itsi Bitsi (1991) told the story of love and friendship between the Odin actress, Iben Nagel Rasmussen, and the first Danish beat poet, Eik Skaløe, who committed suicide at the age of 25. Their relationship evolved in the early 1960s, among travels, rock music, drugs, the illusion of a revolution of the mind and the despair of a personal shipwreck. The narrative thread – the text was by Iben – was interrupted by scenes from some of her performances in which she commented on her own artistic process and the characters to whom she had given life. On the level of concatenation, the performance unfolded, through oppositions, an autobiographic testimony which was both a story of self-destruction and one of personal growth.

It was the theatrical dimension (the organic dramaturgy and the intertwining with the physical and vocal actions of the other actors) which eradicated any form of pathos from the text, giving it new perspectives. Like a grotesque, indifferent or cheerful counterpoint, two musicians (Jan Ferslev and Kai Bredholt[4]) in elegant grey suits and ties, kept an eye on the actress and assisted her, parodying her sufferings. Were they policemen, guardian angels, nurses or a couple of clowns?

The biographical and professional episodes narrated by the actress (concatenation) and the contiguity of the actress with the musicians (simultaneity) produced a kaleidoscopic effect which multiplied the possibilities of interpretation. What was the exact framework of the performance? A theatre where an actress narrated her autobiography? A psychiatric hospital with a delirious patient? The memories of an elderly woman who confused episodes from reality and fiction? Or a cabaret where we were entertained musically with the story of a drug addict who had committed suicide?

The kaleidoscopic theatrical tale addressed spectators who each had to extract their own story. This didn't mean that the performance was open to anything, shapeless and multiform as a cloud. It was composed of a calibrated profusion of vocal and physical stimuli – *sats* – whose correspondences and discordances were carefully interlaced to narrate explicitly or suggest several stories. Their relationships were not always exhibited overtly. They often remained hidden, not obvious, yet not random.

I didn't plan all this in advance. I understood it *a posteriori*, as director and responsible spectator. Now, with the passing of time, I could express it in a formula: nothing was left to the unforeseeable so that the unforeseeable might happen.

Kaosmos

In the reality of the atom, its particles move backwards and forwards in time, indifferent to the laws of cause and effect. I had the feeling that a rash decision, a sudden idea or a spontaneous impulse, causing a row of consequences for me and others, were the fulfilment of a prescription arriving from far away. Somewhere, an ancestor, a person who loved me, had traced a road. I followed it and this choice gave me an unbearable heartbeat and a sense of endless power.

I experienced this condition as a sign of the dark forces within me which held my hand, and also as a meeting with destiny. Or maybe I should call it Chance. The latter was a champion of blows below the belt, capable of knocking me out instantaneously if I didn't predispose a rigorous strategy to avoid its blows and rebut them.

In an artistic process, Chance is not a mother cat which grabs you by the nape of the neck as if you were its kitten, and carries you to where there is food. Chance is an aggressive monkey jumping from tree to tree and you – her unprotected tiny offspring – must hang on to her for dear life in order not to fall, while she climbs, shaking you violently, towards a treetop loaded with fruit.

I wanted to turn into theatrical reality descriptions of events, stories and biographies from the past and the present (which were symbols written on paper) or to give body and voice to ideas, desires, obsessions and emotions (which were impalpable electrical and chemical processes in my head). I devised this metamorphosis according to the rules of *serendipity*: like a game of dice with Chance. In order to win, I had to know the technique to exploit to my advantage the impenetrability of fortuitous situations and accidental tangles which arose in rehearsals. I prepared myself through efforts which were unreasonable but deeply rooted in my personal mythology. I will mention just one of them.

This effort consisted in reading attentively any printed paper I received: thick and thin books, manuals, articles, collections of poems, theatre programmes, artistic manifestos, religious booklets, advertising materials, festival brochures, electoral lists, political pamphlets, dedicatory volumes, academic dissertations, compendia of lectures, marriage invitations, tourist information, sports announcements, publishing house catalogues, magazines and yearbooks. I painstakingly read from the first to the last word. It was not a small-time investment. I received printed and written papers of all sorts: books as gifts, prose, poetry, essays, biographies, texts to be commented upon and manuscripts in search of a preface or a publisher. They dealt with subjects far from my own interests and tastes. Nevertheless I didn't shun this effort. And I was richly compensated.

In 1988 Christian Ludvigsen, a close friend and Odin Teatret's literary adviser, sent me a book. Its title was *Pietà*, and the author was Georg

Klein, a Hungarian oncologist who had taken refuge in Sweden after the failed insurrection against the Soviets in 1956. This scientist, with the vulnerability of a language learned in adult life, described the precarious coexistence of viruses and the human organism amid the reversals of science shifting between enthusiasm and discouragement. Klein also described his feeling of estrangement and his personal strategies in order to adapt the baggage of his own culture of origin to the Scandinavian reality.

A chapter of *Pietà* was devoted to the biography and the literary production of Attila József, a poet unknown to me. Among the poems translated by Klein from Hungarian into Swedish was 'The seventh'.

If you dwell in this world
your mother will give birth
to you seven times.
Once in a burning house,
once under icy waters,
once in a sea of wheat,
once in an echoing monastery,
once among sows in a yard.
Six times you will scream,
but what can you do?
You will be the seventh.

If you meet an enemy on the road
he will find seven enemies against him.
One starting his day of rest,
one ending his working day,
one teaching the poor for free,
one thrown into deep water,
one is the seed before the forest,
one is protected by crazed ancestors.
But no deceptions will help you.
You will be the seventh.

If you seek your loved one,
seven will pursue her.
One gives her heart for words,
one pays for herself,
one plays the dreamer,
one is on guard under her skirt,
one fingers her garters,
one stamps on her handkerchief.
Let them hover like flies around meat.
You will be the seventh.

If you can afford to write verses
seven poets will go to work.
One builds a city of marble,
one is born in deep sleep,
one calls the Word by name,
one measures the heavens and nods,
one gambles away his soul,
one dissects a live rat;
four scientists and two bold warriors.
You will be the seventh.

And when everything written is fulfilled
seven will go together to the grave.
One is cradled by a bursting bosom,
one reaches for a firm breast,
one throws away the empty goblet,
one incites the poor to victory,
one works as though possessed,
one only stares at the moon.
You walk under the tombstone of the world.
You will be the seventh.

Attila József was admired for his prodigious faculty to transfer the most complicated intellectual images into intoxicating rhythms and musicality as in popular ballads. Also in Klein's rough Swedish version, 'The seventh' seeped into the crevices of my mind, humming enigmas. My first reaction was: 'I will decipher the enigmas. They will be one of the sources of my next performance.' Odin Teatret was still presenting *Talabot*, and at least a couple of years would go by before I started a new project. 'The seventh' waited patiently.

Attila's father had abandoned the family when his son was three years old. The child grew up in an orphanage, and as an adult he earned his life as porter, waiter and sailor on the Danube. At 14, he lay down on the railway lines waiting for the goods train which passed at the same time every day through the village where he lived. Time went by and the train didn't arrive. Attila walked along the rails in the direction of the train. But someone else had had the same idea a few hundred metres ahead of him. Attila used to say: 'someone has died in my place.' Survivors always feel guilty.

Goods trains became a leitmotif in his poems. One evening in November 1937, 32 years old, in Szárszó, on Lake Balaton, Attila walked up to the station. The locomotive began laboriously to move. Attila ran after it, knelt down beside the railway line and, as the train passed, he stretched out his right arm between two wagons. The arm was found intact, neatly severed, at some distance from the body which had been dragged and crushed by the train. In his room, on the bed, a shirt was laid out from which he had cut the right sleeve.

December 1988: the Odin is on tour in Chile with Talabot. *Eugenio watches a video about the death of a 'poor' priest, Romero, perpetrated by Pinochet's police. His words impress him: 'People only deserve to have what they are able to defend,' and also the comment of Carolina, a nun: 'We hear the noise of the walls tumbling down, but not the sound of the wheat which grows.'*

Eugenio already thinks about the next performance: Jesus returning to earth in South America. Perhaps Iben could be the Chilean singer Violeta Parra. Another character could be Borges. Later, watching the four veteran actresses of his group at work, he imagines them in the roles of Stanislavski, Brecht, Artaud and Craig meeting on the top of a mountain.

February 1989: We are in Milan in the desecrated church of St Carpoforo. The director tells of the video he has seen in Chile to his actors touring with Talabot. *He makes them listen to the recorded song of a woman and asks in which country and under which circumstances it takes place. Every actor gives his or her own answer. The song comes from a television documentary on Afghanistan, with interviews of the parents of Russian soldiers who are fighting there.*

A mother who sings, images of war, the noise of collapsing walls and the silence of wheat which grows: a performance is fermenting in the head of the director.[5]

I always felt rejuvenated when I finished a performance. It would be played two or three hundred times around the world for at least a couple of years. As the moment approached for the preparation of a new one, I contrived other projects in order to postpone the period of exhaustion and uncertainty, the confrontation with the sphinx, the rehearsals for the performance which would become the flagship in the repertoire of the Odin.

In February 1992, circumstances didn't allow me to procrastinate any longer. I was forced to get down to work. Three young actors had to be introduced into our group through the test of the rehearsals. Roberta Carreri, busy since 1987 with her responsibilities as a mother and with her one-woman show *Judith*, had been long separated from our collective performances. It was important for her to be reinstated in the ensemble. But three actors, Iben Nagel Rasmussen, Jan Ferslev and Kai Bredholt, were away with *Itsi Bitsi* on a long tour. To exorcise these constraints, I exploited an expedient already used on other occasions: a preparatory performance to the true performance.

We had made The Million, *we could now make* The Billion. The Million, *in our repertoire from 1978 to 1984, was a musical performance for up to 400 spectators. Spectacular, rich in melodies, rhythms and colours, grotesque and lyrical, it blended dances, music and costumes that we had picked up during our travels all over the world.* The Billion *should be even more grandiose and with more spectators. The director organised an orchestra with string and wind instruments. We started composing and learning new melodies.*

When standing in front of the actors in the working room, the rehearsals slid in a totally new direction. I abandoned *The Billion* and let the actors improvise on a short sentence which stirred despotically in my mind: 'a ghost wanders through Europe: the ghost of communism.'

I had witnessed profound historical transformations: the demolition of the Berlin Wall, the dissolution of the Soviet Union, the return to 'democracy' of half a dozen countries under a socialist regime. Everywhere I turned my gaze, the wandering ghost of communism was present, repudiated by everybody, knocking on locked doors, rejected on every frontier. It resembled King Lear: a hoary venerable old man, by now blind, insane with despair and incapable of understanding. He clasped to his breast a block of ice, whose heart was a frozen book: Marx's *Communist Manifesto*. He was accompanied by a flock of women – mothers, sisters and wives of Lenin's and Stalin's victims – who all sang an adaptation of the *Requiem* by Anna Akhmatova:

They took you away at dawn,
I walked behind you, as at a funeral,
In the dark room the children cried,
On your lips the cold of the icon,
Deathly sweat on your forehead.
Seventeen months I've been shouting,
I threw myself at the executioner's feet,
All is forever confused.
I no longer understand
Who is beast and who is man.

We improvised starting from nuclei of words which we turned into songs and poems. We came with proposals on the death and the grave of a book. We worked on a dance whose footsteps were like sea waves. [. . .] We spread the sea on the floor: a huge bluish sheet. Ragged women danced upon it to the rhythm of joyful music. They stripped off their rags, revealing white dresses: they were the Russian mothers who had lost their children in the Gulag. One of them was a poetess. The old ghost, dragging himself through piles of rags, slowly became a woman dressed in white, a scarf on her head like a babushka. We accompanied this transformation singing a poem by Nordhal Grieg:

Death burns like a field of wheat.
Every life whirls purer
In its immaculate suffering:
They are the best who die.

The best are slaughtered in jail,
Seized by the fire and the sea.
The best won't be our future.
The best are busy dying.

The women rolled up the sea scattered with rags and memories, put it on their shoulders and walked out. The sea was dead. On its arid bed lay a book – Marx's Communist Manifesto – *encapsulated in a block of ice.*

All materials, songs and entire scenes were put aside when Jan and Kai returned from their tour. Iben took three more months free to finish a book she was writing. We all met again, however, during one weekend in Italy.

March 1992: we are in Padua, guests of the group Teatrocontinuo, for a session of the University of Eurasian Theatre. The discussion concerns the terms 'score' and 'subscore'. We actors work practically on a text proposed by Thomas Bredsdorff, selected among many suggested by the participants. It is the short story by Frans Kafka, Before the Law, *which he later inserted in* The Process. *It tells of a Doorkeeper who prevents a man from the country from accessing the Law. The man waits in vain a whole lifetime. The text is analysed and commented upon by the scholars, then the actors recount it in a theatrical way following the routes of their personal dramaturgy.*

It seems impossible that a director can say to his actors: give the best of yourself and stretch your bow to its maximum. But you must know, however, that the purpose of all our efforts – yours as mine – is to gain time. They are not aiming at the objective for which we have long been preparing ourselves: a new performance. We must let Iben finish her book. You know that for me the theatre loses its sense if *my environment* is not complete, if the nucleus of people to whom I am tied is not present in its entirety, some of whom have shared with me the adventure of all our performances. But what should we do in the meantime, while waiting for Iben to come back? How can we sensibly fill the waiting time before the performance for which we have been preparing ourselves for months? What is sensible or foolish in a creative process, when each of us is part of the thread holding together the necklace of our wishes, aspirations and needs?

I must have said something of the kind to my actors back in Holstebro, after the parenthesis in Padua. It was my task to turn this feeling of suspension into a personal value for each of us. I had the idea to start on a children's performance with the whole group. I would subsequently select and assemble the most interesting scenes with our three youngest actors. In this way, they would have a performance of their own. This time, the source was just one: *The Jungle Book* by Kipling.

I started with an improvisation about 'wolfness': being, feeling like and being seen as a wolf. I fixed every individual improvisation and elaborated each of them into a mini-performance. I added costumes and objects, and encompassed them in music and songs. At times I introduced one or more actors to solve some functional tasks: to lift a body from the floor or to follow an actor as a shadow.

May 1992: The director wants to prepare a children's performance based on Kipling's The Jungle Book. *He proposes an improvisation: 'On a carpet, a wolf is born three times. The first birth is the biological one. The second is the transition which places the anonymous person among those who have a name. Through a rite of passage lasting eleven days and eleven nights, you become a wolf. The third birth happens in old age. It occurs when the others recognise in you the authentic wolf, when you emanate 'wolfness'. The small carpet under your feet limits you, yet it is boundless, ready to fly. The carpet is the jungle.'*

The actors improvise on the three births that must correspond to three poems – from poiein *(to do, in Greek). Their improvisations are performed first as ideograms in space and then set down as words/poems on a sheet of paper to be given to the director.*

Each actor has fixed her own improvisations which have taken place on the cloth, fur or veil which has been chosen as the flying carpet/jungle. The cloth-carpet is a vast territory, an animated companion-partner and a spatial limit. The director treats the improvisations as if they were several mini-performances with only one actor and with a well defined beginning, development and conclusion. But his technique of elaboration is new for everybody.

I found myself with a series of small performances that I structured one after another in a long sequence. There was little which recalled *The Jungle Book*. I didn't give up and persevered on this trail in the hope that it would lead to a children's performance. I knew by now how decisive it was to watch the structured materials over and over again, retouching the details daily, altering the rhythms, introducing new objects or turning a scene around to make it say the opposite.

Tina's actions[6] *are introverted and addressed to herself. The director asks her to repeat them doing the contrary. She must reverse their direction: the actions towards herself are now aimed outside, the floor becomes the ceiling, what was in front becomes behind. Tina seems to be a computer in full swing while she cautiously calculates where to place each foot and hand.*

Roberta is sustained and led by two puppeteers. Torgeir and Kai move her with the help of two long bamboo canes as if they were giving her the impulses for her actions.

Julia must eliminate the carpet on the floor, repeat and adapt her improvisation sitting on a chair, then standing behind it.

Isabel[7] *has difficulty in finding her balance. The director replaces her 'flying carpet' with Hisako,*[8] *whom Isabel lifts, embraces and shakes as she had been doing with the carpet. Hisako is the carpet and must do nothing. Then Jan, taller and heavier, assumes the role of the carpet. In the end Isabel has to perform her score with Hisako and Jan together. Isabel struggles, is sweating, exhausted. We all feel for her back when she lifts her two colleagues from the floor, hugging them to her chest or dragging them.*

One day the masks of Talabot, *our previous performance, reappear. The actors wear them while sitting doing nothing, but remove them when they get up and act, thus inverting the usual rule.*

One day Roberta must distribute coins to the observers who are watching our rehearsals. Later, they must put the money back on the plate when she holds it out to them, then she places it in front of Torgeir who is kneeling on his carpet.

One day the director complains about the way his actors are dressed. The following day they arrive in evening wear, in smart shirts and trousers – the garments they like best. Torgeir wears a grey suit. The costumes start to decide who we are. But who are we?

I welcomed the summer holidays with a sigh of relief. I had some weeks to let the materials settle in my mind, detecting their cul-de-sacs and possible outlets. When we came back, Iben was in the working room. We showed her the fixed sequence and to induce her to join our rehearsals, I proposed to her the role of the man from the country, protagonist of Kafka's short story, *Before the Law*, on which we had been working in Padua. This idea struck me as soon as I noticed the bewildered expression on Iben's face after seeing our materials. Thus Kafka's text blended together in the retort with 'The seventh', the materials about the 'ghost of communism wandering through Europe', and those about *The Jungle Book*.

August 1992: We are back at rehearsals. First we decide our daily schedule: from 7am to 10am bobbletiden *(boiling time), in which the actors concentrate autonomously on their individual work; from 10am to 3pm we rehearse the structured materials from before the holidays, which the director now calls* The Process. *Hisako is no longer with us, she has left with a Danish boy she met in Japan.*

We show our materials to Iben and shortly afterwards we have a meeting. Iben accepts to join us with a cautious yes. Next day she is active, changing the future. The other actors have materials, scenes, days and weeks of rehearsals behind them. Even if they don't know why, they know what to do. They follow an inner logic which is inherent in the working process. Iben has nothing. The director tries to give her some support. He encourages her by speaking about the character of Kafka's short story: 'You should not be theatrical. You should behave casually, dress as a maid who tries to be nice, a sort of Giulietta Masina from Fellini's La Strada, *or Madeleine Renaud in* Happy Days, *in the best acting style of the Royal Theatre in*

Copenhagen. You should let yourself be inspired by the fashion of the 1950s. You must have a hat – a hat always helps an actor.'

The director explains that the performance is about The Process *by Kafka. He also gives us the text of a poem, 'The seventh', by Attila József. He speaks at length about this Hungarian poet, a communist who committed suicide in 1937.*

Kafka's short story was disturbing, but static, excessively symbolic and with only two characters. It didn't help me to explain who the other figures were – the other seven actors with their vast amount of materials. I divided the text of the entire short story in four parts which I inserted in different places in the sequence of materials so as to interrupt their succession and rhythm. It was my intention that the spectators should understand the text in any country in which we toured. I asked Frans Winther, our composer, to put the short story into music as an oratorio. During the performance, the text would be sung chorally in Danish and an actor would simultaneously translate it into the language of the place. Thus Kafka's tale became a leitmotif which disappeared and re-emerged in a flood of events involving many different themes and stories. Frans also composed the music for Attila József's poem. Each verse, sung and danced in different parts of the performance, should burst forth like a geyser, upsetting the landscape.

I struggled to extract a plot from the actors' organic materials. In purely narrative terms, Kafka's short story described waiting, with an epilogue which overturned the sense of the facts previously narrated. In this way I explained to myself the jungle of actions and situations that we had structured: a man from the country begs to enter the door of the Law; he is asked to wait; he turns his attention to the events happening around him, to the coming and going and the vicissitudes of unknown figures executing actions which are incomprehensible to him. He longs to be admitted to the clarity of the Law, but finds himself engulfed in chaos.

Here another source surfaced, a title which I had been carrying within me for years waiting for a performance: *Kaosmos*, chaos-cosmos, confusion-creation.

My story justified only part of the materials. Many scenes were interesting at an organic level, but I was unable to tame them to the logic of my narration. I felt myself dragged by waves in a starless ocean. It is true that during the rehearsals, this ocean is a *deliberate maelstrom* of contexts reciprocally dissociated and incompatible, created *on purpose* as a challenge to my expectations and logical categories. Chaos-cosmos. For the time being, confusion had the upper hand and mocked my reason. I succumbed to the inevitable sense of uncertainty.

August 8, 1992: It is the day of revelations. The director says: 'Till this moment we have followed the will of the sea, distancing us from the land. Now it is time to find our route. In our materials, conflicting strengths, antithetical situations, tensions and incoherence are tossed about. We have to safeguard this tumult and vigour which appear to us as chaos. We know that chaos has its inner coherence, hiding the bud of creation, of cosmos. *How can we reach a creation which maintains its nature of chaos? James Joyce, in* Finnegan's Wake, *calls it chaosmos. Our performance should be like this: Kaosmos. Iben is the man from the country from Kafka's short story. Julia is the Doorkeeper of the Law. I could give names to the "chaos" which we have created: Jan is wings of a butterfly; Frans is storm in Lapland; Roberta is crest of a wave. "The seventh" by Attila József is a political manifesto, a credo of existential revolt, the refusal of the fortuitousness of one's own birth – Sarajevo, Bangladesh, a psychiatric hospital, the Nazi regime. His poem describes the chaos-cosmos.*

A man from the country wants to accede to the Law, its Doorkeeper says he has to be patient and wait. So he waits, surrounded by chaos and events which make no sense to him. This is as far as I have got.'

As often happened in similar situations of stalemate, I focused my attention on a concrete problem: the costumes. I thought about clothes from everyday life in Denmark, but with theatrical features: for example, a cook's or a postman's uniform (a flaming red jacket). When Jan wore the chimney sweep's uniform – a black suit with gold buttons, a wide leather belt, a red handkerchief around the neck and a top hat – he looked as though he came straight from the universe of Hans Christian Andersen. We looked for ideas for costumes in this author's fairy tales: the tin soldier, the paper ballerina who burns; who could be the naked king? Thus Andersen slipped into the retort in which so many ingredients were already boiling. I re-read his tales and *Story of a Mother* exploded within me with its cruel truth. Death has abducted a child and his mother pursues it to get him back. Death describes for her the probable criminal destiny of her child if he should return to life. The mother renounces getting her son back.

I experienced a moment of relief, almost enthusiasm: I had found the narrative link between the story of the mother and that of Kafka's man from the country. To kill time while waiting, the man from the country, sitting on a stool, takes a book and reads aloud Andersen's fairy tale. As in a Japanese Noh performance, the ghost of the mother appears and performs her story.

September 1992. The director explains: 'There are characters who are so strong that they can escape from their own context and keep on living with all of their strength. They cannot, however, behave as in their original environment. What happens if Hamlet trespasses into King Lear? *What are the consequences when one of Andersen's characters slips into Kafka's absurd and inexorable kingdom of the Law? Roberta, you are the mother searching for her child who has been abducted by Death.'*

We spent a lot of time looking for, creating and trying on the costumes. Some were decided rather quickly, others took weeks. Torgeir continued to wear his elegant grey suit and Jan the chimney sweep's uniform. Tina looked like a nymph-amazon with boots, a white tunic and a crown of wheat on her head. I took out from my 'secret' cupboard some skirts, shirts and finely embroidered aprons which I had purchased a few years before in Hungary, distributing them to Iben, Isabel and Roberta. Roberta added a heavily embroidered coat found in Greece and built a wig made of woollen threads. In the same cupboard I fished out a black and white felt jacket, also embroidered, originating from a market in Chiapas, Mexico. It became part of Kai's costume. Julia became a grandmother, bought a long white wig and sewed a green costume adorned with black lace.

How could I make the Door of the Law in front of which the man from the country waits theatrically effective? This was another nut to crack. I imagined it with a frame, hinges, handle and a particular thickness and colour. But how could I give it presence and life? And what sort of voice and nervous system should it have? Travelling in Spain, I was seduced by a door with the patina of age and embroidered by woodworm. I took it on the plane to Holstebro. Too refined. After many brilliant, but theatrically sterile ideas, we agreed on an ordinary wooden door, painted white and bought in a supermarket. The actors started playing with it (how many ways could it be used?) and the solutions arrived, amazing, grotesque and hilarious. It was not difficult to insert them in single scenes or fragments, provoking associations and ambiguities. Nevertheless the whole structure still lacked coherence, refusing to melt into a complex living organism.

I became irritated over my tendency to procrastinate, avoiding definitive decisions. I persisted in the belief that this working process, similar to sea currents, would drag me towards unknown shores. Days passed with no land in sight. I mixed and remixed the scenes' succession, reassembling the whole structure, in search of a plot able to integrate the many elements, threads, stories, contradictions and obviousness – all the rivulets each flowing in its own direction. A plot which convinced me.

What did this fermenting universe *say* to me? I had to be able to formulate it in one sentence. The connection between the story by Andersen and that by Kafka was not enough to create the density which I struggled to attain in a performance. I needed *a thought* which justified each detail in the thick web of interactions and circumstances, making them believable for me. The difficulty consisted in discovering (guessing?) a story which, like a vast frame, could contain various themes and perspectives. Like a tapestry, the story-frame provided the possibility of contiguous yet different tales, while at the same time demanding discipline in their execution. For an outside observer, this story-frame incorporated the actions and explicit or hidden links between the characters of different narrative contexts. As director, these diverse narrative contexts – my sources – inspired me to further changes enabling the characters and the various performances within the performance to grow in an organic wholeness which was convincing for me and, hopefully, for the spectator.

At a certain moment, in despair, I said to myself: 'I'm making a performance for wolves. I will explain this in the programme, and the spectators will put their minds at rest. The events which are incomprehensible to them concern the existential condition of these animals, and they are incommensurable with those of human beings. The spectators will not struggle to understand. They will be seized by the tide of the music, the atmosphere of the songs and the modulation of the voices. They will react to the dynamisms, to acceleration and immobility, to quivers and languor. At times they will feel happy, gratified by a sudden comprehensible fragment.'

We are at the end of September and signs of tiredness are in the air. Roberta comes with a rolled up shawl to produce the image of a child, but the director doesn't want children. The actress protests that the work lacks soul: the director makes the actors go from one place to another, changing character and story and yet they must always do something interesting to prevent the result being cut out.

Julia complains: her knees and back hurt. Her costume, shoes and hat are impossible.

Torgeir, during a seminar with Clive Barker, breaks his Achilles tendon. He must have an operation and remain in plaster for two months.

Jan, who has played the guitar in the last two performances, would like to change instruments. Leo Sykes,[9] *the director's assistant, has the idea of using his spade as a musical instrument. The sound of the cello string fixed to the spade is low and penetrating, effective as an accompaniment to the actors'* sats. *He manages to change the tone by pressing the string against the handle, and to vary the rhythm by beating on the spade's metallic part.*

Julia is no longer the Doorkeeper of the Law. The director has given this character to Jan. She has been given another character: Doña Musica. This is the director's description of her role: 'Doña Musica believes she can hear music which no one else can hear. She follows it, dancing, because angels are playing for her. People who look into her eyes feel like dancing.'

History invaded my life: Yugoslavia and its civil war. When in 1954 I arrived in Norway, my friend Fridtjof Lehne used to tell me about his stay in Yugoslavia after World War II with a brigade of young communists. He described the pride of the population who had withstood the Nazis, the dignity of poor and generous people and the warmth of their hospitality towards foreigners. A couple of years later, I had the same experience while hitchhiking in Yugoslavia. Much later, Odin Teatret was invited several times to the BITEF Festival in Belgrade. Some of the actors and I visited monasteries and mosques in Kosovo, a sleepy world blending cultures and customs. I recognised the names of the places which daily appeared on the television and in the newspapers. Sarajevo weighed on me like a ghost wandering in search of refuge, but no door was open to it. How is it possible, I wondered, that a country which was a living and motivated organism could suddenly disintegrate? The destiny of Yugoslavia, and of the people I had known and loved, infiltrated the rehearsals.

'The seventh' set to music, sung and danced by the actors; the vision of the ghost which crosses Europe among a host of women in mourning; the scenes originating from *The Jungle Book*; the man from the country waiting in front of the Law from Kafka's short story; the story of the child stolen by Death from Andersen; the real and tragic dismemberment of a country: these narrative substances, with the respective materials created by the actors, macerated in the retort. Unconnectable destinies of living and dead people, of historical and fictitious characters who can speak to each other only in our imagination, met in the absolute reality of the theatre.

I bought some coloured chalks and asked the actors to divide the floor between them, sketch the contours of a personal island and draw on the ground an episode from history which had influenced their biography. I was struck by their skill and speed. In less than an hour they had changed an expressionless wooden floor into a many-coloured fresco with the icons of their epoch: the naked child burnt by napalm in Vietnam, portraits of Che Guevara and Mandela, processions with red flags, the Beatles. The actors literally walked on history and their footsteps dissolved recognisable tragic and hopeful events into a colourful mess. It was not a good idea, however, because when the actors lay down on the floor, the costumes were spoilt.

Jan and Tina build a score, trying a variety of postures as statues: a man and a woman who clutch each other, embrace and make love. Then they build another score showing various ways to murder someone: stamping on, strangling, breaking the neck. Then they must mix the two scores and each of their postures belongs to a tango they are dancing. But they must follow the rhythm of another melody which they decide for themselves. Tina and Jan clasp each other tenderly, cling furiously, roll on the floor fighting, then get to their feet in a voluptuous embrace in a flow of impulses and bursts of brutality and passion.

The man from the country cried. He had a handkerchief in a bag, used it to dry his tears and threw it away. The director asked Julia to find out what that abandoned handkerchief meant. Julia bought all the beautiful handkerchiefs she found in town, but the director didn't like them because they reminded him of 'reality'. She then spent many weekends sewing new ones: of lace, cotton, silk and with embroidered borders. She used these in various ways. One day the director asked all the actors to improvise with the handkerchiefs. The result was dolls, hats, sails, napkins, snakes and mice. Roberta created a butterfly. Thus the butterflies entered into the performance. At once the director imagined the final scene: a room invaded by butterflies. The whole floor swarming with caterpillars which became butterflies filling the space with their fragile and many-coloured flight.

I hit my head against the wall of the materials, but no opening appeared. We had found the costumes, composed melodies, theatricalised 'The seventh', structured a succession of scenes in a rhythm which convinced me. Yet I felt as if I was walking on the spot. I was facing the problem inherent to *labyrinthine science*: telling many stories simultaneously, detecting the points of contact between their various episodes and characters, strengthening these connections and letting them grow in a *bios* which convinces. It was not difficult to organise scenes or fragments in a narrative perspective loaded with allusions and meaningful echoes. But I was distant from the result: the whole thing was watery and didn't succeed in coagulating into a breathing organism.

I tried with another source, a text from *Le Soulier de satin* by Paul Claudel on the nature of the theatre:

'I'm searching for the land where no one dies.'

'You have arrived. Here time no longer exists. This is a theatre, and as you know, in theatre we manipulate time as we please, like an accordion. Hours last for days and the years become minutes. Nothing is easier than making different times run together in all directions.'

I introduced these dialogues in the existing structure, extracting some scenes out of them, similar to another leitmotif. It was an intellectual stratagem to explain to the spectators the 'magic' of the theatre and the 'dance' of contiguous and simultaneous scenes. I deluded myself that Claudel's description might help me to escape from the mute horizon which imprisoned the materials. I stimulated the actors with long descriptions about chaos theory and infinity in an effort to convince myself.

'But who is the protagonist of this performance?'

'The one who dies at the end.'

'Is this theatre?'

'Yes, this is theatre: a thread made of mischief and guile. The character dies and the actor returns to life.'

This source turned out to be a sterile guile, a pure conceptual subterfuge, and after some weeks I abandoned it. The performance rejected it: it had not been able to produce new results or an emotional coherence. With the exception of a few sentences, I couldn't find anything which attracted the 'animal' director. It strengthened my belief that the thread made of mischief and guile, in theatre, is only legitimate if it convinces the spectator's nervous system.

Two essential elements were missing: the characters and a story which, like a giant elastic Chinese box, could contain all the other boxes with a multiplicity of tales and plots. I had found two characters relatively early: the man from the country who begs to be admitted to the Law (Iben); the second was the mother searching for her dead child (Roberta). In a late phase of the rehearsals Jan became the Doorkeeper, a role which originally had been given to Julia. The consequence was that Isabel became a 'double' of the Doorkeeper, his twin sister. I imagined them like those striking couples in the villages of southern Italy, the sister serving her brother like a maid or a wife in a dried up marriage. Frans, our composer-musician, had been long absent from our rehearsals through illness. When he came back, I concealed him behind a screen and he became the invisible disinherited son of the Devil who complained about his fate playing the fiddle. Kai, actor and musician, became a sailor who, on returning to his village, told a pack of lies about his travels and sang of his encounter with a mermaid. Julia, who from one day to the next had been deprived of her character, had to invent a new one starting from a name: Doña Musica.

The characters for Torgeir and Tina continued to elude me. Only after months did I succeed in finding them in *The Gospel according to Jesus* by José Saramago: the Son refuses to assume the task his Father has given Him. Thus Torgeir became Christ who lives in a contemporary village in the Balkans, made biblical prophecies come true and accomplished miracles amid general indifference. Only the village prostitute followed him, carrying on her shoulders the Door of the Law to alleviate his suffering. So Tina, too, had a character. We were at the end of the rehearsals.

Christ, doing useless and unrecognisable miracles in a collapsing world, was the detonator which opened a breach in the structure on which I had worked for months. But I didn't reveal this to the spectators, not even through the character's name. He became the secret narrative fulcrum of the performance. I adjusted accordingly all the reactions of the other characters in relationship to this sickly Christ, and filled scenes with allusions to episodes from the Gospels.

The actors were only partly aware of it, but every action of theirs was calibrated in accordance or discordance with this character who, in the final scene, is resurrected as a radiant androgynous paralytic.

By now I was able *to think the thought*: the performance was the story of an anonymous Christ, living in a village in the Balkans held together by a stale tradition and a superficial solidarity. The community fell apart, wiped out by modernity and nationalism.

The director has suggested to the actor the image of a fish quivering in a net. Torgeir, the Man who doesn't want to die, seems shaken by the pangs of a change of conscience. Doña Musica dresses him with a white skirt and a band around his naked breast, while the Doorkeeper buries his grey suit.

Tina, the village bride, has intertwined the ears of wheat in a crown which holds her bridal veil. The director asks the actors what can be done with the wheat and the door. Leo turns Frans into a scarecrow, covering his face with wheat. Iben puts ears of wheat around the framework of the door which is lying on the floor, and then shuts the door. The wheat stands up. A miracle has taken place; we had the performance's final 'knot'.

As was the case in any village in Yugoslavia, also in *Kaosmos: The Ritual of the Door*, every actor spoke his own language. The text was spoken, whispered and sung in Danish, Italian, English, Norwegian and Spanish. Suddenly, when least expected, the performance fell to pieces and the actors, with vitality or lyricism, sang the words of 'The seventh'. They danced what had been happening during the many months of work: the extraordinary events of history, and the trials and hopes of our small personal histories. Thus, from the pages of *Pietà*, the book by a Hungarian emigrant in Sweden, Attila József entered into our lives and still accompanies us.

It is often asked how long Odin Teatret works on a performance. It is always difficult to answer. There is an active time and a passive one, a time which works on us and one with which we work. There is a calendar time and a personal time, a time which speeds by and a time which never passes.

We were in the working room in February, May, August, part of September and October of 1992, and then February and March of 1993. Kaosmos: The Ritual of the Door *took shape during these months. But all the information which imbues it belongs to a time which cannot be measured.*

We had finished working on *Kaosmos* and toured with it for four years. At the last performance in Holstebro we contrived its 'shipwreck'. We presented it without costumes, props and lights between two rows of tables where our friends sat eating and drinking. From the wreckage which had resisted the collapse – the actors' organic actions and relationships – I built a new performance, *Within the Skeleton of the Whale*.

Chained to an oar

How far could I go with a dramaturgy which narrates-behind-actions and places several stories side by side, mixing them? How much could I contradict the need which each of us has as a spectator to slip into the theatrical illusion, in a fictitious reality where we recognise the chains of cause and effect, intentions and finalities, thereby finding the kind of order which life doesn't offer and which art and artifice can rebuild?

Up to what point was it possible to liberate the tale-through-actions from the logic of the tale-through-words? How could I prevent contiguity turning into gratuitousness, disorientation into redundance, confusion into entropy, the experience of not-seeing into blindness and the principle of overturning into fragmentation?

I repeated the same advice to myself: put yourself aside. Forget your certainties and tastes, what gratifies you and makes you confident. Pursue your different identities and cover your traces. Stray without ever letting go the oar of the craft to which you have voluntarily chained yourself. Live in Henrik Norbrandt's *Troy*.

> Each day I am someone different than the day before
> and day by day I move further into darkness:
> before me is a long line of people I have been –
> those nearest, still wrapped in twilight,
> those farther away, in the light, casting shadows
> and the farthest ones, wholly transparent
> like the husks of insects or rock-crystal statues
> fallen forward or completely apart
> exposing their hidden flaws and defects.
> Those I will become stand behind me
> a line of figures equally dark, equally vague –
> I do not know how long it is –
> clumsy, struggling, half-conscious bodies
> waiting to take my place.
> Each day I am someone different, and each day the same:
> the figure in the middle that blocks the view
> keeping those ahead from understanding
> the wild energy and longing for light of those behind,
> and keeping those behind from learning
> from the flaws and failings of those ahead.
> I am Helen, and at the same, the Hellenes
> the rowers who row the carved prows into daybreak
> and each separate rower who, chained to his oar,
> rows with the feeling of never getting anywhere at all.[10]

I have often said, mentioning the dark and elusive forces which led my steps, that I felt like a rider carried by a blind horse galloping on the frozen edge of a precipice.

Zola also spoke of blind horses working in the mines. Like the blind horses that trudged kilometre after kilometre turning around the same threshing mill or the same well. Their image brings to mind the inanity of action. For me it depicted the creative path: a treading and re-treading of my own tracks, until I no longer recognised them. Then I discovered in them the traces of other passages, of footsteps which were no longer mine.

THIRD INTERMEZZO

Stories of passion make sweet dust,
Calm water, grasses unconcerned.
At sunset, when birds cry in the wind
Petals are falling like a girl's robe long ago.
Tu Mu (T'ang Dynasty)

Twenty years later

In the autumn of 2000 I received a small packet. It was sent by an actress, the wife of a director who had participated in ISTA in Bonn in 1980. During the following years we remained in contact and met often. He died in a car accident and his wife, while putting her husband's papers in order, found a notebook which she sent me. These notes – she wrote – which had meant so much in their professional life, belonged also to me.

They constitute an intermezzo which introduces a familiar stranger: the director I was 20 years ago. It was a person who, in words which are unrecognisable to me today, confronts and comments on the heterogeneity of constrictions, problems and aspirations, in an attempt to forge an environment that unites and, at the same time, individualises. This environment was engaged in exploring the possibilities of a dramaturgy structured on levels of organisation. I had just begun to be inspired by biology, and these were my first steps in applying its way of thinking to the theatre craft.

Odin Teatret had already existed for 14 years, twice as long as the average life of a theatre group. I had just finished *Brecht's Ashes*, probably the performance I have loved most. Our group was spurred on by new needs. Some actors were pursuing individual activities which seemed to estrange them from our theatre. Involved in projects they had created and were directing independently, they lived the tension of a double loyalty towards their new needs and the group in which they had their roots. I reflected on the injustice which struck an actor when her group no longer stimulated her. If she decided to leave, she lost the environment in which she had grown and to which she had contributed. Theatre history was full of similar examples:

actors who became 'orphans' when they detached themselves from their director and group. The directors who abandoned their actors survived and historians considered them audacious artists, ready for new adventures.

I wanted to avoid this injustice. It became possible by changing the name of our theatre. Instead of Odin Teatret, whose subtitle was Scandinavian Theatre Laboratory, it became only Scandinavian Theatre Laboratory and included many autonomous activities: Odin Teatret, Odin Teatret's Publishing House, Farfa directed by Iben Nagel Rasmussen, Basho by Toni Cots, Odin Teatret Film by Torgeir Wethal and The Canada Project by Richard Fowler.

As for myself, I proceeded in a solitary adventure accompanied by my actor Toni Cots. It was 1980. I transformed the proposition to direct an international meeting of theatre groups into a project with an unknown outcome. I called it ISTA, International School of Theatre Anthropology. 'School' because at the time everybody wanted to be a 'laboratory', while I wanted to point out that ISTA was a place in which to acquire a basic knowledge; 'international' to indicate a professional country without frontiers; 'anthropology' because it was a term which awoke associations of practical investigation and academic seriousness, although nobody – myself included – had ever heard of a discipline called 'theatre anthropology'. My intention was to introduce artists and friends who meant a lot to me to about 50 'third theatre' directors and actors from all over the world. I wanted them to meet Jerzy Grotowski, Dario Fo, Clive Barker, Keith Johnston, Ingemar Lindh, as well as a few Asian masters and theatre historians, biologists and other men and women of science.

I had previously led courses without my actors. But this was my first experience, lasting a whole month, surrounded by masters I respected and loved, and a large group of young people who I wanted to guide through a storm of stimuli and technical revelations – all to be discovered.

The notebook which I received after 20 years

Thursday, 2 October 1980, 5am

It's our first meeting. Tomorrow we will gather at 6am. Yesterday was the first day of ISTA. We introduced ourselves and watched the artistic presentation of the masters from the Asian theatres. Barba introduced his assistant, the Spanish actor Toni Cots: together they will direct the training sessions in the morning. We are all responsible for the cleaning of this empty school in which we are living. Barba says that it should be extra clean, gleaming like a battleship. This is the schedule: wake up at 6.45am. Quick breakfast. We divide up into small groups and run until 7.30. Then in the gym: acrobatic and vocal training until 8.30. We must not enter the gym wearing shoes. During this first part of the day we must not speak. 'Silence gives energy' says Barba and explains that it is also so as not to disturb the Asian masters who live with us in the school. At 9am the different classes with the Asian masters begin. We are divided into 4 groups, working alternately for a week with each of the teachers (Sanjukta Panigrahi from India, Katsuko Azuma from Japan, Tsao Chun-Lin from Taiwan, I Mades Pasek Tempo from Bali). From 11.30 to 13.30 we are again in the gym for individual training. Barba and Toni Cots will take up what we have learned with the Asian masters in the morning. 13.30–15.30: lunch and rest. At 15.30 the activity of the groups which have been formed around one director starts. Every group – 5 or 6 actors and a director – works during the afternoon on *Hamlet*. In the late afternoon and evening, there are lectures, performances and demonstrations by the Asian masters or actors/directors who have been invited, meetings with the researchers of ISTA: Fabrizio Cruciani, Jean-Marie Pradier, Franco Ruffini, Ferdinando Taviani, Ugo Volli, Moriaki Watanabe. Grotowski will be with us for two weeks. He will not hold lectures or participate in the research, but will be available to speak with whoever of us wants to consult him. 25 and 26 October there will be an international symposium in which Barba intends to clarify his concept of Theatre Anthropology. We are 50 participants, actors and directors from 23 different countries. Barba finishes by underlining Nicola Savarese's significant role as ISTA chronicler. He will document our work with photos, interviews and sketches.

After the initial meeting, some of us who are directors complain to Barba that he has not set aside a time with us for dealing with the problems of directing. He recognises that we are right. He says: 'Tomorrow we will gather at 5am,' that is, today.

Barba comments on the implicit or explicit doubts which some of us expressed yesterday when we introduced ourselves as directors: 'I am a director by chance, I wanted to be an actor, but there was a need for a director and so I assumed this task. But I don't feel like a director.' 'I define myself as a director, but I don't know if I really am one.' 'I often have a clear idea of the performance, but I don't succeed in realising it.' 'I propose something, but the actors don't accept it: to them it seems ugly or wrong. Does a director have to know how to impose obedience?' 'I am a director, but I don't know what a director needs to know. An author, an actor or a stage designer knows what they ought to know. But a director?'

Eugenio Barba:

> What makes a director convincing in the eyes of his actors? That he knows how to speak? That he has an ideology or a clear aesthetical or political vision? That he is theoretically articulate? That he has read more books than the others? That he has a diploma from a theatre school?
>
> If his authority is based on this, he can create a group, but sooner or later the actors will certainly abandon him.

The director doesn't share the experience of the actors, one of the most difficult conditions that can be imagined. Liv Ullmann has described her collaboration with Ingmar Bergman in this way: when day after day you are asked to 'do this; look over there; move slower; lift your chin a little more; your hand . . . not the left, the other one,' and so on, time and time again, the director may be a genius, but in the end you feel like killing him.

The director is a leader. He has a unique power: he turns human beings into people who accept his least desires. But they accept only if they know that the director is able to give them something in return. This consensus doesn't last long. After a while the director no longer has the same attraction. Then he becomes suffocating, and the actors leave him.

Of course, there are actors who love their director and are ready to sacrifice themselves for this person who stimulates and represses them. But I don't believe that love, in theatre, is spontaneous. It grows little by little, as in arranged marriages. It blooms with the years, when the actors have proved day after day that even if their director demands the impossible while remaining sitting in a chair, he has already been up for two hours to prepare whatever can facilitate their work.

The power of the director is that of the example. I don't believe in a director chosen democratically by the group. Some of you said: 'I would like to be an actor, but my group needs a director. So I sacrificed myself.' But how can this be possible? If you feel the need to be an actor, you don't become a writer just because the group needs a play. What is the particular trait of a director? A personal need which makes him choose a role of power: the ability to make decisions, to implement them and take responsibility for them. This entails commitment and effort.

I know I have great power. Everything I do leaves traces: how I speak, with whom I speak, if I keep silent, if I smile or am serious. With a word or a grimace, I can depress a person for a whole month. If I allow my personal problems to take over, these will spread like an epidemic.

Power, or authoritativeness, is necessary for the director to incite, not subdue. To create mutual stimuli. I must be fascinated by an actor, admire his dedication, tenacity or naivety. Not for his physical beauty or talent, but for his will to work, to make sacrifices, for his desire to change and, by so doing, change me. This is the mutual stimulus. If there is not the need to practise this sort of power – to dominate our inertia and conditioned reflexes and to surpass the condition in which we normally live – if there is not this quasi-animal instinct, an inner lash which forces us to surpass what we know in order to live – however briefly – beyond the daily reality . . . if we don't feel this need to climb to the summit of the mountain together with all our actors, then we are lukewarm directors. In this case it is fair that our actors abandon us.

The world of theatre is full of lukewarm directors. But you lead small theatre groups. You do not have the defences of the directors of a 'normal' theatre: economic hierarchy, cultural prestige and contractual guarantees. Your only guarantee is your effectiveness, and your effectiveness depends on your actors. Your capital is their motivation, their will to give, to go in depth, to endure adverse material conditions and to continue even when they are exhausted.

It is not the art of speaking that a director must master, but that of rejecting the obvious and the clichés. It is not only the information provided through words which is important, but even more so is their temperature, their inner energy and faith in what the director is pursuing within himself.

A director is obliged to learn the technique of moulding his own energy: how to recount, how to create a wide or a concentrated space around himself, how to awake a sense of complicity and the enthusiasm for adventure. It is not our ideas which touch the actors but the manner in which we present them and live them out at a personal level. The way to generate trust is a technique and a discipline which the director must develop as second nature.

Friday, 3 October, 6am

Eugenio Barba asks us for our impressions about our first day of work. First he refers again to our way of speaking and expressing ourselves as directors:

Yesterday I stressed the importance for the director of being able to shape his energy just as an actor does in front of the spectators. So I expect you know how to express yourself by giving essential information, summarising the problems in concise sentences without vague or superfluous words. When we meet at 6 in the morning, your very first words must show me the degree of your readiness, just like the actors do with the first exercise of their training. I want to hear precise sentences, said with the necessary motivation to hit the target, with no hesitation, without humming and hawing between one word and another, showing your lack of resolution.

Now let's talk about your impressions of the first day. The organisation of the working day is decisive for the results. If people are motivated, in the course of a few days they will assimilate the most rigorous rules, and the external discipline becomes self-discipline.

Problems of discipline will always exist if personal motivation is lacking.

I know that our schedule is heavy. I could achieve a pleasant and relaxed atmosphere by changing it. But I don't look for joy in the work. Bruno has spoken of the difficulties of his group in Argentina. It was not joy that made them gather at 8 o'clock in the evening after a long day. It was something else. An inexplicable inner motor. The programme of the daily activity corresponds to the building of a wall that can only be climbed over by those people with a stubbornness and determination which is twice what they consider to be normal for them. Self-discipline helps to strengthen this inner motor. Without this motor, we slow down and give up.

The Asian actors that are here with us are super-specialists. They are conditioned to working in only one way: to go to their guru or *sensei* and adapt to his or her demands, blindly following for years what they prescribe. Sanjukta Panigrahi, and all the other oriental teachers, find it difficult to understand why here they have to limit themselves to teaching only basic positions which are the most elementary notions of their knowledge.

As I have already explained to you, my task has consisted in establishing the conditions which would avoid their teaching you all the beautiful things they know. They will show you and repeat only what they, as children, learned during their first three days with their teacher. Their work with you doesn't aim to teach something which is Oriental, but to point out the path toward a quality of energy which is yours alone, and that you can mould individually where and how you wish.

We must become accustomed to rigour and monotony. The daily work is not always interesting. It is a grey mantle hanging over our heads. The pleasure of this work is that, at times, the grey is punctured and we see the blue of the sky, and make others see it. Then the sky disappears again behind a grey blanket.

Saturday, 4 October, 6am

Eugenio Barba:

Over the last few days I have asked you for your impressions of the work and the way the day is organised, what functions and above all what does not function in the environment we are trying to create during this month. A month is a long time. It is a great gift. Yet it is short. We have no time to lose.

We live a unique privilege, although the logistic setup is uncomfortable, we sleep in dormitories with no privacy and we have to do all the cleaning and cooking. The Asian masters are celebrities in their home countries and, one way or another, they enjoy the privileges that celebrity involves. Here you see them cleaning and cooking like the rest of us. I imagine they accepted this because we all work hard. They are used to that. They know that if you want to do the theatre which you have chosen, you cannot wait for help from the outside. You have to pay for it out of your own pocket. The actors of Odin Teatret also know this. Anyone who wants to work at the Odin must learn to do everything, without distinction between artistic, administrative and technical tasks. Of course, particular competences are needed. We have a bookkeeper and a secretary. They receive the highest salary in our theatre, according to Danish trade union rules. The actors' and my salary are equal and correspond to the minimum prescribed by law. But we feel we are privileged, because we have a small yet sufficient space, musical instruments, the opportunity to meet people more knowledgeable than ourselves and have the necessary time to follow our work rhythm.

Our meetings in the previous days have partially disappointed me. I too would enjoy chatting leisurely with you, inquiring about your experiences, the places where you live, the difficulties you meet and the solutions you find, what you plan to do and how you make your plans become real. But we don't get up an hour before the rest of the ISTA participants just to converse among friends. Conversations among friends are pleasant. But under present conditions, I would prefer an extra hour of sleep.

It is different if we work creatively: in other words, use our energies to the maximum. When I describe to you a director's work on the basis of my experience – and I strive to recount it so that you may deduce something profitable in your own practice – this for me is work: a particular way of engaging my energies.

I am asking you to work, to help me organise and fill with meaning the life of this precarious island that we are inventing for thirty days in this school building in Bonn. When I ask you for your impressions, you take me literally and speak to me in an impressionistic way. You are kind and respectful, but you don't come with serious criticism. If you are dissatisfied, you keep your discontent to yourself. I have a feeling that you consider criticism misplaced.

Therefore, every morning before dealing with matters which are more interesting or necessary for you as directors, we will examine the general situation of ISTA. One of our tasks is to protect this environment that we have succeeded in creating. We must make it grow towards a goal or an ideal, organising its space and time, inventing its working language, forging norms which should become the professional superego of each of us, and surprising everyone, especially ourselves. You have to safeguard your results and at the same time be ready for radical changes. You have to watch out for the details that seem meaningless but that, left to themselves, risk becoming avalanches. A leader is always in *sats*, attentive to what happens around him, ready to react instantaneously, knowing how to detect the crises that crouch in the silence or in the euphoria, and face them when it is still possible to do so. If you wait for them to grow, you will succumb to them.

Sunday, 5 October, 6am

We list the things which, according to us, don't work: tight schedules, exhausting days, lack of time to discuss and exchange opinions. We experience our days like a race, with no time for reflection.

Eugenio Barba comments:

Do some of you feel like leaving ISTA because of all these drawbacks? They are the same things which made four people decide to leave yesterday. They explained that the whole activity here follows the clock; that the meaning of the work is all in my head, but is obscure for the participants. They were the same arguments I have heard from you, almost word for word. But the consequences that you and they draw are different. One of the necessary faculties for a director is the skill to decipher what is concealed behind the words that are addressed to him.

Yesterday I discussed for three hours with those people who were leaving ISTA. They repeated some of the points which enrage me: for example, that you are failures, incapable of understanding the 'perfume' of the oriental masters and passively accepting the day whereas they did not, but refused it because it was organised like a factory schedule.

I answered them: the people you criticise don't think differently from you. If they accept, it means that they glimpse the possibility to extract some profit from the situation. I don't believe people are masochists or want to be slaves. Why do they remain?

They replied: because they believe you will perform a miracle, and turn them into creative actors and directors.

They were right and it made me think. For many years I felt I was not creative and had no artistic identity. I was blindly following Grotowski, even at a distance. Not his way of speaking or working with the actors, but the way he protected them in order to protect the creative process.

This is the key: without trust in another, we cannot awaken our capacities. Only by committing ourselves to another can we surpass what we believe are our limits. If we work for an idea or an ideology, our engagement doesn't last long. Routine will soon reveal the pointlessness of our efforts.

The danger doesn't consist in the fact that the director is blind, but that he blinds. This is the ambiguous power of the leader: the actors trust him and follow him. A false step, for the director, can be a fertile experience. For his actors it can end in disaster.

One of you asked whether it wouldn't be better to invent exercises which are not so exhausting as those we do at 7.30 in the morning and with the oriental masters.

But work is the spring board enabling us to reach another quality of energy. When it seems that we cannot take any more, we suddenly discover that it is possible to go on and we meet unsuspected reserves of resistance and vigour. In sport, athletes call it the 'second breath'. The only absolute limit is a biological one: death. We learn a lot by persevering in our work. I speak of 'creative work' aiming at the summit, as opposed to what usually takes place in daily life.

Yes, the director imposes points of reference, rules and goals. However, he should be careful not to apply too rigid criteria. He must be vigilant and judge cautiously what is happening, using a particular form of justice, at times severe, at times indulgent. Above all, he must be aware whether he is still able to stimulate or if this capacity has been eroded.

Tuesday, 7 October, 6am

We start by a thorough examination of the problems. We retouch the timetable. We discuss how to use our day off, Monday. Anybody who wishes can make their own activities. On Sunday evening, some of us held a party. We improvised music and danced until 3am, knowing that the next day we could get up late. 'The amusing thing – says one of us – is that we all complain about the lack of sleep. But on Sunday night nobody felt like going to sleep.' 'Nevertheless, some did go to bed,' replies Barba. 'If you have a party, try to respect the others' rest. Luckily we have space enough not to disturb each other.'

Then Barba answers the question as to whether a group can work without a leader or a director:

> In the dynamics of a group which affirms not to have a leader, in fact there is always one, although not explicit. According to circumstances, there is always a person who influences the behaviour or the opinions of the others. You want to make me believe that all are equal in a theatre group, with the same abilities, competences and stamina. You don't want one single person to take the responsibility

for painful decisions or errors committed because of superficiality. When we are all responsible, in practice nobody is responsible.

If a group disintegrates, the responsibility falls on the director. He is the cement holding together different individualities. The tendency to dissolution is inherent in a group. In theatre, when we talk about 'resistance', we mean withstanding the tendency towards entropy and disintegration. It is the leader's task, the obligation of the man or woman who takes decisions that embitter or comfort, to apply a strategy against the group's irrevocable decay and consequent breakup.

Every time that my group has a problem, I increase the workload. Thus the problem accelerates and demands a solution. For example, if an actor is in doubt whether to stay or leave and I augment my demands, he makes up his mind quickly. I eliminate the period of uncertainty and opposition, when the one in conflict with himself or with me discharges his tensions on the group.

I ask Barba whether he rehearses with his actors 'around a table'. If yes, in which way? And if he doesn't, why? When as a young actor I played in the professional theatre, I found this type of rehearsal very interesting. Why don't we speak about it in our morning meetings?

Eugenio Barba:

I don't rehearse 'around a table', in the sense of reading the text together with the actors and laying out my interpretation. Usually, at the first rehearsal for a new performance, I expound its theme as I feel it. It is a sort of oral improvisation through which I try to inflame the actors with images, associations, historical facts and the contradictions which the theme of departure inspires in me. For example, in the case of *Brecht's Ashes*, I recalled the life of Bertolt Brecht, his plays and poems, his exile, the rise of Nazism, his friendship with Walter Benjamin – the friend who committed suicide – the years in America, his return to Berlin, a free city in ruins which is immediately suffocated under the yoke of a Stalinist dictatorship. It occurs that I tell the actors how I imagine certain scenes. But I seldom succeed in creating them as I had imagined them.

My oral improvisation is the harbour from which to set sail. It is not a project for a performance. My actors know this. I could say that our table is as big as the floor of our performing space. Each of us, however, sits at the table in his own house: he reads, chooses texts, imbues himself with photos, images and music which are related to the theme. The actors do a preliminary work that corresponds, perhaps, to the rehearsals of a company together around a table. I could say that at Odin Teatret the preparation 'around the table' exists and has a reserved space, but is developed independently by the director and every actor.

The reason why I cannot show you my work 'around a table' is that it cannot be done on command, for didactic purposes, as an example or an exercise. The text, a situation or a character from which I start a performance is a vortex which overwhelms me. These imply an exclusive way to question them and be questioned by them, to extract their heart, their nervous system, their enigma, the coded message addressed only to me, that which leaves me indifferent, which I mock but makes me uneasy, the secret motives for which I have chosen them. I don't select a text for its literary value. In such a case I would read it and be satisfied. If I want to work theatrically with a text, it must propose, alluringly, something that I don't grasp and that challenges or irritates me, motivating me for the fatigue of a long and tortuous peregrination without a pre-arranged route.

In rehearsals, during the work on the text or the theme of the performance, I put to the test my ideas and beliefs, filter them through a sceptical sieve and put them on the fire to boil in order to see what remains after the evaporation. But all this mental process will not be transferred to the performance. It is a first spilling over of ideas and intentions that the rehearsals and the actors will upset. I feel it like a gigantic Hercules, one of the world's largest transport planes, which advances slowly, seemingly for ever, on the runway. I have the suspicion, almost the certainty, that it won't succeed to detach itself from the ground. One of the reasons why doing theatre still possesses such a deep attraction for me is the dizziness at the moment when the performance *takes off*, I feel it swaying, suspended in the void, borne along by its strength, and interrogating me in a language which is neither mine nor that of my actors. A language which I must strive to decipher every time.

Wednesday, 8 October, 6am

Most afternoons are devoted to *Hamlet*: we are divided into groups, each of which has chosen a director, and we prepare a scene or one of the themes of Shakespeare's play. At the end of ISTA we will present the result. Barba watches the groups but never intervenes.

Thursday, 9 October, 6am

Many questions about improvisation. Some speak of the 'Barba method'. There are two main points: 1) it is not easy to understand this method, and still less easy to apply it; 2) it deals with an extremely personal procedure, inherent to Barba and his theatre. Does it possess, however, aspects that could be extended to others and make them understand a little of the theatrical art in general?

Eugenio Barba:

> I speak to you from my own experience with words and expressions which are mine. But the substance of what I say is not at all a 'Barba method'. Any technique, when applied, assumes personal, even autobiographic, features. But no technique is exclusively a biographical peculiarity. We often speak about the 'secret of the craft', a craft with its problems, pragmatic solutions and also enigmas. But these secrets have an objective character. The different ways of individually facing and resolving them can be transmitted. The subjective experience includes implicitly objective technical features which I call principles. Someone who is autodidactic – as you are and I have been – must be able to detect the various technical aspects which the secrets assume. The secrets are the same although they hide behind words or theories which are different. This prevents us from starting from scratch, as if nothing could be handed down from one generation to another.
>
> When we follow the so-called methods – norms and suggestions – of those we call masters, we feel we are on the right road. We believe that it is enough to apply them faithfully and they will take us to our destination. Unfortunately, this is not true. We always have to find a way to make them work for us. Reinvent them, that is, extract the objective technical nucleus that allows us to use them in our own way, to redraw them according to our historical situation and biography, our professional and emotional appetites.
>
> I never give an actor a theme for improvisation which has a direct connection with the text or the story we are rehearsing. I know from experience that in most cases this provokes illustrative actions. If I don't disorientate the actor, it is difficult for him to disorientate me, and thereby surprise me.
>
> Generic themes of improvisation, like the one you gave to an actress yesterday (you run as if being pursued), don't help an actor to react with precision and nuances. For me, a valid theme of improvisation must (A) be concise as a telegram; (B) contain a contradiction, a polarity; (C) include several indications; (D) present obscure and ambiguous points; (E) make use of active and transitive verbs that suppose specific actions: to push (what? how?), to eat (what? how?), to nibble (what? how?); (F) avoid the verbs 'to be', 'to have', 'to think', 'to remember' and 'to feel'.
>
> The theme of the improvisation can be a sentence which is unclear, yet suggestive like a line of a poem. Or a coded message, whose code both I and the actor are searching for. I would never give

> the task 'you run as if being pursued'. I would rather formulate in this way: 'you walk on a road covered by snow. It is on a slope. Beyond a bend, a shadow advances towards you. You have difficulty in identifying it: it is a wolf with blood on its mouth. You run in search of the wind.'
>
> The actor receives a range of distinct suggestions to which she can react through actions in her own way.
>
> While the actor improvises, the director too must improvise. He must master a technique of his own. For me, an improvisation has no meaning if I don't recognise something that I have experienced or I can imagine experiencing. It has nothing to do with aesthetics, political ideas, the interpretation of the text, the beauty of the scene, the suggestive forms that I may have dreamt of. I must improvise in the first person reacting to the actor's actions, by entering into a zone of obsessions and truth, memories and desires which belong to my experience and fantasy. I am not interested in the psychology or the biographic facts explicitly expressed by the actor.
>
> There are actors who consider their improvisation as something intimate and sacred. They suffer when extraneous hands distort it into a meaning different from the original one. They don't accept that the actions which for them have a particular sense, assume a different, even opposite, meaning in the director's montage. They live this intervention as a violence and cynicism with regard to their truth and inner life. These actors refuse the most fatiguing and necessary condition in the creative work: complementarity. The actor must be nourished by his own experience, images or visions, manias and ideals, and be faithful to them. At the same time he has to fulfil the artistic demands from the outside. One of the tasks of the director consists in protecting the ubiquity of the actor, allowing him to live in his own world and at the same time to share the world of his companions, his spectators and the performance. If the actor doesn't want the director to change the sense of his improvisation, he sacrifices ubiquity and threatens that of the director.

We keep on asking questions, and there is a particular one which recurs, formulated in various ways: Why don't the actors at Odin Teatret improvise together, only individually? Doesn't this imply a danger of introversion and egocentrism?

Eugenio Barba:

> It's true, I always begin to work with one actor at a time. Or rather, I usually concentrate only on a part of him: a foot, a hand, the hips, the eyes. Whenever I have thrown myself into collective improvisations, or in couples, the results were uninteresting and I

was unable to develop them. It has happened that I have made collective improvisations to sketch a scene, to discover the possible ramifications of the actors in the space or to find combinations for couples or groupings. But in order to achieve results that stimulate me, I must concentrate only on one actor. Why?

While improvising, the actor composes a poem with words made of flesh. These words-flesh spring from his mental, psychic and sexual life and only preserve a strong radiation for him if they safeguard these deep roots. Pay attention: deep doesn't mean sacred, ineffable, unconscious. Only that they go down enough into the ground.

When two or more actors improvise, they live in real time, and the natural tendency is to adapt themselves to what their companions are doing, turned towards the outside in order to understand what is happening and behave accordingly. Often this extemporaneous process assumes the traits of false aggressiveness or superficial eroticism. In spite of himself, the actor 'plays'.

The individual improvisation is of a totally different nature. It is an oneiric vision taking place in a very personal temporal frame which is directed by the actor himself. The latter is free to linger for a long time on a detail, advance at will in the future or move back into the past, repeat the same situation several times, confront autobiographic or imaginary people and real events, bring intimate memories to life, do what he craves or what he doesn't dare to do in real life. An individual improvisation is a childish and extreme daydream which, starting out from a situation of illustration, can sink into a succession of instinctive reactions, without worrying about contradictions. It is an inner journey expressed in a language of reactions which, as a director, I am often unable to decipher at a narrative level. But their organic radiation impregnates their materials, which I interweave with the improvisations of other actors.

Friday, 10 October, 6am

This morning Eugenio Barba, contrary to his habit, doesn't ask us questions or to sum up the situation. He smiles placidly and speaks first:

The situation is becoming interesting. We are besieged by difficulties. Above all fatigue. It is not the sort of tiredness which helps to mobilise our energies, but sheer exhaustion.

You work hard from early in the morning to late at night. Yet many of you are discontent. You must revolt and, by so doing, reverse the situation, yet safeguarding the integrity of the work. A theatre group can't exist if its members don't have a personal reason to carry on. There is always a moment when one wonders whether it is worth continuing. One says to oneself: 'I have lost faith.' Let's consider this expression seriously. What is faith, in our practice? It is certainly not the adhesion to shared ideas, aesthetical theories, an orthodoxy or a school. It is simply what pushes you to get up punctually one hour before the other participants, after only four or five hours of sleep, every day except Monday. We lack oxygen here. It is as if the atmosphere of our habitat has altered.

How can we work together, with a common goal, protecting the different individualities and their various paths and needs? I know that nobody can work 12 hours a day without being obscurely convinced of why he is doing it. I also know that five or six years are needed in order to 'shape' actors and directors who are both experienced and independent. Here at ISTA, all alone, I have had to set up the conditions for your personal Copernican revolution during only one month, and to proceed without creating dependence. I knew from the very beginning that I would have to deal with everything: give courses, devote myself to the Asian masters and take care of each of the participants, encourage the single orbits and maintain the unity of the route, be an administrator and manager, keep up relationships with the German ISTA organisers, program the Asian performances and watch them, prepare my food and check that cleaning was perfect. In ISTA, I find again the same mesh of contradictory and often uninspiring tasks which absorb the leader of a group. Saskja is right: frustration is an experience which belongs to the work, and we must learn to take it into account. However, at least once a week, it would be nice to experience something vivifying, a mouthful of fresh air.

I clearly see the two horns of the dilemma and can describe them to you. But my explanation is not enough to prevent them from poisoning one another. One of the two horns says: you must accept me totally. There is a book, The New Testament, in which this experience is summed up in the expression: in order to acquire a new life, you have to relinquish the old one. I believe deeply in this experience which is the foundation for the relationship between master and disciple, where the latter completely accepts his or her guidance. This has been my experience *during several years*. Without passing through it, I would not have guessed my path. I would not have 'shaped' myself, discovered the form that is mine alone. The other horn of the problem affirms: you have little time. Since the days are limited and filled with activity, the risk is that those who have accepted you don't develop autonomously and remain, professionally, obedient students.

Maybe this contradiction could be avoided by organising a real school, with a varied learning programme. But I believe this would

> be a worse solution than the evil from which we try to escape. At ISTA there is nothing to learn. We are here for *learning to learn*, each in his own way, in an autonomy which often involves solitude.
>
> I don't want people practising my supposed method. I want to give life to an unrepeatable theatre, an environment in which some of my longings and aspirations can come true together with those of a few other people. Our individual needs are particular and incommunicable, and we want to fulfil them through a common activity: an unbeliever's collective prayer and a solitary unarmed rebellion. Just like when we train together in the morning and each of us performs a different exercise with his motivation, his rhythm, moving wherever he wants in the space, together with others, but without conforming to them.

At this point, in my notebook there is a hole of 10 days, during which from 6 to 7.30am I have concentrated all alone on rearranging my ideas for the scene on *Hamlet*: I make a series of drawings – a strip – of the scene I intend to do. On Tuesday evening, 21 October, I ask Barba if I can come back to the directors' meeting next morning. I tell him that my absence was not a whim and that I have kept on working. He answers that the whole group of directors will decide. As far as he is concerned, he is against it. If one springs over part of the process, on one's return one risks being like a fish out of water. This, as well as being disagreeable for the person involved, can also have a negative effect on the group dynamics. I object that others have also been absent for one or two days. He replies that there is a big difference between 10 days and one or two days of absence. He asks me if I have kept myself informed about what they have been doing in the morning. I answer negatively. I have the absurd impression that he likes my answer.

Wednesday, 22 October, 6am

As he had told me, Eugenio Barba refers my wish to the other directors. He mentions that three or four other people have also withdrawn and that I am the only one who has expressed the wish to come back. He explains why he is against it. But the majority will decide. The others welcome me back unanimously. Eugenio Barba exhibits one of his smiles in which he shows all his teeth:

> We all enjoy feeling generous and kind. Unfortunately we can't always afford it. Remember the poem by Brecht about the Chinese demon mask, which he always took with him during his exile, and whose swollen vein on the forehead revealed how tiring and strenuous it was to be evil. Today we can indulge in being good.
>
> This morning, C.Z. has given me a letter and asked me to report

its content to you. She writes that she will no longer come to our meetings because she is unable to keep a distance between what we say here and her work, in which 'I am alone and must be left alone.'

Would you say that I manipulate you? Would my actors say the same? Certainly. Would a boxer say the same when speaking of his trainer? Or a ballet dancer of her teacher? Or a pianist who has begged to study with a particular artist? Could Sanjukta say it of her guru? Today, she is a queen of dance, in India and elsewhere, but in front of her teacher Kelucharan Mahapatra she still behaves like an obliging child. She is certainly manipulated. The ballet dancer, the boxer, the pianist – they are all manipulated. At times they make huge sacrifices in order to be manipulated, to submit to someone who not only teaches them excellence, but demands discipline and an intransigent attitude toward the least facets of the craft. They pay this person in order to be demanding and use authority, without any argument.

We can use the word 'manipulation', but we should understand that it hides opposite options, and they should not be confused one with the other.

An actor accepts to be manipulated for personal reasons, if he has a feeling of breaking the limits of his ignorance, if he knows that there are no privileged colleagues in the group and if he is convinced that the director doesn't decide on the basis of selfish interests. People allow themselves to be manipulated if they aspire to give their maximum and have reciprocally chosen each other. In this case, manipulation is an agreement, an acknowledgment of an affinity aiming at independence.

In the school system things are different. Students don't usually choose their teachers, nor do the teachers select their students. Under these conditions, manipulation assumes another meaning, usually a negative one. This negativity makes us suspicious. It generates automatic reflexes and we don't distinguish between different types of manipulation. This superficiality in our way of thinking produces unnecessary problems in our learning. Especially in an autodidactic process, it is crucial to understand that the same term may comprise diametrically opposed meanings, processes and situations.

Thursday, 23 October, 6am

We start the meeting by commenting on the lecture by Jean-Marie Pradier yesterday afternoon. Eugenio Barba stresses the connection between *form and information* that Pradier has related to scientific thought. Then Barba speaks of the images which condense the contradictions he tries to vivisect in his performances and which withstand his attempts. He depicts the human being as *mysterium tremendum et fascinans*. He tells us a love story. Franek was an adolescent robber and murderer in the perfectly organised hell of Auschwitz. In this extermination camp, he became a kapo, famous for his pitilessness. He was nicknamed *krwawy*, the bloodthirsty one. He always carried a stick, maintaining order and inflicting punishments with it. He had a particular way to jump on his victim, make him fall to the ground by striking his legs and then sinking the stick into his mouth and perforating his throat. He was a human beast, but he fell hopelessly in love with a Jewish girl. While continuing his normal activity, the kapo lived to serve his love. He secretly protected her. He made sure that she was not given heavy jobs and that she had enough food. He stole perfume for her, at risk to his own life. He brought her sweets taken from the SS canteen. He was happy as is any person in love, blindly. Meanwhile he continued to beat up and kill any prisoner who contravened the least of the camp's endless rules. One cold morning Franek saw his love in line with other women in front of the 'shower' building. He knew only too well how people died in the gas chamber. He was often among those prisoners who had to clear and clean it. The dead bodies showed the signs of a desperate struggle to breathe. The most fortunate were those who died immediately after the first few breaths. The bloodthirsty Franek drew near the line of the naked women and accompanied his Jewish girl as far as the door of the crematory. Then he whispered to her the final proof of his love: 'when you enter, breathe quickly, breathe deeply.'

Barba speaks for a long time, differently from when he talks as leader and director. He pursues his images and thoughts. Perhaps this is one of his oral improvisations, similar to those that precede his work on a performance. He relates some indelible memories from his childhood, his hitchhiking travels, a few theatre experiences, episodes from novels and biographies. He describes life in socialist Poland, where he has studied for four years, and life on the Norwegian merchant ships on which he was a sailor for a couple of years. He dwells on his condition as an emigrant, an individual who has lost his language, and how it has coloured his way of living in the world and in the theatre. He doesn't speak of technique, dramaturgy or montage. He speaks of the performance as an experience that concerns him directly, and not the spectators in general.

The meeting draws out and we don't go to train in the gym.

Friday, 24 October, 6am

Tomorrow and the day after tomorrow our meetings will not take place. During these two days a Symposium on Theatre Anthropology will be held. The guests come from different countries: theatre critics and scholars like Xavier Fábregas, who lives in Barcelona. Others are scientists like Henri Laborit, the renowned French biologist who has just finished shooting a film with Alain Resnais, *Mon Oncle d'Amérique*.

Eugenio Barba presents the content of the symposium: he will introduce the results of his research, of which ISTA is a fruit. He wants to give special emphasis to the pre-expressive level in the actor's work by leading some demonstrations with the Asian masters and Toni Cots. There will be performances by the Asian artists and their orchestras and a work demonstration by Iben Nagel Rasmussen from Odin Teatret. Henri Laborit will speak of his research. Barba explains why meeting scientists, especially biologists, has been so important for him. He has not applied their research to the theatre in general, but has related the paradigm of the levels of organisation in a living organism to the organic structure of the performance. This is the reason why both theatre scholars and neuropsychologists like the Danish Peter Elsass and the Yugoslav Ranka Bijeljac Babic are part of ISTA's scientific team.

It is important in our work to know how to distinguish different levels of organisation, each of which has its own logic and can be treated independently from the others. The pre-expressive level of organisation determines the effectiveness of the actor's presence. It is a necessary condition, but it doesn't suffice. It has a meaning only if it succeeds in integrating coherently in the performance's entire organism. Therefore, Barba concludes, I have asked you to prepare a scene on *Hamlet*.

Tuesday, 28 October, 6am

Today's meeting has been short. It is the day when we will show the results of the *Hamlet* groups. Eugenio Barba introduces Roberto Bacci, who has founded a theatre group in Pontedera, a small town in Tuscany, Italy. He will be the organiser of the next ISTA session in Volterra, an ancient Etruscan town. The 1981 ISTA will last two months, the double of this one.

Wednesday, 29 October, 6am

We had agreed to celebrate Eugenio Barba with a surprise (we had found out that today is his birthday). But he beats us to it: this morning we don't have a spare minute. He wants to comment on yesterday's small performances one by one.

Eugenio Barba:

> There is something in your *Hamlet* that has touched me: it is the way you lay bare your solitude and your longings. But as theatre, they lack substance, structure and formal variations. You are still weak. You must confront this weakness as a pressing problem: how to plan solutions so that the spectators are not disturbed by our technical frailty? Especially those who look at us with indifference or distrust.
>
> Think of Napoleon. From the point of view of strategy, two Napoleons exist. The first one is a young general: remember his

> bursting campaign of Italy, the originality with which he upset the precepts of war, inflicting defeat after defeat on the Austrians. He dictated the rules of the game, contrived pretences, ambushes, agile offensives and mock attacks. He resolutely dictated his orders, and his colonels and soldiers performed them with an enthusiasm that overwhelmed the enemy. There are *mises-en-scène* whose strategy conceals the decisions of the director, and the spectators experience the performance as the ardour of the actors.
>
> The Napoleon emperor, advanced in years, behaved in quite another way. He deployed his Grande Armée in front of the adversary armies and a *corps à corps* took place. His marshals didn't appreciate this brutal way to wage war, the often useless slaughter of thousands of soldiers.

Barba comments at length on each performance. He expounds on the few fragments and details where the directors have behaved like the young Napoleon. He indicates where and how the directors' ideas have been smeared on the actors like glue, with the consequence that these are stiff, move in strange ways and use exercises from the training. Too many improvisations have been left in a raw state, treated as holy cows, shipwrecked in a sea of accidental effects and superfluous movements. He points out the director's inability to oppose the actor's clichés. Interesting solutions have been exploited for too long and have lost their incisiveness. We have not succeeded in establishing connections between the improvisations and the story we are telling. From the point of view of dramaturgical interlacement, we are frail.

Eugenio Barba:

> This afternoon, when I will talk to the participants of the *Hamlet* performances which I have watched yesterday, I will apply another point of view. I will not stress the deficiencies, but the positive aspects. I will focus on what has struck me favourably: discipline, dedication and variety. It was impossible to notice a uniform style or a common tendency. I will also explain that I am not a reliable spectator because, in front of the groups' performances, I have a tendency to be impressed by the human qualities and personal needs which have motivated you, the disinherited, to become part of the micro-culture of a theatre group.
>
> But it is not to enjoy human qualities that people go to theatre.

Thursday, 30 October, 6am

It is the last day. We exchange greetings, addresses and promises.

4

EVOCATIVE DRAMATURGY AS A LEVEL OF ORGANISATION

My favorite time to write is in the late afternoon,
weekdays, particularly Wednesdays.
This is how I go about it:
I take a fresh pot of tea into my study and close the door.
Then I remove my clothes and leave them in a pile
as if I had melted to death and my legacy consisted of only
a white shirt, a pair of pants and a pot of cold tea.

Then I remove my flesh and hang it over a chair.
I slide it off my bones like a silk garment.
I do this so that what I write will be pure,
completely rinsed of the carnal,
uncontaminated by the preoccupation of the body.

Finally I remove each of my organs and arrange them
on a small table near the window.
I do not want to hear their ancient rhythms
when I am trying to tap out my own drumbeat.

Now I sit down at the desk, ready to begin.
I am entirely pure: nothing but a skeleton at a typewriter.

I should mention that sometimes I leave my penis on.
I find it difficult to ignore the temptation.
Then I am a skeleton with a penis and a typewriter.

In this condition I write extraordinary love poems,
Most of them exploiting the connection between sex and death.

Afterward, I reward myself by going for a drive at sunset.

Billy Collins: *Purity*

The Trans-Siberian

I had always dreamt of travelling on the Trans-Siberian Railway. In 1982 I succeeded. It was in second class since foreigners were forbidden access to the third class. The lines of demarcation in the Soviet Empire were still difficult to cross.

I remember the litany of the stations: Moscow, Iaroslavl, Danilov, Buy, Poloma, Sharya, Kotelnich, Kirov, Balesino, Perm, Shalya, Sverdlovsk (where the Urals begin and Europe ends, according to General De Gaulle's political geography), Kamishlov, Tjumen, Ishim, Nazivayeskaya, Omsk, Barabinsk, Novosibirsk, Taiga, Marinsk, Bogotol, Achinsk, Krasnojarsk, Uyar, Savjernaja, Kainsk-Jenissieiskj, Ilanskaya, Resheti, Gaishet, Inzhneudinsk, Tulun, Zima, Cheremkovo, Angarsk, Irkutsk, Sliudyanka, Misovaya, Selenga, Ulán Udé (capital of Soviet Mongolia), Pietrovski Zavod, Kilok, Mogsoi, Iablonovaya, Lesnoi, Chita, Darasun, Karimskaya, Prinskovaya, Chernishevsk Zavod, Silovo, Ksenevskaya, Mogocha, Amasar, Erofiei Pavlovich, Urusha, Taktamigda, Skorovodino, Bolshoi Never, Taldan, Madgagachi, Tigda, Ushumun, Shimanovskaya, Bielogorsk, Zavitaya, Bureya, Arkara, Kundur, Obluche, Isviestkovaya, Bira, Birobidzhan (capital of the territory chosen by Stalin as a state for the Jews and to which many of them were deported), In and Khabarovsk, capital of Soviet Central Asia. Here we foreigners were made to descend and get on a special train to Nagodkha, from where I proceeded by sea to Japan. The Trans-Siberian continued as far as Vladivostok, almost a day's journey away, a military port which was closed to all but Soviet citizens.

I have only to repeat this list of names for images and episodes to spring to mind.

The guard at the Soviet frontier: a young woman with an impenetrable expression and long hair hidden beneath a military cap. Out of my bag she pulled the pears, picked from the tree in my garden at home and carefully wrapped in paper by my wife, Judy, so that they would keep for a long time and accompany me on my journey. She took a knife from its sheath and cut them in half one by one, searching for hidden forbidden substances. Then she applied herself to the books she found in my baggage. She made out the title of one of them: The Brothers Karamazov *by Dostoevsky. She stopped rummaging and her expression melted, as though I were a friend with whom she did not have the time to converse.*

The forests of birches were like golden icons at sunset.

The gentle grandmother from Achinsk who had crossed the whole of Russia to visit her grandchildren in Odessa, and the tubercular balalaika player from the Irkutsk Symphony Orchestra who was returning from a state sanatorium in the Crimea.

Fjodor Pavlovich, a fastidious and bony old man who did nothing but eat. He made fun of me every time they came round with free tea because I didn't buy the lumps of sugar. He blankly refused my explanation that I never used it. In the corridor he blocked my way and pushed me against the window. From his wallet he pulled out a faded, greasy calendar, with pictures of girls in bathing costumes. He wanted to share with me the pleasure of looking at them. As the days went by he became a more and more odious presence. Finally we arrived at the station where he was to get off. We were all asleep in our bunks. As he was about to leave, he shook me and pressed my hand as if to scratch it. The train left. I felt something between my fingers: a few rubles so that I too could pay for sugar for my tea.

That little temporary community in a Trans-Siberian Railway carriage became a fragment of oral underground history. My travelling companions exchanged information linked to the geography of the land we were crossing and denied to them by the political powers that be. One taciturn passenger told that here, in Ussurskaja, there were big goldmines where he had worked for 15 years as a deportee. The nurse from Vladivostok pointed out the factory in which a strike had broken out, only to be quelled within a few days. The train driver from Bielogorsk asked repeatedly to see my passport. He scrutinised it, weighed it in his hand, refused to believe that it belonged to me personally and that I could use it at will. Nor did he believe me when I told him that Denmark had a queen as its head of state. Nowadays queens only existed in fairy tales.

A pair of shy young newlyweds on their honeymoon boarded the train. The groom's mother accompanied them. Him, her and his mother – a typical farce situation. The bride felt hot. Standing, barely touching each other and swaying to the rhythm of the train, the husband slowly removed her jumper. An erotic caress that transcended any sense of decency.

Not all of these images are confined to the train which crosses the Siberian steppe. Some of them reappeared in Mythos, *a performance which I prepared 15 years later. A mountain of severed hands – carved in wood and looking like bones or stones – invaded the performing space like pebbles on a beach or the flotsam of history.*

These severed hands stemmed from the Trans-Siberian.

Mikail Chusid was an artist in a Russian puppet theatre. We had met at a friend's house in Moscow. He wanted to continue our conversation, but the next morning I had to leave on the Trans-Siberian. There was no time.

The train had barely left when Mikail appeared in my carriage. He accompanied me for three days as far as Sverdlovsk. It was the easiest way, he said, to take the 'liberty' of talking together. Mikail had with him a pair of small wooden hands for a new puppet he was carving. He gave them to me. We said our goodbyes with the intention of meeting again.

With the fall of the Soviet Union, Mikail Chusid and his family emigrated to the United States. There, at a theatre congress, we met fleetingly. Once more we promised to correspond, to meet again to talk about the things that were closest to our hearts, apart from theatre. We heard nothing more of each other.

But his small hands continued to live and speak in Odin Teatret's performances. They were symbols of the abuse of power in The Gospel according to Oxyrhincus, *the childlike prosthesis which concealed the claws of tyranny. They proliferated in* Mythos *as severed hands which materialised the horror from which the spirit of the time averted its gaze, worn out by the will to change the world.*

Memories of the Trans-Siberian do not end here. The freckled girl in our carriage boarded the train at Darasun and was going to Birobidzhan. She was patient because she knew that three days must go by before she would meet her fiancé. She talked of this discreetly, with a shy smile and gleaming eyes. There were still about a hundred kilometres to go before our arrival and she calmly began to pack her suitcase with the things she had used during the journey. The landscape the train passed through was nothing but snow. 'When we reach Birobidzhan it will already be pitch dark – she said – but they are coming to fetch me.' Behind this impersonal form of speech was her beloved. For a long time she stood, waiting, near the carriage door. When the train stopped, I couldn't help following her with my gaze. There he was in the frosty air, white with mist. He was enveloped in a large fur coat with a fur hat – a huge motionless bear. She rushed into his arms.

Through the white veil of icy vapour shrouding the station, I watched the bear's tenderness and the patient girl's embrace explode with passion. In the exaltation of the moment, her hand knocked his hat to the ground and out of the voluminous fur coat emerged a smooth bald head. Its nudity contradicted the cold and insulted the surrounding world with the obscenity of a huge phallus exposed to the night.

There are dark forces which make us blind, and dark forces which make us see. They dance like snakes in the torrid zone of memory which is evocative dramaturgy.

The torrid zone of memory

We also travel inside our memories. Some of them become vast vertical landscapes. At times we sink into them. First we cross the cold zone of distance. Once we have succeeded in gathering together some of the circumstances surrounding a piece of information we say: 'Now I remember.' But what we remember is not yet a part of us. It begins to belong to us only when we enter the 'humid' zone of the emotions, or rather of our present reaction towards past emotions.

The journey through the vast country of memory confronts us with the confusion between the feelings of the present and those of the past. We can seldom differentiate between the emotions which belong to the past as we remember it, and those which belong to the actual moment of remembering. This second zone of memory's boundless vertical landscape is such a conglomeration and intricate web of moods and humours that I refer to it as 'humid' rather than using the word 'viscous'.

When we manage to disentangle ourselves, we enter the fertile zone in which actions, passions and past circumstances release their pollen towards the present day. Memory no longer belongs to what we were; it is no longer sentiment, but flesh and blood. It is an integral part of what we are and will be.

From there – in rare cases – we cross into the 'torrid' zone where extremes meet in an embrace. Here the sun is both a divinity and an inferno in the heavens, appearances burn up and apparitions emerge. We are dazzled, seduced and sometimes burnt.

In my theatrical work, the torrid zone was the zone of the *wound*.

The *wounds* are stories which do not wish to be told. Whenever we try to tell them, they turn their backs on us and distance themselves. We glimpse their bent backs, like greyish or radiant humps: our rucksacks. Our wounds refuse to be danced or mimed. Perhaps because they know their destiny is elsewhere, to be poured into another story, the smokescreen which allows us to evoke and conceal them at one and the same time.

Each of my performances has opened my eyes. Sometimes with regard to technical problems. Usually, seeing them again and again has made me aware of other zones of myself. There were traces of autobiography in them, but not of confession. I have never spoken consciously about me. I once made a production whose title was the name of the Norwegian ship on which I was a seaman. This was *Talabot*, but its main theme was the autobiography of Kirsten Hastrup, a Danish anthropologist who had agreed to write a series of episodes from her life.

When we travel, we are struck by novelty, but we never forget what we have left behind. The horizon of our knowledge widens but it is not a question of genuine discoveries. The true discovery happens when the invisible hump – the wounds from which the journey seems to liberate us – slowly resurfaces. Our eyes are opened at the very moment when our gaze is directed elsewhere.

I ask myself if this is an experience common to all who practise a craft we pompously call 'creative'. What did I create? A few dark corners and a few moments of silence. Small rooms in huge buildings and brief moments out of an hour. Darkness full of the expectation and threat of a sudden flash of light. The intimate resonance of silence.

The rest was craft. Without craft nothing can be achieved; there is no departure, no journey, no arrival. Craft means composing performances which are capable of renouncing the usual theatre audiences and inventing their own spectators. In other words, patiently constructing a specific physical, mental and emotional bond with the spectators and the texts without conforming to the well-assessed models which are valid in mainstream theatre.

My companions and I were not accustomed to asking ourselves many questions. *We treated the points of departure as definitive.* We knew very well that they would change and others would be added. We were used to showing care and attention as though everything was clear, even though we knew we were working in the dark. The material accumulated and became a collection of prospects, stories, texts, scores, songs and accessories that were dear to us. The time came when we realised we were navigating in the superfluous.

This was the moment to change course. What was the purpose of this great abundance? Only to be discarded, pared down. It formed the mass on which the axe and the chisel would work. Only then could I begin to sculpt time, space and the *necessary* relationships. There was much peeling away and cutting down to be done. Complexity, at times, was what remained.

Often, the scenic space became overburdened, filled with props, some humble, some precious. A professional love of objects urged us to dig them out from the theatre's storeroom, from old family trunks, to pick them up on our travels and put them to one side saying, 'I want to work with this in the next production.' 'Prop' is the wrong word. They are trusted friends, lovers, accomplices. They are not mute and passive, as may appear from the outside. When the moment for the axe and the chisel arrived, separation from them was hard.

The *humus* of our profession is made up of these loves and idiosyncrasies which may seem infantile to the uninitiated observer. But without them nothing can grow.

The performing space could become so overloaded with objects-partners as to become suffocating. The actors were like fish swimming in an aquarium that was too small. The eyes were satiated, but the heart and the mind received no nourishment. In such cases the axe must be particularly merciless. Was it me wielding the axe, or the axe manoeuvring me? At times it was disconcerting and painful because the director seemed to be moved by a sort of cynical enthusiasm for slaughter.

Something similar has happened with all my performances. In *Mythos*, we fell in love with too many of the poet's lines. We became aware of it when work on the production was finished. Thus many of Henrik Norbrandt's impressive images were sacrificed. For *Andersen's Dream*, the actors had prepared 24 hours of materials. I condensed them into 80 minutes.

What is the use of explaining this? It can't be taught. It can't be programmed. After years of experience I lived the *time of the axe* as a last resort, an angry reaction against the impasse into which the work process had driven me. Talking about it only serves to point out that this phase in the work is bound to arrive.

The important question, however, is another: why is it complexity which remains?

Among Thomas Hardy's last poems there is one entitled *Convergence of the Twain*. Literature is full of stories telling of the disastrous consequences of the encounter between a man and his double. Thomas Hardy's poem does not deal with this theme. For him the 'two' are different and distant, never meant to meet. The subject of his poem is, in fact, the tragedy of the *Titanic*. It consists of 11 tercets and begins as follows:

In a solitude of the sea
Deep from human vanity,
And the Pride of Life that planned her, stilly couches she.

He describes how the sea eats away at the luxurious wreck of the transatlantic liner, raising mute questions about the will which had built her to satisfy a desire for glory. Then the poet turns his gaze in quite another direction. He sees at work, amid the polar ice, what he calls *the Imminent Will that stirs and urges everything*. This Will makes an iceberg grow in all humility while, at the same time, the transatlantic liner is taking form amid the din of the shipyard. These two foreign bodies are then viewed in the light of the future – a destiny that no one could ever have imagined. No mortal eye could have foreseen how the two stories could merge so as to become *twin halves of one August event*. The last tercet reads:

Till the Spinner of the Years
Said 'Now!' And each one hears,
And consummation comes, and jars two hemispheres.

Thomas Hardy's poem about the unforeseeable collision between the iceberg and the gigantic liner, built to cross oceans like an unsinkable city, comes from a collection of poems published in 1914 which the poet named *Satires of Circumstance*. They demonstrate the quintessence of an important aspect of creative work. It is not pure coincidence that ignites unexpected meanings, unintended connections and clusters of images that surface from time to time and question us on things about which we do not speak. We have to increase the *probabilities*, especially the unsuspected ones, and work meticulously in order to materialise them.

Chance, especially if we denote it by such an exotic and learned name as *serendipity*, evokes the impression of luck. We talk of being smiled upon by fortune. But in Odin Teatret's practice fortuitousness was deliberate. A main aspect of our creativity consisted in *generating circumstances in which 'two', who do not appear to be destined to meet, collide*. It belonged to my know-how to contrive conditions which allowed my actors to interact in such a way that they made a mockery of my way of thinking and feeling.

This mockery did not *merely* arouse laughter. In the torrid zone, laughter blended with pain. The mocking attitude destroyed the reassuring distinctions and the distance which anaesthetised my wounds. Extremes clung to one another, obliging me to stare, wide-eyed, while at the same time I wanted to look away. It was the moment of *evocation*, of a changing state.

When my work presented me with moments like these, it was as though it was saying 'now!' As they clashed, the actors' actions suddenly acquired an unimaginable force, welding together two hemispheres which were never intended to meet. They deflagrated as Disorder in my senses, in my memory, in that part of me which lived in exile within me.

This is why I had to subject myself to the exhausting experience of waste by following the long path of accumulation and then destruction. The shorter path, from planning to realisation, from the director's intentions to their implementation, could produce excellent results but it did not easily allow me suddenly to step into the torrid zone of that *art of memory which is theatre*.

Winds that burn

At dawn, a surge of gratitude flows through me on seeing the window, radiant with blue sky. On the Mexican beach, a Japanese woman waves her arms as though signalling to the horizon. It is reiki, a way of communicating with one's ancestors. I go downstairs anticipating the pleasure of reawakening my remote origin of lizard in the sun. In my hand is a thick biography of Elizabeth I of England, the queen who protected the theatre from the anger of her puritanical parliament. In the afternoon, in front of my computer's bluish screen, I will continue the struggle with this book which has gone on for more than 10 years.

Usually, the sound of horse's hooves and the creaking of carriage wheels woke me. They brought back the memory of the night which lasts a whole lifetime. Only a few peasants went to the fields with this anachronistic transport; the others set out later on their 'bees', motorbikes with a trailer. The dawn glowed. Lying on my bed, I let the lukewarm air caress me while I smelt the sharp odour of tobacco leaves drying in the sun. June 1974: Odin Teatret had just settled in Carpignano for five months to begin a new performance, Come! And the Day will be Ours. *In this village in southern Italy – so different from the safe refuge of our black room in Holstebro – we trained and rehearsed in a gloomy ex-warehouse for tobacco whose deafening acoustics made any vocal training impossible. Thus at about six in the morning, the actors spread out in a field outside the village 'to give voice' in the open air.*

That morning, Jens Christensen[1] *was waiting for me in front of my house. He was sorry, he must leave the theatre. He was in love with a Norwegian girl and wanted to marry and live in her country. A numbness, already sensed in the past and always feared, took hold of me. A hand squeezed my stomach, while panic and incomprehension made the moment unreal. His face expressed regret and at the same time was bright, as if a burning wind warmed him from the inside. I told him to train with his companions. On our return, we would tell them of his decision.*

I followed the vocal actions of the actors scattered in the field so as not to disturb each other. They addressed themselves to clouds, to a nearby bush, to the trees on the horizon, touching and caressing with their voices stones and rocks in the red earth of Salento.

Jens was concentrated on his training. The hand grasped my stomach tighter. He had come to Odin Teatret by chance, in 1969, to visit Ulrik Skeel, his school friend from Copenhagen who wanted to be an actor. We had shared the long and laborious preparation of My Father's House, *toured together for two years playing 322 times in 20 countries. He had been the only actor of the group to support without hesitation my plan to turn Odin Teatret into a theatre-farm. In addition to our theatrical activity, we would have cultivated the earth and raised pigs, independent of any subsidy. The other actors were sceptical with regard to our skill in tilling the earth and looking after pigs. After many months of discussion, which took place on Saturdays at the end of the week's rehearsals, common sense prevailed and my bucolic idea was dropped. Jens was already integrated in the rehearsals of the new performance and flashes of scenes animated by his actions and voice passed through my head.*

I gathered the group, surprised by the interruption of our daily routine. 'Jens has decided to leave us. He will tell you the reasons himself.' I burst into tears, something which had not happened for years. I sobbed uncontrollably. I felt the immobility and the bewilderment of Jens and the other actors discovering the defenceless child in their director, always so confident. Nobody uttered a word; my tears fell on the floor impregnated with years of dirt.

It has been one of the mournings in my life: a beloved actor was leaving me for his 'vocation', the voice which called him to a destiny far from me. I have relived a similar agonising pain every time one of the actors dear to me has gone on his or her way. When Ulrik did it, because he wanted to be a writer. When Else Marie left, because she felt the need to escape from discipline. When Tage created a theatre group with his wife. I have waited patiently for the opportunity to propose their return. It happened for Jens, but it didn't last long; his family situation didn't allow it. In turn, after some years, Ulrik was again with us in Brecht's Ashes. *Else Marie returned after one year. I waited for Tage for 10 years, and twice my offer was turned down. Then I had the joy of seeing him again in the group. I need warmth more than light, love more than clarity.*

> *Amithaba, child of a lama,*
> *listen to the invocation of Tara, the Red:*
> *wear boots with seven stars*
> *and come to me in the night*
> *clothed in love, late to my tent.*
> *Moons will rise*
> *from the sky's dusty chests.*
> *We will rest our love*
> *like exotic animals, tired of fleeing*
> *among the tall reeds where the world ends.*
>
> Elsa Laser-Schüler

'Were you in love with my father when you married him?' We were sitting in the kitchen, in her flat in Monte Mario in Rome. With her customary vivacity, my mother confided in me: 'I was 17. It was my last year at high school and my father was the admiral commanding the naval base in Brindisi. I was the centre of every party, courted by the young officers and my schoolmates. Your father belonged to another world; he was 15 years older than me, an enormous difference in age at the time. I thought he considered me a child. I was astonished yet flattered when he made me understand that he liked me. Without delay he asked for my hand.

Your father was general of the fascist militia and commanded a legion of black-shirts in Brindisi, a position of power during Mussolini's dictatorship. He was handsome and a well-known Don Juan. His adventures with the music hall dancers were the main gossip of the town. I married him as soon as I was 18. My father – your grandfather – was against the marriage because of the age difference. But also because he maintained that the officers of the fascist militia were parvenus, the navy has always considered itself aristocratic. Accompanying me to the altar, he whispered: you still have time to change your mind.'

But my mother was carried by a wind that burns.

'Admit it, mamma, you too have had some escapades, while the consul was away on his ideological duties.'

She pretends to be scandalised, and asserts that she found sex irremediably boring. She breathed a sigh of relief when my father went to his music hall dancers and left her in peace. She had never seen her husband naked. In bed, she wore a nightgown with a 'tiny window' in front. When my father wanted to make love, she unbuttoned the little window and he leaned inside. I laugh, incredulously, and my mother shares my merriment. I have a doubt that she may be pulling my leg in spite of her bourgeois attitude belied by a cheeky glint in her eye. She has a peculiar sense of humour. Once, in a bus, I saw her smiling kindly to a child. When he reciprocated, she opened her mouth wide in a silent grimace and loosened her false teeth.

One of my actors says that I resemble my mother. It is true; I too have a particular sense of humour. I like to begin a performance as if it were a hamster and end it as if it were a hyena. Undoubtedly the peculiarity of my humour is a gift of my mother, but the temperament of the wind that burns stems from my father.

My sentimental education took place in the military college of La Nunziatella, in Naples. I was 14 and ignored almost everything about sex. The older cadets took pleasure in explaining its mysteries. They bribed the doorman of a brothel who let me in despite my age, and they celebrated at my expense my initiation to Venus. My accession to manhood was a distressing failure, but the girl was kind and consoled me like a judicious older sister. At 16, when I visited Denmark and Sweden for the first time, the girls were the ones to take the initiative. I was stunned and I lived again the experience of that first time.

I hitchhiked in Scandinavia during the summer vacations, earning my living as a dishwasher or helping the farmers in the fields. Picking strawberries and apples on a Swedish farm, I met Miriam. Bashful and taciturn, she had just returned from a kibbutz in Israel where she had stayed for a few months. She was the daughter of a rich Jewish family from Stockholm and suffered from depression. Her wrists showed the marks of a suicide attempt. On the farm, the students of different nationalities revolved around her, attracted by her impenetrable reserve.

A bond was established between Miriam and me. It was expressed through rapid glances and a sense of complicity when we sat apart, each reading our own book, while the other young people chatted or danced. In three weeks we exchanged only a few words.

I continued alone to Lapland and took a job in a coal mine in Kiruna. When they found out that I had no work permit, I was escorted by the Swedish police to the Norwegian frontier. In Oslo, on my way back to my university studies in Rome, I met a French boy with whom I had picked apples on the Swedish farm. He told me that Miriam was employed in an old people's home in town. That same evening, driven by an unknown wind, I went to visit her.

Miriam and I planned to live together in sunny Italy. Oslo was under a mantle of snow and ice when we hitchhiked south in December. In Rome we stopped at a youth hostel. My mother was living in the house of her father, the admiral. My grandfather had given shelter to his two daughters, who were both war widows, and also to his son, my uncle, who had survived a German concentration camp. Knowing my grandfather's intransigence, I didn't dare to face him arm in arm with a Swedish girl. It was better to seek my mother's advice. I phoned her and we arranged to meet at the central post office.

Goodness knows what impression we made on my mother: Miriam 19 years old and me 18. She was 39, and had been a widow for seven years. She embraced Miriam and bombarded her with questions, making her smile. Sitting at a coffee bar, we spoke at length about my journey and our future intentions.

'You love each other, want to live together and don't intend to get married at once,' concluded my mother. My grandfather would never accept my living together with a girl under his roof. I had no possibility of a job and becoming economically independent. It was better that I returned to Norway. Sacrificing the desire to keep her son close at hand, my mother urged me to set sail and let burning winds carry me away.

Thus I left Italy and settled in Oslo. I achieved my economic self-sufficiency in Eigil Winnje's workshop, where I learned to weld. Through the rigour of the winter and in the splendour of the Norwegian spring, I lived my first love with breezes and whirlwinds of passion, pride, jealousy, animosity and indifference until the final separation.

This happens not only to individuals, but also to theatre groups. The main motive for their crises and subsequent disintegration is boredom. This word conceals situations very different one from another.

Boredom creeps in because an actor is no longer stimulated by the director or the latter by his actors.

Boredom surfaces when an artistic activity has become routine. The challenges are by now well known and, as a rule, take place under the same conditions of material precariousness.

Boredom can be sexual: the interest towards your own partner fades and a sudden attraction throws you into the arms of a colleague. Couples fall apart and unpredictable relationships spring up. When this happens, there is always someone who leaves the group. The new passion lives in another town or else you want to escape from the milieu you know so well. From this point of view, the dynamics in a group are like skating on ice, which inspires the most reckless figures. Suddenly the surface gives way and you find yourself soaked in icy water, almost always alone.

Also at Odin Teatret many people have left for these reasons. Many of the changes and solutions which have enabled the same core of people to collaborate for more than 40 years originate from an endogamous tendency: the rotation of partners inside our small enclave. It is amusing to read theatre historians expound on the values and the artistic, political, even spiritual motivations keeping a theatre group together. They forget, however, the gusts of winds that burn, the various manifestations of Eros. For a director, the choice of an actor as a favourite, replacing another, has also to do with this internal meteorological perturbation.

Finally I was in Warsaw. In January 1961, walking in this town in the grip of a harsh winter and a cheerless socialist regime, I was euphoric thinking of my imminent theatre studies. I asked a young man the way. I didn't speak a word of Polish, but Wlodek answered in fluent French and guided me to the student house where I lodged. He was an electrician but at home he spoke French. As the son of an aristocratic family, he had been precluded from the university, which gave priority to young people of a proletarian origin. We agreed to visit that evening a student club of which his fiancée was a member. The place was pleasant, a jazz band was playing and the students danced freely or conversed animatedly at the tables. I asked my new friends a thousand questions, surprised by their openness and the 'decadent' American influence in their socialist country. I glanced at a girl at the nearby table: black hair and turquoise eyes. Our gazes met, mine escaped at once. A burst of laughter forced me to turn around: six or seven people sitting with her were staring at me in amusement. The girl got up with a camera in her hand and, approaching, said something. Wlodek translated: she wanted to take my photo. Before I managed to mumble an answer, she bent over like a half moon and 'click'.

Now you have to dance with her, Wlodek's fiancée commented. Lilka – the girl with turquoise eyes – accepted happily. We danced for a long time, communicating politely in a rudimentary German. She had made a bet with her friends that I would invite her to dance within five minutes. Her delight at winning the bet encouraged me to ask if I could take her home. Or rather, to a street close to where she lived. She wanted to walk alone for the last part. In this way my love story with Lilka began.

A few months later, in the mid-spring, the window of my room was inundated by the sun while Lilka and I chatted about our families, our past and childhood. Lilka asked if I was Catholic. No, Jewish, I answered. She scrutinised me as though she had never seen me before. I repeated: Yes, Jewish. She got up, dressed and left in silence.

I am not Jewish. I have grown up in a Catholic milieu which has deeply marked my imagination, but not my faith. It had a meaning, for me, to call myself a Jew after meeting the Polish mother in the kibbutz in Israel, the one who had asked the question which was still vivid in my memory. At times the need for an imaginary and alternative life has the same strength as the fury of burning winds.

I looked for Lilka at the university, in the student clubs and the kawiarnas *where we used to drink tea and in the neighbourhood of her house whose exact address I had never known. I felt constant pangs in my stomach. Wlodek and his fiancée could not explain her conduct, nor were they able to console me.*

She stepped into my room one afternoon a couple of weeks later. She liked to be elegant, but I hardly recognised her. She was casually dressed, with hair dishevelled, her face swollen and no lipstick or nail varnish. She made no attempt to come near me. Intimidated, I crouched on my chair.

She abhorred Jews. She was stunned when she heard I was one of them. At home, she had isolated herself. Her mother couldn't understand her behaviour. Why didn't she go out or go to the university? Why did she no longer meet her Italian friend? Why did she cry all day? Lilka refused to confide in her. Finally she opened up. In reply, her mother had said: 'I have always told you that your father was killed in the war against the Germans. But he died in a gas chamber. He was a Jew. I survived because I am Catholic.'

I have never understood whether her mother had not confessed the truth to her daughter because she too was anti-Semitic, although she had forgotten her prejudice with the man she loved. Or perhaps she had remained silent in the hope of sparing her daughter if the apocalypse should be unleashed once again in Poland.

Lilka and I found each other again and only radiant memories are left with me now. Lilka, Lilienka: the diminutives of Lea in Polish. We never mentioned the episode or the consequences it had for each of us. But its effects fluctuate as infected cinders within me: we don't live contempt without impunity.

In December, I took the sudden decision to leave the theatre school and move to Opole, to Grotowski's small theatre. I had a date with Lilka and she came with two friends. She thought we were going to the cinema. I explained briefly my intentions. Her astonished face was ugly: is this the expression of pain? I turned my back and went away. That was the last time I saw her.

A 17-year-old girl, my mother, falls in love with a mature man. This is my origin. Today this girl is an old woman, 96 years old, and inhabits senile dementia. Her body has shrunk and she advances unsurely, leaning on the furniture and the walls. She stares at me in surprise when I take her hand. She responds uncertainly to my smile. I tell her of her parents, of Ernesto, her first-born son who died years ago, and of my family and my job in Denmark. I find again expressions, diminutives, intonations, words in the dialect of Gallipoli and fragments of melodies she sang to me. They belong to our confidential language, that bond that has united us since my childhood and that no distance has erased. Her behaviour changes. From a remote zone to which I have no access, the cheeky glint reappears in her eyes. She pretends to bite me as when we teased each other, gestures and traces of the unique intimacy between mother and son surface again.

I see ghosts: when she visited me at the military college and my companions made vulgar comments about the young widow; her protective embrace for Miriam; the soft touch of her hands while, blessing me, she tucked me in my bed; when she leant over the sun-drenched balcony and waved to her son who left her once more.

What was my mother's favourite colour?

The spectator's dramaturgy

The performance is not a world which is equal for everybody; it is a reality which every spectator experiences individually in the attempt to penetrate into it and appropriate it. The definitive substance of the theatre is the spectator's senses and memory. It is this substance which is attacked by the actors' actions.

The *heart* of my craft, as a director, was the transformation of the actor's energies in order to provoke the transformation of the spectator's energies. The one could not happen without the other. It was essential to work in depth on the individual actors so that they, in their turn, might provoke a reaction in depth in the individual spectator.

I wanted the spectator to watch stories of fictitious characters and, at the same time, glide into a world of her own. I had seen that it was possible. When this happened, the performance not only had succeeded in whispering a secret to her, a premonition or a question, but also in evoking another reality. The performance was no longer an appearance, but an apparition visiting her inner city. This evocative experience involved a leap of consciousness in the spectator: *a change of state*.

The evocative dimension – the level enabling the performance and its spectators to go beyond their own limits – has been the passionate longing of part of the theatre of my century. It was what gave it value as well as meaning.

There could be no leap without a suitable platform. This platform was the organic level which struck the spectator's senses, as well as the narrative level which implicated his emotional and intellectual sphere. The platform was the *necessary* condition for the leap, but it was not *sufficient*. Only if I dedicated myself to the building of the platform could I hope to produce a leap of consciousness.

I could knowingly structure the organic level and lay down the conditions for the narrative one. But I could only wait for the evocative level, in the double sense which Simone Weil attributed to the word 'waiting': to wait, but also to engage one's full awareness. The evocative level had nothing to do with emotions, memories and associations which the performance could and should arouse in the spectator. But it didn't end here.

It is one thing to compose materials for ourselves, a succession and a simultaneity of actions and circumstances with a sense and value for us who have created and elaborated them. It is yet another thing to affect the spectator through these materials in a stratified orchestration of conflicting and discontinuous relationships, while 'waiting' for another reality to manifest itself.

The evocative potentiality of a performance depended also on the capacity to safeguard, beneath a recognisable skin, the independent life of other logics: that of each actor, that of the director and that of *each spectator*.

But of which spectators am I speaking? Of *spectators-fetishes* whom I addressed while rehearsing.

These spectators-fetishes were a few concrete people, with recognisable characteristics: a child carried away by the euphoria of rhythm and wonder, but unable to appraise symbols, metaphors and artistic originality; Knudsen, an old skilled carpenter, who knew how to value small details; the spectator who thought he did not understand, but danced sitting on his seat; a friend of mine who had seen many of my performances, and lived again the pleasure of recognising what made him love them, and at the same time was bewildered by distasteful scenes; the blind Jorge Luis Borges, who enjoyed the least literary allusions and the thick layers of vocal information; the deaf Beethoven listening to the performance through his eyes, appreciating the symphony of its physical actions; a bororo from Amazonia who envisaged it as a ceremony for the forces of nature; a person I loved and whom I would like to be proud of me and my actors.

Work on the dramaturgy of the spectator for me meant operating on the different levels of his attention through the actions of the actors.

I behaved like a first spectator, with a double mind-set of estrangement and identification. Estrangement from the 'audience', but also from myself. And identification in the dissimilar experiences of my *spectators-fetishes*, who reflected the diverse ways in which a performance is alive.

I justified every detail and action in the performance through the reactions of each of these spectators. I passed from one to the other, I noticed their resistances and appreciations, imagining the ironic smile of one of them and the dismay of another, harmonising or sharpening the various emotional responses, and always taking care that whatever enabled one of them to react didn't block the reactions of another.

Technically, when I worked on the dramaturgy of the spectator, I decomposed the reactions and the mental behaviours of my spectators-fetishes into a few possible basic attitudes. I mixed and attuned their reactions the same way I did with the actions of the actors.

This procedure offered a potential variety of reactions which gave the performance the freedom to bloom in different memories. Each spectator who might have watched my performance was considered an individual made up of a blend of my spectators-fetishes.

But I had also some spectators who were 'absences' vividly present, although many of them were not alive. The non-living were not only those who were dead, but also those who had not yet been born.

I could reach those who had not been born only through those who were alive: the spectators who visited me. These came with an extraordinary gift: they gave me two or three hours of their lives and, full of trust, placed themselves in my hands. My actors and I reciprocated their generosity by giving our outmost, the rigorous result which characterises *excellence*. But I also tested their intentions. With their naivety, indifference and scepticism, they had to face a gust of conflicting situations, of allusions and contradictions, clusters of images and meanings which grappled with each other. They had to resolve the enigma of a performance-sphinx ready to devour their energies until boredom.

I wanted my performance to inflame the memory of the spectators and caress a wound in that part within them which lived in exile. The spectator had the right to be cradled by the thousand subterfuges of entertainment, by the pleasure of the senses and the stimulation of the intellect, by emotional immediateness and aesthetical refinement. But the main point was the transfiguration of the ephemeral performance into a virus which took root in him, provoking a particular way of seeing: an upside-down look, one which was addressed towards the interior.

Vision is the upside-down look. Disorder (with a capital D) irrupts, and the performance becomes an empty ritual because it has burst its chains: theatre-in-liberty.

While preparing a performance, I had to be loyal to my actors. This loyalty didn't seek their success, the interest of the critics or the consensus of the theatrical milieu. It consisted in establishing the conditions for the discovery of a personal meaning in the performance in progress, without being totally subservient to my demands and visions.

On the other hand, I wanted to be loyal to myself, to my needs and nonsensical questions. This second loyalty could not suffocate my loyalty towards my actors, just as the loyalty of the actors towards themselves should not smother their loyalty towards their director.

This meant that my associations and narrative sources – my subscore – was not a direct channel to communicate with the actors, but with myself. My subscore was a reality which made my work with the actors fertile because it remained secret and personal. This discretion was essential to give the work the value of a collaboration *in depth*.

The aim of the creative process was not to discover the points of contact or to enter into a communion with the actors. It was a particular way to collaborate with them in order to discover a different route to communicate with myself while being loyal to the spectator.

I wanted the spectator to sense the reality created by the actors as a personal message addressed only to him or her, splitting the field of evidence and conscience. For me, to be loyal towards the spectator meant to explode the unity of the audience at a mental level.

While rehearsing, each decision of mine had consequences for the dramaturgy of the actors, for my dramaturgy and for that of the spectators who were still not present. These three dramaturgies flowed contiguously but autonomously through my work. I could not neglect these three loyalties, although they reciprocally inhibited each other during the creative process.

The loyalty towards the actors dominated the first phase of rehearsals. I granted them absolute freedom to propose any idea and develop it into scenic materials. I gave them time to fix the improvisations, encouraging the growth of independent and individual logics and contexts.

The loyalty towards myself took the upper hand in the following phase of the story-behind-actions. I intervened on the cells, the organs and the systems of the future organism-performance with the caution and the decisiveness of a surgeon on whose hands the life of a human being depends. I have already described this situation which I have called *the moment of truth*.

In the final phase of the rehearsals I passed to the other side and became the depository of the artistic rigour and the interests of the spectator. I strove to protect the autonomy of the performance to leave a place for the dramaturgy of each spectator, for his intimate experience of Disorder.

Then a series of problems came to the fore. They had to be resolved with the lucid methodology of a theatrical architect and with an incoherent faith in superstition: a technique whose goal was the creation of an *elusive order*.

The elusive order

There was the face of the patterns and the face of the knots.

I wove the performance like a carpet, with a right and a wrong side. One automatically thinks that the right side, full of beautiful pictures and colours harmoniously blended together, is the one which appeared to the spectators; and that the wrong side is the one which showed itself to the director: threads laboriously knotted together in order to produce pictures and colours.

However, when we speak of dramaturgy, we should always reverse the image. I wanted my spectators to see the clots of twisted threads: asperity, contradictions, ambiguous meanings which were toppled and entangled, thus changing value and nature, *knots*.

The creation of an *elusive order* involved a performance with two faces. One belonged to the gaze and the sensibility of the spectator, comprising what he would see and experience during the performance. The other turned towards my inner world and concerned the justifications and the emotional logic which I projected onto the actors' actions and onto the performance as an autonomous living organism.

The autonomy of a performance resulted from the contiguity of these two faces, from their friction and forced cohabitation, from the net of relationships they had established coincidentally or deliberately, from their differences and separate destinations.

I could call them the sun and the moon. In the very moment when the performance presented itself to the attention of the spectators, the inner face became invisible, as the moon fades at dawn, concealed by the light of the sun. It fades but doesn't disappear.

I didn't intend the spectator to decipher a performance by finding out the sense given to it by its hypothetical author (writer? director? actor?). I laid out conditions enabling the spectator to question himself about the sense. The true sense is always personal and not transferable. There are spectators for whom the theatre is essential because it doesn't confront them with solutions and recognisable patterns, but knots.

The dialogue between performance and spectator reminded me of the tactics of a tribe with which Alexander the Great had clashed on his way to India. These nomads, who excelled as riders, used to fight with two horses. They constantly jumped from one to the other, protected themselves from enemy arrows by sliding down on the side of one horse or, galloping to the attack hidden under the belly of one of the animals, they sent the other away in order to confuse the adversaries. Suddenly they appeared again in the saddle in an unbridled attack that didn't stop even if one of the mounts was stricken.

As director I manipulated and mixed actions and peripeteias from different stories in order to avoid them being transfixed by the understanding of the spectator. I jumped from one narrative thread to another. At times, I favoured the development of one, leaving the other to evolve more slowly, then allowing them to unite and unravel the interlacements of the two stories in the same space. I exploited the possibilities which simultaneity and concatenation offered me to achieve a kaleidoscope of relationships, actions and reactions, causes and effects, illogical coincidences and gaps.

Both at the sensory and narrative level, I struggled to establish a dialogue between spectator and performance in which not everything was overt. This apparent entanglement was effective when it was the consequence of an order hidden in the meanderings of a labyrinth, meticulously built up through the director's montage. This *elusive order* was the performance's resonant cavity. From this cavity a shadow extricated itself.

The shadow was the evocative dramaturgy projected by the living organism of the performance, one which might cause a change of state in the spectator. It is impossible to create a living shadow. We need first to feed and let an active body grow. Then we may hope that time, the conditions of light and sun and the position of the body-in-life will enable an observer to sense the reality of an immaterial 'double'.

I have never been able deliberately to shape an evocative dramaturgy. It was ever present in my thoughts. I knew of its existence because I had experienced it in many performances, both my own and those of others. But in rehearsals, it was like hunting a ghost beyond the performance's horizon. If I succeeded in ensnaring it in the labyrinth of organic and narrative dramaturgies, this ghost instilled life in personal and collective mythologies, in historical experiences, in superstitions and wounds which belonged to me and a few of my spectators. I only knew that the outcome depended on the actors' scores of real actions and the smelting together of different stories, on my wish to favour contiguity and reversal while I explored simultaneously in many directions.

I protected and appraised every detail, every situation and every scene, the effects of their concatenation and the consequences of their simultaneity. I scrutinised the materials that emerged from the rehearsals, at times *as if* they were merely a living structure which danced, supported by the organic coherence of its dynamisms; at times *as if* the materials were only narrative plots with the single purpose of orientating the spectator through the actions' meanings. I manipulated and upset the images, sounds and words of the different threads from the stories I was telling.

I observed first from the perspective of the organic dramaturgy, and then from that of the narrative one. I continually shifted from one to the other, striving to discover possible bonds and correspondences, underlining assonances, contrasting their similarities, meaningfully structuring cacophonies and false notes, ramifying and compressing the connections between organicity and narration in a density from which the long-awaited 'ghost' might materialise. Then a third 'look' was activated, one which pursued a shadow beyond what I was seeing: *another performance*, limpid yet abstruse, which was mine alone but not born of my will. It was a performance which gradually *freed* itself from the demands of my energy and my needs.

Without warning, another vision lacerated my senses and my memory. Like doors, some of the intentional or accidental connections opened up to situations contradicting the results accumulated so far. An unforeseen sense shone as a small familiar and unexpected prodigy. I sailed on a stream which returned to its source.

My groping work on the evocative dramaturgy meant *unconsciously* invoking in the belly of the performance the shadows of the greater history and the small history from which I came.

Shadows like roots

I have tried to answer the question 'from where do I come?' quoting names and facts, moving backwards in the vast forest of shadows which populate the present. Shadows like roots. In real life, shadows draw their origin from the bodies which project them. In fairy tales, which follow the realism of another way of seeing reality, the contrary is the case: the shadow is the root. And he who loses it, loses himself.

'You are magic! You cast three shadows.' These words were whispered to me. But they didn't belong to a fairy tale or express admiration. They were said with irony.

It was late in the night. The rehearsals for Ur-Hamlet *dragged on. Armed with patience, actors and collaborators watched me and Luca Ruzza, creator of the scenic space, fiddling with the lights of the performance, all of which had to be modified. After a long day of work and a run-through, we still had four or five busy hours ahead of us.*

After a while, exasperation due to tiredness and unexpected extra activity turned into a comradely and resigned mood. We were all sleepy, but the trying and re-trying of the projectors no longer provoked impatience and vexation. A bivouac atmosphere was taking over. It was a night of summer and mosquitoes, after a performance in the open air where we had noticed that the lights and the shadows were not as they should be. They needed adjusting. Those who were not involved in the task dozed or chatted in low voices. Some giggled discreetly when they saw that the lights were still wrong. This was in Ravenna, in the heat of 2006.

'You have become a man with three shadows.' I was standing in the middle of the space to check the lights, keeping myself awake and encouraging my companions. I looked at the three shadows. Yet again a spotlight was misplaced.

We should be grateful for a job in which even technical errors can tell fairy tales. The three shadows seemed like tentacles. Then I grasped the truth concealed in the paradox: shadows like roots. Our origins are to be found in what moves away from us. They don't come before, but afterwards. They don't belong to the past, but to the future.

FOURTH INTERMEZZO

The music critic was one hundred and fourteen years old
and, at his side, the woman who looked after him had gone mad.
José Lezama Lima: *Paradise*

What a notebook says

I have a drawer full of small notebooks with thoughts, epigrams, news, true and imagined facts, comments, jokes, quotations and plays on words. I open at random one of them and reproduce here a few pages.

The action of an actor, like the adjective of a poet, if it doesn't transmit life, kills.

Poetry is the struggle of words against their meaning (Octavio Paz). The actor executes an action by denying it.

The effectiveness of an action stops the flight of a bird. Yet there is neither flight nor bird. Power of persuasion of the actor, organic effect on the spectator.

A mental exercise for directors: to disrupt the succession of the scenes or their segments and recompose them according to various yet coherent combinations.

Arundathy Roy: stories attract writers as carcasses attract vultures. I was not moved by compassion, but by greed.

Flaubert, in a letter to a friend whose mother has died: 'Tomorrow you will go to the funeral of your mother. You don't know how much I envy you. You will really see the reactions of the people and, what's more, you can scrutinise yourself, know what one feels in such a dramatic situation and in front of the attitudes of others. What marvellous material to write about.'

Take care of the details as if they contained a whole scene.

Sats: the nervous vibrations which ripple on the skin of a gazelle in the instant before flight.

The theatre is a style for inhabiting the world.

Notes for a meeting with directors:

- performance = to think by actions in a shared space/time
- compose different materials
- ramify the story or stories; text/context; how we tell the story to the spectators and how we tell it to ourselves
- mixing past and present: tell in the present tense; suggest, evoke, keep one's distance
- work on the attention and on the memory of the spectator
- the spectator's participation, his personal execution of the performance's score = the story as he tells it to himself
- *mettre en scène/mettre en forme*; form/information; the director puts-into-form a simultaneity of sonorous, semantic, rhythmic, political and associative information, quotations, references to other genres and spectacular traditions, etc.
- performance as a living organism = organicity and organisation
- induce an organic effect in the spectator, make him believe in the illusion and then shatter the illusion
- rhythm: it creates tension, organises, transports, excludes
- how to act with sound and light
- how to make space breathe
- costumes and objects are endowed with temperament, voice, backbone, likings and antipathies
- visual reality and auditive reality
- allusions, associations, suggestive narration, metaphors, evocation, literality
- flow = manipulation of several simultaneous and divergent rhythms
- the two-dimensional space of the text on paper *versus* the tri-dimensional theatrical space.

The theatre allows the actor to become a 'twice created' individual.

The sky, the earth and what is in between: the theatre.

The pupil who has met a master wants to fulfil only the master's precepts. It is possible. Provided that it is impossible.

Adapt the poem by Sophie de Mello Breynen Andersen as a mantra for directors:

> O poema è // A libertade. // Un poema não se programma // Porem a disciplina // Sillaba por sillaba // O acompaña. // Sillaba por sillaba // O poema emerge // Como si os deuses os dessem. // O fazemos.
> The performance // is freedom // A performance cannot be programmed // but discipline // action after action // accompanies it. // The performance emerges // as if Chance gave it to us. // We are the ones who do it.

To tell in theatre = to seduce *the biography* of the spectator with a disorientating montage of gestures, sounds, words, silences. Irony and compassion.

The spectator's mental state: neither awake, nor dreaming.

All of a sudden, the performance must flow backwards.

They don't know that we bring them the plague (Freud to his disciples).

Magnet-scenes: they attract the straying fragments of the performance.

A performance full of wind. The wind is not seen, yet everyone notices its effects.

The performance grows when the director dreams it. It is a dream which he guides while awake, eyes wide open. He concludes it by letting the spectator dream it. The difficulty is not to dream, but to put himself and the spectator in a dream state. Give an anatomy to the dream: ligaments, nervous tensions, articulations, blood circulation and pressure, epidermis and features (of both Anna Karenina and Quasimodo).

Practice and experience make work easy, but produce automatisms.

From potatoes to aquavit: the secret is the fermentation.

Choose the actions of the actors with precision in order to create ambiguity.

The invisible doesn't exist. There is only something visible which hides something visible. The invisible is a mental state of the spectator.

To improvise: to enter a territory which cannot be dominated. *How* to create this territory: concrete conditions, premises, rules, material factors that don't allow spontaneously (i.e. mechanically) to use one's own experience.

There is a memory which forces us to repeat (without our awareness); and a memory which helps to elude repetition (needing all our awareness).

The actor doesn't walk; he takes one step after another.

First make the spectator smell the perfume, then pick the flower.

Conspicuous oil deposits have turned the territory of a small tribe of pygmies into a modern technological enclave cut up by highways and infoways, hypermarkets and discotheques. The pygmies, unperturbed by these radical changes, continue enjoying their ceremonies. These take place between two rows of participants facing each other in order to celebrate life which, according to their beliefs, is a river flowing between two banks. Each participant dances, first himself and his 'double', and then the revered presence of an ancestor and the uncertain destiny of a descendant. They speak and sing in an invented idiom that contains the roots of their present language and its future developments. They address the spirits of the dead and of their yet unborn children. They declare with solemnity: 'the whole world belongs to the others, but this ceremony belongs only to us.' Watching the ceremonies of this tiny tribe, the critics call it 'theatre'. When at night the critics return home in the rain they admit, perplexed, that they no longer know what theatre is.

What are the origins of Pinocchio?

A tree trunk suitable for burning in the fireplace?

A pile of logs?

The workshops of two carpenters?

The abdomen of a shark – or was it perhaps a whale as for Jonas?

A donkey? (because for a period he was also a real braying donkey, with long ears and a tail).

The sky with its stars from where souls are sent down into the jails of the bodies?

All his escapes from the houses where he was made welcome?

His desire to return?

A rebellious puppet, which preceded him, but was not his father?

Pinocchio is himself, only because he is no longer what he was.

What would Pinocchio find, once he became a respectable adult, if he returned to his origins?

A pile of ashes in a fireplace?

The door of an old cupboard?

A small hand, carefully sculpted, as a reminder of the past?

A long pointed nose like a billiard cue?

A wedge beneath the leg of a wobbly table?

An old clog containing a flowerpot?

Experience: word-box of treasures hiding boredom, exhaustion, disappointments, indifference. It is difficult to live with experience and have a successful old age.

The anti-Borges: Eratostenes, in charge of the library in Alexandria under Tholomeus III Evergetes. At 80, he becomes blind and lets himself starve to death since he can no longer read.

Performances bleeding colours, images, sounds and black humour. A blind man enters a shop, led by his dog. He grabs the animal by the tail and swings it around above his head. A shop assistant comes running and protests. The blind man: I am just looking around.

Rules for composing a Chinese quatrain. The first line contains the initial theme; the second expands it; the third line separates itself from the theme in order to begin a new one; the fourth unites the previous three lines. Example:

> In Michin, a silk merchant lives with his two daughters
> The oldest is twenty, the youngest eighteen
> A soldier kills with the sword
> These girls slash men with their eyes.

Actions half embers, half ash.

It is my perfume, not my thorns, which protect me, says the rose (Claudel).

The pearls don't make the necklace, the thread does (Flaubert).

The difference between acting and showing the acting.

In theatre, time is created artificially. One possibility: to imagine time is neither outside me nor does it flow around me: *I am time*, it is me who flows. Then time is no longer an abstract dimension, but it is matter endowed with senses, directions, impulses and rhythms. Time becomes a living organism which may be moulded into actions felt as rhythmical units by the spectator.

The dynamics of our body are perceived by any observer as a succession of apparently foreseeable actions, but whose course and ending are unpredictable: someone pours me a drink; I know how this action will end, but I cannot guess the rhythm, the micro-pauses, where and how on the table the bottle will be placed. To be scenically alive, every action ought to contain a change, although microscopic, with respect to the preceding one. Just as every inspiration varies, and every snowflake is different from all the others in the same storm.

Rhythm is experienced as continuity, which is at the same time repetition and alteration. It sets the spectators in a state of expectation, pulls at them, makes them foresee the next step and surprises them because of its variations.

May your next performance resemble the description you have of it in your head.

Theories are rootless bushes flying with the wind. At times, however, they pollinate other plants.

Science and theatre. A scientist takes a flea and speaks to it while it freely moves around. Then he pulls off its legs and orders it to jump. The bug doesn't move. The scientist writes in his diary: when its legs are cut off, the flea becomes deaf.

For a young actor, the environment in which he learns to fight obviousness and the conditioned reflexes of the mind and body is decisive. Every exercise in the training is a mental and physical action to incorporate the reflex of reversal. For the actor and director, the theatrical technique manifests itself through a paradoxical way of thinking and acting. In literature, the master of this is Witold Gombrowicz. The novel by Mark Dunn, *Ibid.: A Life. A Novel in Footnotes* (Methuen 2005), is also a good example. It could be an inspiration about the way a performance might be imagined and made to grow. The book tells of an author who has lost the only copy of his manuscript: a biography of Jonathan Blashette, a circus artist with three legs who became an industrial magnate in the field of deodorants. The publisher publishes the part of the text which has been saved: the footnotes. The whole biography is revealed in flashes through these footnotes, which give information narrated 'in hiccups'. Here are two examples among many:

> *Chapter 3. 'Jonathan passed part of the summer in the house of his Aunt Gracelyn in Clume.' Note 9:* In a letter to the author, the local librarian explains: 'Some say that our town held the world record for lynchings. This simply is not true. There were only a handful of lynchings and the rest were trick lynchings in which the rope would break in just the nick of time and everybody would go home chuckling at the cleverness of it all. The real lynchings were not funny, of course, and I am not defending them, but remember also that the intendees weren't always Negroes. There were two Chinamen, an Italian who was mistaken for a Negro, a parrot who wouldn't stop saying dirty

words, and a Romanist (which is different from an Italian in that Romanists display Catholic arrogance). After a while we started to lynch the ones who had done all the lynchings because we began to feel that the whole thing was wrong and the wrongdoers needed to be appropriately punished. And in so doing, the town of Clume demonstrated that it had a conscience.'

Chapter 15. 'They are the pretty twinkle stars of my twilight years.' Note 4: Jonathan's diary, 2 September 1958. Among the female companions who brightened Jonathan's final years was Venetia House. Venetia was an active member of a small Christian sect that believed that Jesus Christ, as lover of both man and beast, had a pet collie which accompanied Him during His last months on earth. A book published by Venetia includes illustrations of the dog being fed table scraps by Jesus at the Last Supper, dog-paddling behind Jesus as he walked upon the waters of the Sea of Galilee, licking the face of Lazarus to help Jesus wake him from the dead, and howling plaintively at the foot of the cross.

The theatre director who thinks paradoxically will conclude: Venetia's assertions sound preposterous, but she was right. Jesus was surrounded by 'dogs' that he loved: Judas was a real dog, Peter followed Jesus everywhere like a dog and the women at the feet of the cross complained, yelping like bitches.

Technically, invisible action means: disseminated in minute doses throughout the performance.

The theatre doesn't continue a tradition, it predicts the future.

Written on a pillar at an archaeological site by the river Amu Darya: 'Remember that when you were born you cried, while everyone around you laughed with joy. Live your life so that at your death you may feel happy while the others will cry in sorrow.'

I prefer this haiku by Kobayashi Issa as an epitaph:

> You are washed when you are born
> You are washed when you are dead
> That's all.

'Tu vois, je dois aller à répéter; et bien! aujourd'hui je déteste ça. Je suis comme le chirurgien qui, las d'opérer, entre au bloc avec une envie de vomir. Je ne connais plus ce plaisir de la répétition. C'est facile d'aimer le théâtre dans l'ivresse de la jeunesse. C'est encore facile lorsque tu as appris ce qu'est le métier. Puis arrive la jouissance d'être un peu sûr, de savoir tout de suite ce qu'il faut faire. Et puis vient le moment où le chirurgien se dit : « Ah, encore un pancréas! » Mais il doit se dire qu'en dessous il y a un être vivant, alors il y va. Le théâtre, c'est la même chose. Tu continues quand même. Pas par habitude, pas par lâcheté. Avec plus de doute, de fatigue, de tristesse. Tu n'aimes plus avec la passion, avec le sang, avec le sexe. Alors là, tu touches au vrai amour du théâtre.' Giorgio Strehler to Jean Pierre Thibaudat, *Libération* 20.9.1995.

We can only talk to ourselves in an untranslatable language.

> All I long for will be fulfilled one day.
> To be at the same time man and boy,
> I'll climax and I wet myself
> When the rope tightens on my vertebrae.
> György Petri[1]

Epitaph on Vicente Huidobro's grave in Cartagena: Open the tomb, at the bottom is the sea.

Body memory: I remember once seeing some young Indian girls dancing. I knew that they were boys, yet I didn't want to eliminate the doubt. A part of me wanted to believe that they were beautiful little girls. They troubled me deeply.

The fifty districts of my inner city.

In a performance, the truth of the narration doesn't depend on fidelity to a pre-existing text, but to the persuasive power of the actor. Only the actor can convert written words, thoughts and fantasies into rhythms, tensions and musicality: flesh which seduces the mind and makes us 'see through'.

The theatre: tenderness and indifference towards an animal threatened by extinction.

The director's indispensable quality: patience. His passion is a long patience. The contrary is also true: his patience is the proof of a long passion.

God can be good both to the man who wants to swim across the river and to the crocodile which would like to eat him. Today God has been good to the crocodile (Peul proverb).

Obviousness turned upside-down: there is no thorn without a rose.

Man and woman: animals with the theatre inside them.

The temptation to say everything and something more.

Mercè Rodoreda (*The broken mirror*). A novel is words. The wild immobility of horses by Paolo Uccello. The slow spasms of a bud as it sprouts from the branch.

Ricardo Piglia (*Crítica y ficción*) quotes this dialogue between Gauguin and Mallarmé:

Gauguin: I have a few ideas for writing a novel.
Mallarmé: The problem is that you don't write a novel with ideas but with words.

In the same book Ricardo Piglia proposes this etymology for theatre: *theos* (god) and *iatros* (physician): a place where we are healed by meeting the divine.

It is amusing to write a book in which a lot of things are recognisable and yet none is imitable.

Fail, try again, fail better.

The theatre, like Moldavian or Guarani, is a marginal language.

Saladin, at his death, possessed 47 coins of silver, one of gold and 17 children. His funeral was paid for by his friends.

The prophets are extinguished in the desert
and angels with drooping wings
are dragged in lines,
piled up in the squares.
Soon they will be interrogated,
executed. What sin
has banished their essence from the heavens?
What guilt? Betrayal? Error?
And they, in a last act of love,
will look at us through the mists of sleep
without finding the diabolic impudence
to confess that angels fall
not from guilt, no, not from guilt,
but because they are tired.

(Ana Blandiana)

The actor moves within the rules and confines that he sets himself. His scenic existence rests on these rules turned actions.

The last Reformer: an old immobile bell-ringer on his stool. Death has entered. So as not to frighten him, it has lowered its hood on the faceless head and grasping the bell rope with bony fingers, bent as if in prayer, it tolls the death of the old bell-ringer – the death of a whole century's theatre. What do we care about this art, this coloured shout, without these tolls of despair?

5

THEATRE-IN-LIBERTY

Think, now: if you have found a dead bird,
not only dead, not only fallen,
but full of maggots: what do you feel –
more pity or more revulsion?

Pity is for the moment of death,
and the moments after. It changes
when decay comes, with the creeping stench
and the wriggling, munching scavengers.

Returning later, though, you will see
a shape of clean bone, a few feathers,
an inoffensive symbol of what
once lived. Nothing to make you shudder.

It is clear then. But perhaps you find
the analogy I have chosen
for our dead affair rather gruesome –
too unpleasant a comparison.

It is not accidental. In you
I see maggots close to the surface.
You are eaten up by self-pity,
crawling with unlovable pathos.

If I were to touch you I should feel
against my fingers fat, moist worm-skin.
Do not ask me for charity now:
go away until your bones are clean.

Fleur Adcock: *Advice to a Discarded Lover*

Burning the house

For centuries, even when theatre performances were appreciated as noble works of art and culture, the actors who created them were considered people who could be denigrated with impunity. The actors themselves often exhibited contempt or rejection towards their own condition. Today, the common opinion is radically changed. Contempt has been replaced by an ample appreciation which exudes officialdom and is nourished by indifference. In Europe, the public façade of the theatre is no longer one of a tolerated craft, but of a protected artistic species, foraged by law.

It is easy to see how both the denigrated profession and the art which has the honour of being protected concern only the surface. In depth, yesterday as today, the need to do theatre – which is the basis of its raison d'être as a milieu and a craft – doesn't derive from its social function or the various ways of being integrated in the surrounding society as art factory and diversion, but from the motives for its separateness. In other words: from the quality of its exile.

We all know the history of the theatre which explains circumstances and facts, theories, hypotheses, interpretations and influences. But under it another history flows, subterranean and anonymous as our dark forces. It is a history of passions, solitude and mirages, stubbornness which looks like blindness or fanaticism, coincidences, loves and refusals, wounds and technical obsessions. It tells of women and men fighting to escape from themselves and from the theatre of their time.

The subterranean history of theatre has been my house. I have wandered in its rooms to discover my professional identity. In its dark corners I have come across my ancestors and the legacy they have entrusted me with: my roots and my wings.

When I began, I considered myself an orphan. In Europe there no longer existed a single theatrical tradition. The Great Reform of the twentieth century, the theatre's 'big bang', had generated many small nomadic traditions. They didn't belong to a culture or a nation. A totem was at the origin of each of them, an actor or a director who, borne by a deep personal need, had invented superstitions and techniques to give life to it. These superstitions and techniques were embodied in individuals. They travelled, proliferated by contagion and spread the 'plague', indifferent to frontiers, fashions and the impositions of history.

For the totems, the theatre has always been an enclave: a handful of men and women united by a rigorous craft in cultivating a garden which, in the eyes of others, seemed exotic or a utopia. In reality all of them, from Stanislavski to Grotowski, have erected a fortress with walls of wind, at the same time an island of freedom and a shelter from the spirit of the time.

The power of the example of my theatrical ancestors came from the motivations which urged them to separate themselves from the values and practices of the theatre of their epoch. In other words: from the continuity of their intransigent professional exile. That's why the stubborn men and women of the 'third theatre', acting often at the frontiers of the recognised playhouses, have appeared to me as a founding element of my craft's dignity. In them I presaged the potentialities and the future of my small nomadic tradition.

I have only been an epigone living in the old house of the ancestors. I struggled to decipher their secrets and excesses. My zeal has set their practices and ideas on fire. In the smoke, I had a glimpse of a sense that was mine alone.

My small tradition has confronted me with a question: how to escape the voracity of the present and preserve a splinter of the past, safeguarding its future?

My answer was: tradition doesn't exist. I am a tradition-in-life. It materialises and transcends my experiences and those of the ancestors I have incinerated. It condenses the meetings, tensions, misapprehensions, dark sides, wounds and the many paths on which I continuously lose and re-find myself. When I disappear, this tradition-in-life will be extinguished.

Perhaps one day a young man or woman, borne along by their dark forces, will exhume my legacy and appropriate it, burning it with the temperature of their actions. Thus, in an act of passion, will and revolt, the unintentional heir will intuit my secret at the same moment in which she apprehends the sense of her heretic tradition.

A dramaturgy of dramaturgies

The premise of my dramaturgy was to think in the plural: more than one meaning, more than one story, more than one type of relationship, a multiplicity and a ramification of elements and lines of development. The density of a performance was not only due to the fact of proceeding by levels of organisation and structuring antithetic organic and narrative materials, but also to the contiguity of different dramaturgies.

My director's dramaturgy was a dramaturgy of dramaturgies.

I have often spoken of the director who weaves. The task of the actors was the creation of individual threads: materials, scores, relationships with space, text, the objects and sources of light inside and outside them. My task was to weave the actors' dramaturgies – their organic materials – into a living 'text'.

In the metaphor of the weaving, what comes to light is the intertwining. This is not wrong. It is what is suggested by this image that is misleading: in other words, the possibility *to extract* the different dramaturgies from the final result of this intertwining, so that it may be possible to analyse the process in detail.

The metaphor of the weaving suggests that the analysis corresponds to the process. Like a woman who starts patiently undoing an old sweater which has become too small for her child in order to make another. The action of undoing a woven fabric somehow corresponds to that of weaving it. When we talk of the dramaturgy of a performance using the metaphor of weaving, we tend to believe that the main point resides in the various threads which must be intertwined and woven.

I should have spoken not of weaving, but of *perfume*.

The process according to which a plurality of dramaturgies interacts is similar to the preparation of a perfume. Precious flowers soak together with unscented or malodorous substances until they become a dense liquid to be distilled into an aromatic essence. Then, different essences are mixed with oils and resins which fix a lasting fragrance. (We could say that a score corresponds to these oils and resins since it fixes the manifestations of the various psychic fragrances of an improvisation.) In mingling, the single aromatic essences lose their autonomous value. They become perfume, an intense indivisible unity.

During the rehearsals, the director distils and blends the dramaturgies of the actors. When the performance is ready, if the process is successful, the different dramaturgies settle and condense into a perfume which acts on the dramaturgy of the spectator.

I am not affirming that the individual thread created by the actor is no longer perceived in the performance. I refer to the obvious fact that any thread *disappears* – if all is as it should be – irremediably erased by the shared process towards an autonomous result. After the process it is no longer possible to go back. It is impossible to extract from the perfume the different aromatic essences which compose it.

The metaphor of the perfume demonstrates an impossibility: *the connection between analysis and process doesn't exist*. Only a chemical analysis can establish which elements are present in a perfume, and chemical analysis doesn't resemble the operations to create it.

* * *

My dramaturgy was also a method to find something I wasn't looking for. At the start of a new performance, there were tacit knowledge and dark forces: a certain degree of artisanal skill, a dialogue with that part of me which lived in exile, revolt and unbelieving prayer. In practice, my dramaturgy established different types of collaboration: of one actor with another, of the actors with the director, and of the actors and director with the spectators.

Whatever the type of collaboration, it was always rooted in a double loyalty: towards myself and towards another, whether actor or spectator. This loyalty came from an ethos, from a type of behaviour and the artisanal procedures which I have described.

The actors' materials were impregnated by vulnerability, with their own story and an emotional sense clinging to personal circumstances. I had in my hands not only pre-expressive materials, but also their *mana* and the fetishism of which they could be the object. I developed them, altered the coherence according to which they had been created and even eliminated some of them. When they changed their nature and the affective relationships which had made them precious, they would be buried, rendering the earth of the future performance fertile. A new avatar would multiply the possibilities of life and meanings in the original materials.

To this effort, I added yet another: my attempt to explore the potentialities of these avatars, organising them into an elusive order, an invisible and unusual structure: an effective dramaturgy. It was the humus in which my personal sense grew.

But my loyalty towards the spectators forced me to alter the nature of my work, to disarrange it and bury the order I had created within a story-behind-actions: the humus that would nourish the personal sense of each spectator.

My dramaturgy wanted to create a dance between actor and spectator in order to let the latter experience a reversal of his relationship with himself.

The theatre was for me the spectator. As the director, I was not only *the first spectator* for the actor: a competent external look, a nervous system and a memory which reacted. I also represented a principle of justice. The true tragedy, for an actor, is not being able to find in his director an individual to whom he can offer his total trust.

Those who collaborated with me not only accepted that I had the last word with respect to their work, but they were even prepared to surrender their autonomy, mixing it intimately with mine and that of their colleagues.

A particular type of creative agreement could be glimpsed, one which renounced the distinction between *mine* and *yours*, and which over a long period of time became a shared awareness. We knew about the necessity to fight individual mannerisms, the crises of trust and the discouragement, the paradoxical utility of inventing difficulties and resistances, of solving them and then overturning the solutions. We knew that each of us had different rhythms of growth and that work is like a defenceless child who must be protected from our private conflicts. This awareness nourished the artisanal commitment and safeguarded the personal motivations during the time-consuming distillation of the materials.

For months and even years, this agreement and a mutual loyalty between actors and director spurred us to distil the materials with dedication and rigour, treat them with regard and scepticism and combine them in apparently irreconcilable doses in order to offer a castle of perfumes to the spectator.

At Odin Teatret, dramaturgy didn't only embrace the techniques to compose a performance. It also involved a web of motivations, relationships, tacit norms and superstitions: an environment-in-life.

Letter from the director to his friend and adviser Nando Taviani

Montevideo, November 7, 2006

Dear Nando,

In your last letter you asked how I got the idea of taking the question of my origins, or rather of my dramaturgy, seriously. And you added that it was a good sign when the most abstruse and pointless thoughts are expressed through apparently harmless words.

I could reply: what makes me feel I am right? What makes others say that I am wrong? The answer to this double question, which is like a koan or a joke, is obvious: my origin.

My questions about origin are a means to detect a red thread in the events of my life. In other words: to capture the elusive order. Today I know it is an error to trace my origin by going back to the beginning. I must alter the chronology, the succession that seems to enclose my existence, whose sense I insist on transmitting in oblique ways.

A week ago in Buenos Aires, while I was waiting to begin my lecture, a man of about 50 approached me. Do you remember me? Help me, I answered. And he: I am Odin's father. We both burst into laughter and hugged each other. Twenty years previously, in 1986, during my first visit to Argentina, a young man had told me he had seen Odin Teatret three years before, while in exile in Europe, and he had given his son the name of our theatre. How old is he now? I asked. Two. I expressed the wish he might be wise and brave like the god whose name he bore. He shook his head doubtfully: 'Let's hope that he will not need to be.' At the end of the performance, he left without greeting me.

He reappeared exactly 10 years later, still in Buenos Aires. This time, too, he introduced himself as Odin's father. How old is he now? I enquired. Thirteen. You should bring him to our performance. But the father would make no promises. I didn't see him again.

'This time Odin will come to our performance,' I told him. 'I doubt it. He is 22 now, a musician fully taken up by his passion.' We embraced knowing there would be no further greetings at the end of my lecture. Around me, many young people were patiently queuing to get in. I call them 'children of the shipwreck', an expression used by a young Argentinean actress in 1996 when, while performing Kaosmos, *Odin Teatret and some theatre groups from Buenos Aires and its outskirts had gathered together in a barter. After this meeting, four directors founded an alliance and called it El Septimo, 'The seventh', after the poem by Attila József which was one of the themes in* Kaosmos. *El Septimo established contacts with other Latin American theatre groups and decentralised many of its activities to Humahuaca, a small town in the Andes, 2000 km from the capital. It had promoted courses, encounters and festivals for Third Theatre groups. It was for the celebration of its tenth anniversary that Julia and I had been invited, and for a whole week we were surrounded by about 100 actors and directors from Argentina, Paraguay, Brazil and Chile. They were so young – most of them around 20 – and they treated me with a thoughtful mixture of deference and intimacy. They aroused in me a carnal*

feeling of being their grandfather, much more than my own grandchildren, as if they had known me from their professional birth and I belonged to their origin. Doubtless, taking their first steps in the craft, they had stumbled on one of my books or heard of the legend of Odin Teatret, and they had appropriated it as a part of their professional mythology.

They are my origin, I said to myself. I was wondering what the precise meaning of these words was, when a flash of lightning struck my brain: origin is a mental state. It is linked to transition, to the need to refuse to belong to a culture, a nation, an ideology. Transition is the permanent path of de-familiarisation and extraneousness. It is the impulse to meet the foreigner inside and outside yourself.

Transition is the consequence of an instinct which is present only in a few. My origin is this: the instinct to separate myself from my native home, from the ideas that gave certainty to my parents, from the criteria giving sense to my actions and from my prejudices that I call values. Origin is the flavour of risk and the euphoria of ignorance which make me travel without leaving my home, and feel at home while on the road. Origin is not 'something' or 'somewhere' from which I move away; it is a hive of dark forces which I stubbornly try to stay close to. The maîtres fous *of the twentieth century theatre remained close to their origins using the art of fiction.*

They came in the morning at eight o'clock sharp to pick us up at our hotel in Buenos Aires. They had travelled all night from Paysandú, a town in north Uruguay, where their group, Imaginateatro, was based. They had come to know of my presence at El Septimo's celebration in Buenos Aires a year previously. During the seven hours of the trip, Marcelo and Dario told how they got the idea to contact me and how they teased each other about the illusion that I would take their proposal seriously. They couldn't understand why I had accepted a détour of 800 km to visit them. Their group was active since 1997, a dozen people who earned their living during the day and gathered three times a week, from nine p.m. to midnight to rehearse or perform. They had won the national prize Florencio in 2005. They are schoolteachers, technicians, truck drivers and distributors of soft drinks. Here, any job is good which ensures economic independence. Baking orange cakes and selling them at local fairs is Marilena's way of earning her living. She is an actress with ResiduArte, a group in Las Piedras, 40 km from Montevideo. On my visit, they arranged their tiny black working room with a huge table covered by an antique lace cloth belonging to one of their grandmothers. These are not sentimental anecdotes; they are small stones in that mosaic of energies in transition which I call my origin.

We might feel tempted to call them amateurs. You like amateurs. You have told me about your grandfather. But they are not amateurs, although they earn their bread with other jobs.

Let me tell you about Ivan who was bitten by the scorpion when he saw Odin Teatret in Montevideo. Together with Quique, they created a group, La Comuna, and followed us to the most amazing places in their continent. Once they came to Holstebro to show their performance and hear our comments. Time separated them. Ivan created Trenes y lunas, rented a venue, sold the house he had inherited from his parents, but at the end he was submerged in debt and had to close down. But he keeps on doing theatre. Quique started Polizon Teatro, rented a small house (de los 7 ventos), turning it into a school and a theatre which are still active. In his house of the 'seven winds' Quique offered a homenaje *to Odin Teatret on the occasion of the twentieth anniversary of our first visit in Uruguay. He had gathered our close friends, about 40 of them, together with the students of his school.*

Quique relates quietly the repercussions of the meeting with the Odin in his life and in that of people dear to him. He recalls the enthusiasm, the mistakes, the refusals, the doubts and the inflexible comments from me and Julia which burnt on the skin of his vanity, but which had led him to discover his road. Today, the path I follow belongs to me, he says with serenity. Close to him, Ivan cries in silence. The faces of my friends are serious. They are commemorating not the presence of a foreign theatre, but something else: an origin, a gust of winds that burn. Quique asks: 'what would we have become if we had not met the Odin?' I answer by asking him a similar question: 'what would I have become if had not met Latin America? Because you and a handful of theatre people scattered over your continent are the voices and the landscapes of my fatherland whose roots are in the sky. You have helped me to remain close to my origin.'

When we break up, three shy students explain to me that they too are part of that Latin America I have described, this fatherland embodied by people, bonds, affections, shared adventures, disappointments and successes. I had been with them from their first day of school.

On the last evening in Buenos Aires, at the end of the El Septimo celebration, we saw a performance by Baldio Teatro. Franco, 10 years, and Federico, 8, sons of directors and actors, hugged me and slipped a piece of paper in my hand. It was a long strip on which they had written in shaky handwriting: 'Eujenio, we love you although you give a lot of work to our parents.'

Dear Nando, you are a rigorous historian and don't let yourself be deceived by sentimentality. Do you think that all this has a place and a meaning in a future subterranean history of the theatre?

Here it never stops raining; I long for Tengri, the blue dome of the sky, the only divinity dear to Gengis Khan. An affectionate embrace
Eugenio

P.S. Draw an imaginary line from Rio via São Paulo up to the Bolivian frontier. You will have half of Brazil. In this southern part alone there are over 200 'group theatres' with more than five years of activity behind them. They insist on this appellation, refusing the more generic one of 'theatre group'. I heard this from André Carreira, director of a group and professor at the University of Florianopolis. He is doing research into theatre groups with his students and, as soon as he finds more money, he will map the north of Brazil.

In Buenos Aires they speak of movida joven (young movement). During the last three or four years, more than 200 theatre venues have been opened. It appears that during the economic crisis of recent years, unemployed parents have discovered that their children were able to earn their daily bread as actors.

Incursions and irruptions

In Gallipoli, in the church of St Francis, the statue of the bad robber crucified on the left side of Christ, tore his clothes at night, in despair, since he did not believe in the Saviour. After sunset I hesitated in front of the church, petrified, waiting for his wild cries.

Henri Laborit, the French biologist to whom I owe so much, used to say that the human being is memory which acts. If I affirm that I did theatre by chance, or that the theatre, as art, has never attracted me, I realise that my words sound false or arrogant. Yet they are true.

Today I must admit that something like the theatre was present on the margins of my childhood. It was the exceptional manifestation of a disconcerting *mana*, of an inexplicable power. As if irresistible emissaries of a people of giants irrupted in my world and overturned its normal dimensions.

Mother and child, in the procession of the Week of Passion. The statue of the forsaken Christ, covered in wounds, kneeling and crushed by a heavy cross, was surrounded by hooded men, in robes of vivid colours and holding long candles. His Mother's statue, Our Lady of Sorrows, all in black, followed him at a distance, accompanied by a crowd of women in mourning, litanies, songs and prayers. During the whole night the flickering flames of hundreds of candles glided through the narrow streets of the village. The shadows grew and crumbled, dancing on the walls which were corroded by the salt sea winds: a theatre of fire.

I must admit that the emissaries of the people of giants had little to do with the religious devotion which I felt at that time. It was as if their irruption disturbed my faith too.

I can compare them to the impression made by the performances I saw in Asia as a sailor, when I never imagined I would be professionally involved with them. In those situations, too, the theatre revealed itself as Disorder: *the irruption of an estranged and intensified reality* which upset the points of reference of my daily existence.

The theatre has constituted – and today I'm well aware of it – a precious tool to make incursions into zones of the world which seemed beyond my reach: incursions into unknown lands which characterise the vertical immaterial reality of the human being; and incursions into the horizontal space of human bonds, of social circles, of the relationships of power and politics, in the daily reality of this world in which I live, and to which I don't want to belong.

Still today I am fascinated by the fact that the theatre furnishes tools, paths and alibis for incursions into a double geography: the one which surrounds us, and the one which we surround. On one side, the external world: with its rules, vastness, incomprehensible and seductive zones, its evil and chaos; on the other, the inner world: with its continents and oceans, its folds and alluring mysteries.

Theatre anthropology has been an expedition into this inner geography, just as the pedagogy, the barters, the street performances, the organisation of encounters and celebrations lasting days and nights have been incursions into the geography of circumstances.

During my apprenticeship, I have lived several times the unexpected clash with a theatrical reality which sowed Disorder within me. *The Mother* by Gorkij-Brecht at the Berliner Ensemble, a Kathakali performance in the tropical Indian night, *The Constant Prince* by Grotowski, all remain indelible in my marrow.

Similarly, I have experienced Disorder in the work with my actors in an unexpected and unwanted way. Since the first years, certain patterns of their physical or vocal actions, by being repeated and refined, leapt towards another nature of vision or a different order of being.

For me the training has been a bridge between these two extremes: between the incursion into the machine of the body and the opening of passages enabling the irruption of an energy which breaks the limits of the body.

I loved to work with organic matter in order to weave silent dialogues with the spectators who needed to satiate a particular hunger. I liked to make use of the living matter in order to trace paths which, once opened, closed again behind me. They allowed me and my actors to remain in transition.

I made theatre, therefore I was interested in the expressive problems of this craft. But it was the pre-expressive level of organisation which fascinated me most, that of the organic dramaturgy; and – at the other extreme – the level of the dramaturgy I have called evocative, causing a change of state: the reversal, the irruption of Disorder in the order of the peripeteias, of the plot and montage.

I know that a craft for the irruption of Disorder is not possible. Yet it is so evident: the whole craft aims at making it possible, even when it only seems intended to render incursions sharp and effective.

Finally, what is dramaturgy for me? An operation to satiate my hunger, a small loaf of warm bread. I dig the earth, I water and fertilise it and sow wheat. I wait. From the seeds, grass and ears are born. I reap them. I let them dry, then grind them into flour. I blend the flour with water, add yeast and salt. I knead it into a dough. I wait for it to rise, watching this tiny miracle, fruit of experience and care for detail. My hands shape the dough into a small loaf. I put it in the oven and check the baking time. I take it out and wait for it to cool a little. Now I can eat my warm loaf.

But from the very first moment I break up the earth, I think *for whom* I prepare the bread, *where* I will eat it, *how* I will share it, and *with whom* or *without whom*. This awareness extends to the way I use the craft, how I keep alive the sense of relationships whatever their duration, and how I live in this world without belonging to it.

The dramaturgy doesn't concern only the composition of a performance. It is a struggle not to be expelled from the present and the refusal of hell.

Hell would be to feel at home in my time.

EPILOGUE

This spring the birds came back again too early.
Rejoice, O reason, instinct can err, too.
Wislawa Szymborska: *Returning Birds*

The slap of a stone on the water.

I was in bed, I heard voices – my wife, my sons, my actors, my dearest friends. It is time to get up, I murmured to myself, but two hands held me back in an embrace. I looked up and saw a youth.

'I have to run, I have a lot to do.'

'You are ill,' my grandfather answered.

'I have never been in such good shape as now.'

'You are old and ill from greatness.'

I gently freed myself from his embrace and showed him a handful of mud, a clog, and a clump of black feathers and claws from a dead crow: 'With this weapon I will win all the princesses.'

A row of young girls was approaching. I recognised them with a shudder of happiness: my mother, Sanjukta, Miriam, Lilka, my grandmother Checchina. '*Puer æternus*, for us you are always young,' they whispered. They held my hands, laughing and caressing my hair in front of a mirror. The reflex of the adolescent had vanished.

Once again the slap of a stone on the water. It had my name engraved on it and floated like a tiny island. It moved away and in its wake shimmered four words: disappeared in the East.

Far away, a house was burning.

Carpignano, Holstebro, Puerto Morelos, Sanur 1994–2009

ENVOI

Before I irrevocably detach myself from this book and deliver it to its readers, I feel obliged to remember a few people and certain circumstances. I'm writing these lines in January 2008. Outside the temperature is pleasant, although it is windy and the sky sometimes cloudy. The tepid waters of the Caribbean Sea lap against an almost empty beach.

I have written most of these pages under a warm sun: the short Danish summers of Holstebro and the scorching ones of Carpignano in southern Italy, the humid tropical heat of Sanur in Bali and the balmy Mexican winters in Puerto Morelos in Yucatan, in a small hotel far enough from Cancun to give me the illusion of being safe from the tourist invasion. And here, every morning of December 2006, I saw Jack C. returning along the seashore from the village where he had bought *The Miami Herald*. He climbed the steps from the beach to the terrace of my hotel, crossed through the garden and went out to the street where he owned a house. This year I have not seen him.

Jack is the first person to whom I want to send my thanks, although I imagine he will never read this. He was an important character in my book up to the penultimate version. Then the pages devoted to him fell away and he disappeared noiselessly. To be honest, I unwillingly erased him after criticisms by some of my first readers. They thought Jack was colourful but anecdotal. I had to admit that he gave this impression, although for me he represented something quite different. I want to thank these readers too and tell them I feel no resentment.

Yet it was Jack who unwittingly suggested to me one of the threads with which I have tried to weave the dramaturgy of this book. Our dialogue had started with the classic question: 'Where do you come from?' I answered that I held a Danish passport, but that my parents were Italian. Danish? Jack began to speak to me in fluent Swedish. He had studied linguistics at the University of Lund in southern Sweden. He had wanted to continue at the ancient University of Uppsala, north of Stockholm. Here a professor explained that this was impossible and invited him to lunch at his house. He had three daughters, the eldest about 20. 'They were very beautiful. They took me to see the cathedral and for a walk through the woods in the surrounding hills. For a whole day.' Jack was 83. Age had bent his tall figure, twisting him into a diaphanous vulnerability. Recalling the Swedish girls, his face so similar to the bark of an ancient olive tree, was illuminated by the sun of Eros.

Every day I saw Jack arrive along the beach, and every day my questions added another page to his biography. As an American, he had fought in World War II in the Philippines, then in Germany. The American army had thanked him by financing his studies. First in Lund, then at the University of Zurich where an Austrian girl hijacked him to Salzburg. He continued his studies in Japan and, after divorcing the Austrian girl, he had directed the school of Japanese language for American soldiers in Tokyo for five years. 'My present wife was a teacher there,' Jack said, and once again his face became radiant. I asked if she was the lady doing gymnastics at dawn on the beach. 'She does reiki, a way of communicating with one's ancestors.' 'Do you believe in reiki?' 'No, but it fills my wife with energy. And this is good, because then she lavishes it on me.' A ray of light passed across his face.

During the war, Jack deciphered messages in code. He didn't need to read the newspapers, he knew everything already. I asked him if he had met General MacArthur. He roared with laughter: 'I read all his correspondence.' When he left the army, he became professor of linguistics in Toronto. He has lived there for more than 40 years and has become a Canadian citizen. 'And the United States?' I enquired. 'It is not pleasant to live on a steam roller.' I liked to converse with Jack. He had seen a world that had intersected my own. Behind his words, I always sensed a joy in life that time had not managed to snuff out.

At the time, I wondered how my book could describe the many facets of the subtle power of Eros, without which no theatrical adventure can be explained. I felt that Jack could be a sort of guide, with his 80 or more years, and because of the light that shone in his eyes every time he alluded to love 'which moves the heavens and the other stars'. Not Artaud's 'black sun', but the simple and mute force released by a stone which is smoothed by water and age.

The conversation with Jack was also interesting because it gave me the opportunity to explore a path of the subterranean history of theatres. I asked him whether in Tokyo he had met Fabion Bowers, 'the American who saved Kabuki'. In the immediate post-war period, Bowers had worked in the US censorship office and it was thanks to him that Kabuki had not been prohibited. The American Military High Command saw in this form of performance a receptacle of feudal values which were incompatible with the spirit of democracy they wanted to install in occupied Japan. Jack had heard of Fabion Bowers, but had not met him.

I then asked him about Frank Hoff, who also taught at the University of Toronto. He roared with laughter: 'Frank? Of course!' I named my other American friends who were experts of Japanese theatre. He knew some of them. Jim Brandon? 'Sure, he learned Japanese at my school in Tokyo during his military service. Do you know Jim's wife? She too was a teacher at my school. I always chose attractive teachers. *They stimulate motivation*.' He smiled happily and I thought how often *Jack's motivation* had steered my life too.

What does it mean to speak about dramaturgy?

If it has taken me 14 years to finish this book, it is also because I started imagining dramaturgy as a theatrical technique. I wanted to write a collection of objective and practical recipes for those who want to do theatre. Some close friends raised their eyes to the sky. 'It is pure madness! You would be like a cook who prepares food according to recipes that only you are able to follow.' I was convinced they were wrong. Those recipes existed and I could put them in writing. I read them: they worked. I re-read them. *For whom* did they work? For me. My friends were right. I gave in, although unwillingly. I would like, however, to thank Pierangelo Pompa who read three versions of this book and whose naive but pertinent questions helped to rid me of my conceit over objective recipes.

I involved my actors, asking them to explain in their own words how I worked with them. Torgeir Wethal, Else Marie Laukvik, Iben Nagel Rasmussen, Roberta Carreri and Julia Varley accepted. After so many years together, each of us knows the other like the inside of their pockets. But sometime we still succeed in observing each other as if we were strangers from far away. For this, I feel I have to express my gratitude.

First Will, The Ritual of Disorder, The Book of Gems, Dramaturgical Recipes, Origins and Dramaturgies, Under the Theatre's Skin . . . These are all titles of the various versions through which I have filtered this book before arriving at the most appropriate one. I have burnt its architectural plan several times. Each time I came closer to the point of departure, because dramaturgy is not *a single* technique, but merges the different techniques of the theatre. And, finally, dramaturgy identifies with the person who does the merging, with his or her biography.

I became aware of this while discussing with some close friends. After years of acquaintance and mutual tolerance, our affection and respect express themselves though the intransigence of a devil's advocate. And here I should mention Lluís Masgrau, Franco Ruffini and Nicola Savarese.

Three readers have followed the many avatars of this book, encouraging me with severe but helpful comments: Nando Taviani, Julia Varley and Mirella Schino. Their words, in the moments of low spirits or euphoria, have provoked a reaction that I know from my theatre practice: to start afresh.

Others have supported me practically or by confessing to a difficulty in finding their bearings through my unusual terminology and plethora of metaphors: Maria Ficara, Rina Skeel, Raúl Iaiza, Max Webster, Andrew Jones, Eliane Deschamps-Pria.

Judy, who has accompanied my theatrical adventure since my apprenticeship in Poland and in India, has helped me to tone down my Italian style by translating bit by bit the various chapters into the sobriety of the English language.

But it was Jack who suddenly showed me the road, when the naturalness of his question – *Where do you come from?* – interrupted my thoughts about a book on dramaturgy which time after time undid itself between my fingers. The directness of his question suggested to me the less conventional and the most sensible solution: to weave technique and autobiography together, the places of origin of every artisan.

During the first weeks of January 2008, I wondered whether Jack, who had disappeared from my book, had also disappeared from our Mexican beach. Unexpectedly he materialised yesterday with the same way of walking, but with a slightly bemused expression on his face. He looked at me as if it was the first time he saw me.

'Where do you come from?'

'From Denmark. But I am Italian by birth.'

'Ah, Italian! I know Italy. I have been in Bellinzona.'

Bellinzona? Switzerland? Do I come from there too?

NOTES

Second Intermezzo

1 Norwegian, among Odin Teatret's founders in Oslo in 1964 and still working with us (2009).
2 Danish, arrived at Odin Teatret in 1966 and still working with us (2009).
3 Juha Häkkänen, Finnish, worked at Odin Teatret during the period 1967–70.
4 Norwegian, among Odin Teatret's founders in Oslo in 1964 and still working with us (2009).
5 Italian, arrived at Odin Teatret in 1974 and still working with us (2009).
6 Francis Pardeilhan, American, worked at Odin Teatret in the period 1976–86.
7 Ulrik Skeel, Danish, arrived at Odin Teatret in 1969 and still working with us (2009).
8 Tage Larsen, Danish, arrived at Odin Teatret in 1972 and still working with us (2009).
9 Julia Varley, British, arrived at Odin Teatret in 1976 and still working with us (2009).
10 Frans Winther, composer and musician, arrived at Odin Teatret in 1990 and still working with us (2009).
11 Master at ISTA, International School of Theatre Anthropology, since 1994. Has worked as actor at Odin Teatret since 2004.

Chapter 3

1 Italian, worked at Odin Teatret during the period 1974–84.
2 Catalan, worked at Odin Teatret during the period 1974–84.
3 German, actor and director, worked at Odin Teatret in the period 1983–87.
4 Jan Ferslev, musician and actor, arrived at Odin Teatret in 1987, and Kai Bredholt, also musician and actor, in 1990, still working with us (2009).
5 All texts in italics in this chapter stem from Julia Varley's *Wind in the West. A Character's Novel*, Odin Teatrets Forlag, Holstebro, 1996.
6 Tina Nielsen, Danish, worked at Odin Teatret in the period 1991–97.
7 Isabel Ubeda, Spanish, worked at Odin Teatret in the period 1990–96.
8 Hisako Miura, Japanese, worked at Odin Teatret in the period 1991–92.
9 British, she worked at Odin Teatret in the period 1991–93.
10 Translation: Alexander Taylor.

Chapter 4

1 Danish, worked at Odin Teatret in the period 1969–74.

Fourth Intermezzo

1 Translation by George and Mari Gomori.